THE LOST REVOLUTIONARY

The Lost Revolutionary

A BIOGRAPHY OF

John Reed

RICHARD O'CONNOR

DALE L. WALKER

Harcourt, Brace & World, Inc.
New York

Acknowledgments

For assistance in research, the authors are especially indebted to Mr. Baxter Polk, librarian at The University of Texas at El Paso, who not only managed, miraculously, to come up with rare source material on the shortest of orders but who demonstrated a keen interest in the Reed project from inception to finished manuscript; to the Hoover Institution on War, Revolution, and Peace of Stanford University for helpful bibliographical information; and to Dr. Haldeen Braddy, of The University of Texas at El Paso, for his critique of the Reed-in-Mexico chapter. They are also indebted to the Houghton Library at Harvard, the repository of the Reed Papers.

In addition, Dale Walker would like to extend loving thanks to his wife, Alice, for not complaining about the closed-door sessions with the typewriter, for her encouragement, and for riding herd on Dianne, Eric, Chris, and Mike, who will, in a few years, understand what it was all about.

Contents

". . . to write my name in letters of fire against the sky.'

—*John Reed*

1

"FORMLESS PERCEPTIONS
OF BEAUTY"

The place of his birth and the place of his burial parenthesized his life in a manner that would be hard to make credible in fiction. John Reed was born in the stateliest home on the highest populated hill overlooking Portland, Oregon. He was buried beneath the Kremlin Wall thirty-three years later and still lies there among the elite of the Russian Revolution. Between those two events lay a career seldom equaled in creative energy, thirst for adventure, and capacity for legend-making. Reed's passage was a brief, gay, and furious one. His unappeasable appetite for life was matched by seemingly inexhaustible energy. He was many things: rebellious Harvard poet, Greenwich Village playboy, lover of women (and of life), war correspondent during Pancho Villa's campaigns in Mexico and on the western and eastern fronts during World War I, revolutionary propagandist and agitator, friend of Lenin and Trotsky, author of the classic *Ten Days That Shook the World*, official in the first Soviet government and its first American "martyr," and patron saint of the American Communist Party—all within the space of a dozen incandescent years. He had been a cheerleader at Harvard; he was the most eupeptic of revolutionaries, one of the few who were able to bring a joy of living to the grim business of overthrowing governments.

By birth and breeding he was eminently equipped to defend the *status quo* rather than assault it. He was born on October 20, 1887, in Cedar Hill, his grandmother's mansion on a hill west of Portland, which he was to remember as "a great lordly gray mansion modelled on a French château with its immense park, its formal gardens, lawns, stables, greenhouses and glass grape arbor, the tame deer among the trees. . . . The lawn terrace below the house was surrounded on three sides by great fir trees up whose sides ran gaspipes grown over with bark; on summer evenings canvas was laid on the turf, and people danced, illuminated by flaming jets of gas which seemed to spout from the trees." [1]

He was christened John Silas Reed in a small but impressive ceremony at Trinity Episcopal Church, but the thing everyone remembered about his birth was the notable binge with which his grandmother's Chinese cook celebrated the event. Lee Sing, as John Reed would recall from family conversation, "lit countless joss sticks in his cellar room, burned a peck of prayer-papers, and gave a feast of dried shark-fins, seasoned chicken gizzards and sam-shui to his Chinese friends. My grandmother found him alone in the pantry, very drunk, with twelve of her Royal Worcester cups lined up before him, drinking whiskey out of one after another." [2]

His father was Charles Jerome Reed—always called "C. J."—a young upstate New Yorker who had come out to the Pacific Northwest several years earlier as regional sales representative of the D. M. Osborne Co. of Auburn, New York, manufacturers of farm equipment. In the few years he had lived in Portland he had established a reputation for wit and energy. The former resulted in his election as president of the Arlington Club, the members of which lunched together daily; the latter, in his prosperity as a busi-

[1] The notes are on pages 311-320.

nessman, at least during the good times preceding the panic and depression of 1893.

His mother, Margaret, was the daughter of Henry D. Green, one of the city's magnificoes, and Charlotte Jones Green, the granddaughter of Christian Wilmerding, a German merchant in New York whose descendants married into some of the East's most prominent families.

In a brief memoir written shortly before he reached his thirtieth birthday, John Reed said, "All that remains to me of my grandfather is his majestic height, his long slim fingers and the polished courtesy of his manners." [3] Actually, Henry D. Green died on a business trip to New York, two years before John was born. By then he had achieved as much in the way of material success as any man in the city, but apparently it did not entirely satisfy him. It was known that Green, in the privacy of his home, drank to excess; but never in public. He was always conscious of his position as a leader of the community who could not afford to be seen drinking immoderately in bars or clubs. As quoted in Green's obituary, a friend named T. B. Merry recalled Green's presence, shortly before his death, at the inauguration of President Grover Cleveland: "In all the countless throngs of distinguished men who walked those streets, embracing the aristocracy of both continents, there was no more graceful figure nor flashing presence than the tall and sinewy figure of this representative Oregon man, who moved through those courtly throngs with the aplomb of an Alcibiades himself." [4]

The "self-poised" characteristics Mr. Merry recalled with such admiration evidently formed the façade that Henry D. Green, when he wasn't brooding among the decanters in his library, presented to the world. With his brother John, Green had gone to Portland in the early eighteen-sixties and established the Portland Gaslight Company. Next they bought the city's rudimentary water system, consisting of a mile of wooden pipe leading to a small stream in Caruther's Canyon; within a few years they had expanded it to thirty miles of iron water mains, three reservoirs, and a pumping station with a daily capacity of twelve million gallons. A few years later they established the Portland Iron Works at Oswego, the first smelter and pig-iron factory on the Pacific Coast, which was subsequently merged into the Oregon Iron and Steel Company.

One of the city's early historians wrote that the Greens "rose to wealth without resorting to oppression." [5] The seed money for their enterprises, however, was derived from a particularly noxious form of commerce, the memories of which may still have bothered Green as he looked down on Portland from his mullioned windows on Cedar Hill.

Green was born in 1825 in Tompkins County, New York. Twenty-eight years later he joined his brother and H. C. Leonard, their partner in subsequent enterprises, at Astoria, Oregon. There John Green and his partner had established the only trading post competing with the Hudson's Bay Company at the mouth of the Columbia River. Years before, the pattern of trading with the Indians for their furs had been formulated by John Jacob Astor's American Fur Company. The method was simply a swindle based on the Indians' ignorance of what their furs were worth in the eastern markets. It was cogently described by Major Thomas Biddle in a report to his superiors: "These traders are continually endeavoring to lessen each other in the eyes of the Indians, not only by abusive words, but by all sorts of low tricks and maneuvers. If a trader trusts an Indian, his opponent uses all his endeavors to purchase the furs he may take, or prevent in any way his being paid; each trader supports his favorite chief, which produces not only intestine [sic] commotions and dissensions in the tribe, but destroys the influence of the principal chief, who should always be under the control of the government. The introduction of ardent spirits is one of the unhappy consequences of this opposition among traders; so violent is the attachment of the Indians for it, that he who gives most is sure to obtain furs; while, should any attempt to trade without it, he is sure of losing ground with his antagonist. No bargain is ever concluded without it, and the law on the subject is evaded, by their saying they give, not sell it." [6]

Perhaps it is sufficient comment on the Green brothers' methods of trading with the Indians to note that within three years they had accumulated enough money to abandon their post at Astoria, transfer their operations to Portland, and set themselves up as the gas, water, and iron magnates of the raw new city. Seven years later, in 1873, Henry D. Green had prospered sufficiently to buy the property at the head of B Street and spend the then lordly sum of twenty-eight thousand dollars to build his château on the sunny slope of Cedar Hill.

From its founding, Portland was a city with rigidly conservative standards. It would never be another San Francisco. Respectability was the essential quality for social acceptance; gaiety was suspect and nonconformity unheard of (at least until Mrs. Green began to spread her wings). It was and is one of the stodgiest port cities of the world. There was an almost Teutonic emphasis on the virtues of public order. The qualities of thrift, piety, sobriety, and hard work—puritanical in their intensity—were required of any citizen who hoped to amount to something. Little wonder that John Reed, once he had escaped from the city swearing he would never return except on the most urgent family occasions, became the antithesis of the worthy Portlander: a spendthrift, a hard drinker, and an advocate of free love who lustily practiced what he preached. His defiance of the standards set up by the burghers of Portland was only reinforced by the discovery, vigorously assisted by his own father, that so much of Portland's wealth and hauteur was footed in the fraudulent manipulation of public-land grants, which resulted in the private exploitation of millions of acres of virgin timber.

In his early boyhood, however, John Reed was made conscious only of the fact that he was a member of one of the First Families. His parents lived in his grandmother's château for the first nine years of his life. For Mrs. Green it was a merry widowhood; she spent the fortune left by her husband on parties and world travel until, twenty years later, there was nothing left. She and all the Greens, C. J. Reed observed, had "no sense at all about money matters." The parties at Cedar Hill were extravagant, large, and boisterous; her social position was so secure that she could afford to entertain on a scale and in a mode that would have made most of her contemporaries outcasts on the upper level of Portland society. Charlotte Green—"Tod," as her family called her—was a willful and high-spirited woman who had little respect for public opinion. Undoubtedly her grandson inherited many of her qualities, particularly her venturesomeness in a day when the Victorian widow was expected to be a vaporous creature living in seclusion with the smelling salts in easy reach.

Widowhood, however, was Charlotte Green's means of personal emancipation. John Reed thought the best one-word description of her was "sprightly." His father would have considered that an understatement bordering on the charitable. Years later, still clinging to her belief that a penny saved was a penny lamentably wasted, she took off on a trip around the world with the little that was left from her husband's estate. C. J. Reed wrote to his son that Tod was blowing the last of the money which might have been used, in part, to help John and his younger brother, Harry, through Harvard. "Yesterday," he added, "came a large photograph of Tod mounted on a camel, holding with a death grip to a Bedouin sheik, who looked as if he could cheerfully chop her with a scimitar. Another son of the desert, remaining carefully out of reach, looks as if he had the best of his partner. In the background stands the Sphinx with a nauseated expression. . . . Surely the long line of Pharaohs were in luck to have become only a memory before Tod invaded Egypt. If Moses could have subsidized her there would have been eight instead of seven plagues." [7]

During the first nine years of his life, John was brought up more under the Green influence than the Reed. The big house on the hill sheltered his "gay young uncles and aunts" as well as his parents and their two sons. The money was still plentiful, and there was a succession of nurses for "Jackie."

His favorite among the relatives was Uncle Ray, a foot-loose and fanciful fellow who "played at coffee-planting in Central America, mixed in revolutions, and sometimes blew in, tanned and bearded and speaking 'spigotty' like a mestizo. Once the tale ran that he had helped to lead a revolution that captured Guatemala for a few brief days and was made Secretary of State; the first thing he did was to appropriate the funds of the National Treasury to give a grand state ball, and then he declared war on the German Empire —because he had flunked his German course in college! Later he went out to the Philippines as a volunteer in the Spanish War— and the tale of how he was made King of Guam is still told with shouts of mirth by the veterans of the Second Oregon." [8]

Despite the ease and gaiety of life at Cedar Hill, John remembered his early years as cheerless and depressing owing to "illness and physical weakness." He was a pale, spindly child, "never really well until my sixteenth year," who had to be protected and carefully nurtured. With his mother or a nurse always present as a buffer between him and life outside the iron railings of Cedar Hill, he grew into an imaginative boy influenced more by the books he read than by what little he could observe of the world. In a single sentence, which shows his loneliness and introversion, he summed up his boyhood: "The beginning of my remembered life was a turmoil of imaginings—formless perceptions of beauty, which broke into voluminous verses, sensations of fear, of tenderness, of pain." [9] He would always think of his mother chiefly as the person who overprotected him, or tried to, even after his health became more robust.

The most fascinating elements in his boyhood, he afterward wrote, were the Chinese servants who trooped through his grandmother's household. They were hard-working but never humble. They would take orders but insist on carrying them out in their own way. Not only coolies, Reed recalled, but "scholars, soldiers, outlaws and those who would be mandarins in their own land worked for our family." He remembered them particularly for "their unfathomable connections with mysterious Chinatown, their calm assumption of superiority over the white race, their sardonic humor and laughable solemnity."

His earliest memory was of the cook, Lee Sing, lordliest of all the servants, ordering Mrs. Green from "his" kitchen. She would approach his domain and announce, "I think we should like mutton today, Sing." Sing would think it over and reply, "No—I guess not. I think I catchee one piece beef." When her personal maid wasn't around, Lee Sing would consent to button Mrs. Green's shoes, but always commented, "You got heap big feet. China lady got small feet."

Lee Sing was more important and more impressive to John, as a small boy, than anyone else at Cedar Hill. All day he tagged along after the Chinese cook, and years later he wrote an essay about him. "He was a thin-faced, slender heathen, attending mission school for business purposes, but a stern devil-worshipper on weekdays. Many a time I used to go out in the kitchen—we children and the dogs were always welcome—and find Sing washing the dishes, his long pigtail jumping as he simultaneously executed a double shuffle, and at the same time singing Methodist hymns with doleful relish." He insisted on decorating cakes with such inscriptions as "Jesus Wept" or "I believe in the Holy Ghost."

Lee Sing was a relatively rich man and owned a store in Chinatown. On Chinese New Year's he would present Mrs. Green with "gorgeous embroideries, bronzes, caravan tea—and heaped upon us children Lichee nuts, Canton ginger and firecrackers all the year around. We retaliated at Christmas although I think Sing had little use for our barbaric gifts."

Sing was a superb cook, the competence of the Chinese in anything they undertook, as Reed observed, being matched only by their independence. His only failings were an inordinate thirst for anything alcoholic and a love of gambling. "Sing's besetting sin was drink," as his young admirer observed, "and he would steal anything that looked alcoholic. Once coming upon a bottle of ammonia in the pantry, he seized the supposed whiskey and quickly up-ended it in his mouth." He clapped both hands to his mouth, "sprinted howling down the drive," and didn't return to "his" kitchen for two months. Occasionally he would give more formal notice of his intention of taking a bibulous vacation from his duties in Mrs. Green's pantry. "Me I go Chinatown. Catchee loom. Go bed. Dlink whiskey. Muchee sleep. Catchee 'nother bottle whiskey. Dlink. Go sleep. Dlink. Sleep . . . One month. I come back." [10]

John's two lighthearted maternal uncles had taught Sing to

play poker, and the boy would never forget their sessions at a kitchen table. "It was a great sight to see them seated behind three stacks of chips, Sing's yellow face quivering with cupidity, and to hear him shout in a squeaky falsetto, whenever he held three jacks, 'Chickpot! Chickpot!' " [11]

During his shut-in early boyhood, John believed, his constant association with the Chinese taught him something of enduring value: that because people were different from him in race or nationality, in customs or outlook, they were not necessarily inferior. It also taught him to accept with enthusiasm those differences in people, and later, whether traveling across the Chihuahua desert with Villa's *compañeros*, through the ruined Balkans of the war years, or enduring the privations of St. Petersburg and Moscow during the revolution, he could share their lot cheerfully. Perhaps it also discounted for him, at an impressionable age, the differences between people of wealth and privilege and those who were far down the social scale.

The other, and more traditional, consolation of his sickly childhood was reading. His mother taught him to read, and soon he was progressing from fairy tales to the stories of King Arthur and Camelot. He "plunged into an orgy of books," as he later recalled, and even then his tastes were catholic. "History was my passion," he said, particularly the Crusades and medieval Europe, but he was "equally enamored" of "Twain, Bill Nye, *Lorna Doone*, Webster's Unabridged and the Arabian Knights [*sic*] and Tales of the Round Table." [12]

At the age of nine he decided that he would be a writer and began composing a "Comic History of the United States" in the style of the humorist Bill Nye.

About that time his parents moved down from Cedar Hill and into a small house, then a short time later into an apartment hotel. The Reeds had decided to cut themselves loose from Mrs. Green's rather hectic household just at the time of the panic of 1893 and the years of depression that followed it, but John remembered that his parents accepted their reduced circumstances blithely. In addition, the Osborne Company, which had employed C. J. Reed as its western sales representative, combined with International Harvester, and C. J. had to scramble for a living. Finally he went into the insurance business. It was hard going for a time, but John recalled "a crowd of gay young people around my gay young father and mother."

John was soon placed in school for the first time, attending the Portland Academy, even though he had to stay home for a week or two at a time when illness struck. A doctor traced his troubles to an ailing kidney but could find no cure for it. The kidney ailment dogged him into manhood, until finally the organ was removed.

School, on the whole, did not appeal to him. The best part of it was associating with other youngsters. Handicapped though he was by his years of isolation, it was the social experience of going to school, he said, which "meant more and more to me until it almost crowded out the study side altogether. . . . I was a small boy, though, and not very well, and I didn't mix much with them (the other boys)." As he explained it later, "I wasn't much good at the things other boys were, and their codes of honor and conduct didn't hold me. They felt it, too, and had a sort of good-natured contempt."

He was never able to shake off an antipathy toward Portland largely because of his early impressions. His unhappy boyhood, he would later say, was "why I have so few close friends in Portland, and why I don't want ever again to live there." [13]

Even more keenly he felt that because of his frailty he was a disappointment to his vigorously masculine father. Now that he had been removed from Lee Sing's influence, it was his father whom he came to admire above all others. "He was a great fighter, one of the first of the little band of insurgents . . . to give expression to the new social conscience of the middle class." The sufferings of the working class, now observed from closer up than the view from Cedar Hill, convinced the elder Reed that something must be done socially and politically to guarantee them a better life and protect them from the rapacity and callousness of their employers. If this placed him at odds with his companions at the lunch tables of the Arlington Club, C. J. was quite unaffected. "His terrible slashing wit, his fine scorn of stupidity and cowardice and littleness made him many enemies who never dared attack him to his face." [14]

Certainly John's preceptors at the Portland Academy did not arouse anything like the same respect and admiration. Admittedly he was an "indifferent" student except when his imagination was involved (as by English poetry and, oddly enough, elementary chemistry) or when he was attracted to the "personality of some great teacher," as later at Harvard. But the teachers he encountered in Portland were "men and women—usually women—whose chief qualification is that they can plough steadily through a dull round of dates, acts, half-truths and rules for style without questioning, without interpreting and without seeing how ridiculously unlike the world their teachings are." He quickly forgot most of what was forced on him before he was ready and retained only what he learned from "books I had the curiosity to read outside school hours." An older John Reed would bitterly reflect that there were "many fine things I have had to force myself to explore again, because school once spoiled them for me." [15]

Even a score of years later he believed that his cavalier attitude toward formal education was justified. "Why should I have been interested in the stupid education of our time? We take young, soaring imaginations, consumed with curiosity about the life they see all around, and feed them with dead technique: the flawless purity of Washington, Lincoln's humdrum chivalry, our dull and virtuous history and England's honest glory; Addison's graceful style as an essayist, Goldsmith celebrating the rural clergy of the eighteenth century, Dr. Johnson at his most vapid, and George Eliot's *Silas Marner*; Macauley and the sonorous oratings of Edmund Burke; and in Latin, Caesar's Gallic guidebook and Cicero's mouthings about Roman politics."

He learned more by what he called the "social experience" of playing and fighting with boys from all strata of society in the streets around the apartment hotel in which he and his family lived. Boy gangs were in "a constant state of fierce warfare." Nearby was a tenement district known as Goose Hollow, which was populated by Irish boys who seemed to come out of their cribs with fists flailing. "I belonged to the Fourteenth Street gang, whose chief was a tall, curly-headed Irish boy who lived across the street —he is now a policeman. My best friend could make sounds with a bugle, and he was the trumpeter. Standing in the middle of the street he would blow, and in a minute boys would come swarming to him, tearing up lawns and making mud-balls as they came. Then we'd go running and shouting up the hill to give battle to the Montgomery Street gang, or beat off their attack. . . ."

But the joy of battle, in John's case, was largely simulated. He didn't really see much sense in throwing rocks at other boys simply because they lived on another street and belonged to another gang. Romantic though he was, then and always, he could not pretend that these set-tos in any way resembled the jousting of King Arthur and his knights. Besides, there was always the chance of getting hurt himself. "I was a good deal of a physical coward," he confessed. "I would sneak out over the back fence to avoid boys who were 'laying' for me or who I thought were 'laying' for me. Sometimes I fought, when I couldn't help myself, and sometimes even won; but I preferred to be called a coward than fight. My imagination conjured up horrible things that would happen to me, and I simply ran away.

"One time, when I was on the editorial board of the school paper, a boy I was afraid of warned me not to publish a joking paragraph I had written about him—and I didn't."

Even the path to school was perilous to him, "peopled with brutal Irish boys, many of whom grew up to be prize-fighters and baseball stars. I was literally frightened out of my senses when I went through Goose Hollow. Once a Goose Hollowite made me promise to give him a nickel if he didn't hit me, and walked up to my house with me while I got it for him. The strange thing was that when I was cornered, and fought, even a licking wasn't a hundredth time as bad as I thought it would be; but I never learned anything from that—the next time I ran away just the same, and suffered the most ghastly pangs of fear." [16]

In 1898, while the country trembled with anticipation of going to war with Spain, the Reeds took their two sons on a trip east to visit their paternal grandparents and various branches of the Green family in upstate New York and New York City. John would always remember the contrast between the cool green-clad hills surrounding Portland and the steaming turmoil of the metropolis, "the awful summer heat, the vermin in our boarding house, the steam engines on the Elevated," and the marching columns of the first troops leaving for their training camps in Florida and the campaigning in Cuba.

It was several years after he was entered in the Portland Academy before he began to feel at ease with other boys. He was still a boy who lived more in his imagination than in the world around him. He read voraciously, particularly among the more romantic novelists, everything from Sir Walter Scott and Robert Louis Stevenson to Marie Corelli; he wrote poetry, stories, and plays which he and his brother, Harry, with a few of their friends, staged in an attic. He left no record of whether he read the work of a young California writer, Jack London, eleven years older than he, whose quick-flaming career was to resemble his own in so many ways. *Call of the Wild*, London's first big success, was published when Reed was fifteen.

In the summer of 1903, when he was fifteen, John and four other boys went on a camping trip up the Willamette River, an account of which he entered in a newspaper essay contest. "We were a tough-looking crowd," he boasted, armed with rifles and knives and equipped with "a canvas wagon-sheet for a tent, five rolls of blankets, six valises of duds, and provisions to last us about a day, with a frying pan, sauce pan, lard can, and three coffee pots." They camped on an island in the river about twelve miles from Portland, and trudged into Oregon City, about two miles away, for their provisions. For about a week it was an idyllic outing as John and his companions sailed on the river, swam, fished, and shot game. Then John fell ill; the stabbing pains in his back indicated that his kidney was malfunctioning again. His mother fortuitously arrived the next day, and "She said right away that she thought the river water which we drank made me ill, because the river was going down, and she said I had to go right home, which I did." [17]

Different as they were in disposition, John and Harry got along well as boys. An age difference of two years seems enormous in boyhood, but John took his younger brother into partnership in the theater they built in the attic. Harry was more of a conformist, as became apparent even when they were boys, and he was somewhat dismayed and puzzled, on occasion, by John's compulsion to dramatize himself. Once, Harry went to school without his older brother and was asked by John's teacher why he hadn't come that day. Harry had to report that when he asked John the same question, the latter told him in a lordly voice, "Don't disturb me. I'm composing a melodrama."

It was obvious to their grandmother that the boys differed greatly in character. "Harry is a lamb," Mrs. Green once remarked, "but Jack is a lion. I prefer lions." It was an accurate forecast of how the two boys turned out.

In John's last year at Portland Academy, the family doctor finally found a successful treatment for his kidney trouble, largely based on a rigorous diet, and for the first time in his young life John knew what it was to be healthy, bursting with energy, and he vowed to make up for the debility that had shadowed his boyhood. Something of the same frailty in boyhood had afflicted Theodore Roosevelt, then the political hero of the Reed household. Perhaps like the valiant "Teddy," who was cherished by John's father more for his political courage in tackling the vested interests than for his charge up San Juan Hill at the head of the Rough Riders, John would enter into a rugged and adventurous manhood. When the two finally met a dozen years later—Roosevelt the former President and passionate advocate of U.S. intervention in World War I, Reed the fiery propagandist of the antiwar forces—they quarreled vociferously and frequently over their opposing views.

At sixteen, during his last year of schooling in Portland, John's greatest ambition was to make himself worthy of his father. To the end of his life, different as it was from C. J. Reed's, John was conscious of the example his father had set for him. From that side of the house, undoubtedly, he inherited his idealism, his search for a crusade worthy of dedicating his life to, his sense of justice; just as from his mother's side he may have acquired the self-indulgence that marked his maternal grandmother's life and the prankish, wayward tendencies of Uncle Ray. Certainly, as a crusader for social and economic justice, John Reed was a split personality. The playboy and the prophet, the profligate and the Communist pilgrim, coexisted uneasily and turbulently in him. He was more a rebel than a revolutionary. He could take his cause seriously, but never, for more than a few moments, himself.

He did not then know how much it would cost his father and mother in self-deprivation to send him and his brother to preparatory school in the East and then to Harvard. C. J. had not been able to attend college himself, but he was determined that his sons would have the best possible education even if it took every cent he could scrape together—as it did. "We never knew until later," John wrote years afterward, "how much our father and mother denied themselves that we might go [to prep school and college], and how he poured out his life that we might live like rich men's sons. He and mother always gave us more than we asked, in freedom and understanding as well as material things. And on the day my brother graduated from college, he broke under the terrible effort and died a few weeks later. . . . He was always more like a wise, kind older friend than a father. . . ." [18]

For John, at sixteen, hardly aware of these considerations, going away to the preparatory school at Morristown, New Jersey, simply meant a break with a past that, except for his family, he wanted to forget. No one there would know of his sickly boyhood or of what he regarded, with a curious overemphasis, as his cowardice as a boy street fighter. He would be starting from scratch. In this self-willed metamorphosis, the pallid and sheltered John Reed became the dashing, daring, mischief-loving, risk-taking Jack Reed almost as quickly as it took to travel across the continent.

2

A REBEL IN
THE IVY LEAGUE

The Morristown School was a small, exclusive academy designed to equip boys of good breeding and preferably Episcopalian background for the best of eastern colleges. Even then it was encrusted with tradition and imbued with the consciousness that it was training young men in the responsibilities of belonging to the upper class. The worst thing you could say about anyone, as was made plain in the flourishing literature about the Merriwell brothers and Dick Stover at Yale, was that he was a "mucker." That meant, simply, that he did not belong; that he was ill-mannered or uncouth, defiant of standards, and probably came from west of Philadelphia. Obviously Jack Reed from Oregon was on trial.

It was a challenge he met eagerly and with initial success. Going to the New Jersey boarding school, he wrote later, "meant more to me than anything else in my boyhood. Among these strange boys I came as a stranger, and I soon found out that they were willing to accept me at my own value. I was in fine health. The ordered life of the community interested me; I was impressed by its traditional customs . . . the sense of a long-settled and established civilization, so different from the raw, pretentious West. My stories and verses were published in the school paper; I played football and ran the quarter-mile with very good average success; I had a fight or two, and stuck it out. There were perilous adventures when a few of us stole down the fire-escapes at night and went to country dances, slipping back to bed in the dormitory at dawn. . . . Busy, happy, with lots of friends, I expanded into self-confidence. So without trying I found myself; and since then I have never been very much afraid of men." 1

As he entered Morristown, gangling and not too well co-ordinated, he stood six feet tall but weighed only one hundred and thirty-four pounds. Nevertheless, he went out for football, won the position of left guard, and distinguished himself on the field more for his enthusiasm than his skill. In dormitory bull sessions he was equally vociferous debating matters of sex, in which he claimed more knowledge than he possessed, and of politics, in which he was a passionate pleader for the administration of Theodore Roosevelt, some of whose measures against "malefactors of great wealth" were almost as alarming to the upper classes as a later Roosevelt's were. His masters would remember him as a leading mischief-maker and practical joker. One of his pranks was particularly annoying: he placed a chamber pot on the helmet of a suit of armor just before a group of visiting mothers and other ladies climbed past it on the staircase.

His unquenchable thirst for experience, his determination to make up for his sickly and sheltered boyhood, made him something of a problem for the school authorities, but they recognized that his pranks stemmed more from exuberance than from an evil disposition. Allowances had to be made for boys from the recently wild West, who were less carefully nurtured than sprigs of the tamer eastern aristocracy. It was a mark in his favor that he showed signs of developing a notable literary talent, and that some of his adolescent energy was channeled into writing poems and stories for the *Morristonian*. One of his efforts in verse for the school magazine recalled his emotions on hearing a violin:

> Sobbing through the still night places,
> Like a little child a-weeping,
> Singing happily, and laughing,
> Laughter like the bells of silver
> Which are rung in Paradise.[2]

As he remembered it later, it was "a period of intense emotion, in which I endowed certain girls with the attributes of Guinevere, and had a vision of Galahad and the Sangreal in the sky over the football field; a furious energy drove me to all kinds of bodily and mental exercise, without any particular direction—except that I felt sure I was going to be a great poet and novelist." [3]

His two years at Morristown, corresponding to the junior and senior years in a public high school, provided him with the self-confidence that was the self-starting mechanism of a notable and unique legend. He learned how to stand out from the crowd, even if it meant making himself ridiculous in the eyes of the less venturesome. He wanted popularity on his own terms, if possible, but at all costs he yearned to be unique. Attracting attention to himself was his constant preoccupation. Even at seventeen he was busy at making himself legendary; "the storm boy," as people would later call him, was always conscious of himself as a public figure.

Again it was his father who offered an example. John never admired his father more than during the summer vacation of 1905 when he went back to Portland and found C. J. involved in a fight against corruption that was shaking the foundations of the city's business and financial structure. It was an act of civil courage on the elder Reed's part which his son would never forget. "As United States Marshal under Roosevelt," John wrote later, "it was he who, with Francis J. Heney and Lincoln Steffens smashed the Oregon Land Fraud Ring." This was a slight exaggeration, since most of the "smashing" was done by federal investigators under Heney's direction, and Steffens came on the scene later as the journalist and muckraker who would describe it for the *American Magazine*.

Nevertheless, it took a great deal of courage on C. J. Reed's part to break away from the city's establishment, of which he had been a vocally dissident member, and join in the government's campaign to end the graft and thievery underlying Portland's long and serene prosperity.

The wealth of many of its most prominent citizens was built upon a system of fraud dating back to the land grants given the western railroads by Congress. The Northern Pacific Railroad alone received fifty-seven million acres of land in the public domain, a strip forty miles wide running along its right of way from west of the Missouri River to the Pacific Ocean. Another huge holding was that of the Southern Pacific through its subsidiaries, the Oregon and California Railroad and the Central Pacific Railroad. The Southern Pacific was granted a strip of territory sixty miles wide and six hundred and eighty-three miles long through the richest timberlands in the Pacific Northwest. Thus it owned, according to a report by the U.S. Commissioner of Corporations, seventy-one billion feet of standing timber in Oregon.

By the turn of the century, the Northern Pacific, under James J. Hill, was disposing of much of its timberlands. A favored buyer was the Weyerhaeuser Timber Company. The founder of this enterprise was Frederick Weyerhaeuser, who had migrated from Germany in 1852 and had quickly built up one of the great American fortunes. He had started out as a sawmill worker in Illinois, moved to St. Paul and set up his own mill, and eventually built a mansion next to Hill's in that city. Partly through the neighborly interest of James J. Hill, he acquired great stretches of virgin forest in the Northwest. Weyerhaeuser, like Jay Gould, preferred to go about his business of amassing millions and gobbling up vast forests without glorifying himself. He cultivated what Gustavus Myers termed the "studious art of extreme reticence." Publicity about his vast holdings was the last thing he wanted. Thus in 1900, according to the report of the U.S. Commissioner of Corporations, the Weyerhaeuser timber holdings had reached a total of 1,945,000 acres, four-fifths of them bought from Hill's railroad. In 1900 Weyerhaeuser acquired a block of 900,000 acres, at six dollars an acre, from the

Northern Pacific. The favored-buyer's status, according to the federal commissioner's report, made Weyerhaeuser and his subsidiaries the owners of ninety-five billion feet of timber. No one was greatly surprised when Weyerhaeuser's fortune was estimated at three hundred million dollars when he died in 1914.[4]

With Hill and Weyerhaeuser serving as exemplars, many of the leading businessmen and financiers of Portland took a rapacious interest in the public lands, which appeared to them to be up for grabs. They apparently did not pause to reflect that Hill and Weyerhaeuser operated within the somewhat blurred and inequitable bounds of the law. With so much of the farm and timber land vanishing from the public domain, they made haste to acquire their own holdings through bribery. Secretary of the Interior Ethan Hitchcock began to suspect that the laws were being evaded and ordered a quiet investigation. William J. Burns, of the Secret Service, was borrowed from the Treasury Department for this purpose. He was soon able to report that "very much, very old and very settled graft" had been uncovered in delving into the administration of the commissioner of the Land Office in Portland.

The law read that to acquire a section of public land the claimant must swear that he had occupied it and improved it for five years. By falsifying the commissioner's records, thousands of timber plots had been parceled out to lumber companies and other interests by the commissioner and a group of politicians. "Senators, representatives, and appointees to Federal office," wrote Lincoln Steffens after conducting his own research for the *American Magazine*, "had built up, protected, and used the Federal departments to further the frauds." [5] The systematic corruption reached into every area of Portland's establishment.

On receiving Burns's preliminary report, the Roosevelt administration ordered its attorney general to prosecute both those who had received the bribes and those who had passed them out. Obviously, a fearless and intrepid man would have to be found to conduct the investigation and prosecution; "very old and very settled graft" can be rooted out only by someone unafraid of shaking the foundations of the community. And the guilty men in Portland would resist all the harder because for decades they had posed with such invincible smugness as guardians of the public morality.

The man finally selected as special prosecutor was Francis J. Heney, a tough ex-cowhand from Arizona who liked nothing better than plowing up corruption in high places. An Irishman with a square jaw, a fine blade of a nose, and a sweeping gunfighter's mustache, he had studied law in the bunkhouse of a ranch near Tucson. His first case on leaping out of the saddle and into his first law practice almost proved fatal. The wife of the political boss of Tucson wanted a divorce and begged every lawyer in town to take her case. None would touch it because the political boss had sent word around the legal circuit that he would personally shoot any attorney who dared to represent his wife. Finally, the woman took her plea to the newest lawyer in town, Francis J. Heney, who immediately agreed to press her divorce action. From then until the case came to trial the politician daily insulted Heney in an effort to make him draw his gun. Each time Heney coolly replied that he wouldn't shoot it out until he'd won that case. At high noon the day Heney won his case he saw the political boss approaching him across the city square. Heney was not carrying a gun. The politician drew anyway, and would have shot Heney if the young lawyer had not grappled with him. During the struggle, the gun was fired, and the bullet entered the politician's chest, with fatal results. Heney was acquitted on the grounds of justifiable homicide.

On arriving in Portland, Heney soon learned that the city's ruling elements were united in placing every possible obstacle in the path of the Oregon Land Fraud prosecution. The special prosecutor, as Steffens recorded, had to ask President Roosevelt to "transfer judges, remove United States district attorneys and appoint United States Marshals before he could summon unfixed jurors, trust the courts, and have an even chance to convict." The incumbent U.S. Marshal was Jack Matthews, who was also Republican boss of Portland. Matthews was determined to block Heney in every way. He was finally removed on Roosevelt's order. By then, Heney's wife had met Mrs. C. J. Reed and formed a close friendship with her. It was Mrs. Heney who suggested that her husband appoint Reed U.S. Marshal to make sure that the subpoenas were served, unprejudiced jurors impaneled, and all the other machinery of justice kept in working order.[6]

At first C. J. hesitated to accept the post because he did not feel qualified, but Heney persisted in urging him to join the effort. A crusade for justice, so long delayed, proved irresistible. Reed was not deterred by the fact that many of his old friends and associates "cut" him and denounced him as a traitor to his class. The Arlington Club removed him as its president. Lincoln Steffens has attested that Reed, as part of the government's team, was "ruined" socially and financially when one tycoon after another was exposed.

Several years after the prosecutions, Steffens accompanied Reed to the Arlington Club for lunch and saw for himself how Reed was ostracized. " 'There they are,' said Reed to me, but for them to hear. 'That's the crowd that got the timber and tried to get me. And there, at the head of the table, that vacant chair, that's my place. That's where I sat. That's where I stood them off, for fun for years, and then for months in deadly earnest; but gaily, always gaily. I haven't sat in that place since the day I rose and left it, saying I'd never come back to it and saying that I would like to see which one of them would have the nerve to think that he could take and hold and fill my place. I have heard, and I am glad to see, that it is vacant yet, my vacant chair.' " [7]

From then until the approaching end of his life, C. J. suffered for having taken up the cause against the city's highly placed predators. Even the marshal's job was his only until the change in administration. "In 1910," as his son recalled, "a man came around to browbeat my father into contributing to the Republican campaign fund, and he kicked the collector down the courthouse stairs—and was removed from the marshalship by President Taft. Afterward he ran for Congress (as a Progressive) but lost out by a slim margin, mainly because he came east to see me graduate from college instead of stumping the state." [8] About the only appreciable asset from C. J. Reed's courageous participation in the crusade against the public-land pirates was the enduring friendship between the Reed and Heney families. More than thirty years later,

John's widowed mother would be asking Francis J. Heney to help her prevent the American Communist Party from exploiting her dead son's "martyrdom" by establishing the John Reed Clubs for recruitment of young people.

The summer he came home from Morristown, John Reed spent much of his time around the marshal's office. C. J. was often in danger of his life, and the respectable people had sworn that he would never be received in polite society again. Despite the pressures on his father and Francis Heney, neither man, he observed, lost his poise or sense of proportion; he would always remember them "guying William J. Burns, the detective on the case, for his Hawkshaw makeup and his ridiculous melodramatics." [9]

Next to his father, the most influential adult in those formative years was the free-thinking and picturesque Colonel Charles Erskine Scott Wood, a Portlander as obnoxious to the established and the overprivileged as C. J. Reed himself, and even more of a gadfly. John had played with the Colonel's sons, and had formed a close if unlikely friendship with him long before he went away to Morristown.

Certainly the Colonel was one of the most curious specimens ever graduated from West Point. It was miraculous that he served long enough to wear eagles on his shoulder straps, considering that he was not only a poet but also an anarchist. "This patriarchal aristocrat and warrior-libertarian, at once histrionic and bellicose, picturesque and warm-hearted, had begun to write verses long years before as a young officer on the plains, in Alaskan canoes and the lodges of friendly red men," wrote Van Wyck Brooks in describing the Colonel's remarkable career. "He had served all over the West beyond the Rockies; then, setting up as an Oregon lawyer, he had been a defender of unpopular causes and a friend of Emma Goldman and working men's rights. He was best known in later years for the dialogues collected in *Heavenly Discourses* in which God was presented in the image of C. E. Scott Wood, the enemy of 'star-sprinkled buncombe' whose motto was 'Freedom is heaven's first law' and who planned to abolish St. Peter's exclusive gate. For only war-mongers and armament-makers, prigs and prohibitionists were unwelcome in this anarchistic heaven, where the favored characters were Voltaire and Paine, Ingersoll, Mark Twain and Rabelais and it was treason to wish to wear a fig-leaf." [10]

Obviously John Reed, in his forays against conformity and or-thodoxy, which expanded in vehemence from prep-school rebellions against authority to leadership of a movement seeking the over-throw of the United States government, was encouraged by the ex-amples set by his father and his father's two closest friends, Francis J. Heney and Colonel Wood. All three of the older men doubtless would have been appalled at the result, yet it may be doubted whether any one of them would have tried, if he could, to curb his freedom of action.

During his last year at Morristown, John was a somewhat soberer young man, responsible enough to be appointed to a student council of seven. Little of his intellectual energy, however, was devoted to his studies, and he finished his last term in the bottom half of his class. Morristown and its traditions no longer seemed so marvelous; he was now conscious of a stuffiness in the academic atmosphere, and contributed a poem titled "Twilight" to the *Morristonian* which reflected a nostalgia for the splendors of the spacious West:

> That wind has stirred the mighty pines
> That cling along Mt. Shasta's side
> Has hurled the broad Pacific surf
> Against the rocks of Tillamook;
> And o'er the snow-fields of Mt. Hood
> Has caught the bitter cold and roared
> Across the prairies, piling high
> The huge white drifts of swirling snow.[11]

After barely passing his entrance exams, he started at Harvard in the fall of 1906. Initially it was a lonely and depressing experi-ence. At Morristown he had cut a rather flamboyant figure, but at Harvard he was merely one of more than seven hundred freshmen trying to find a foothold in a cloistered society not easily impressed by, or particularly welcoming to, the newcomer. "For the first three months," he would recall, "it seemed to me . . . as if every one of the seven hundred had friends but me." As he strolled the crisscrossing paths under the elms of the Yard, he determined to make his mark on the indifferent throngs brushing past him. "Desperately lonely," he fought against any tendency toward self-pity.[12] Perhaps to rally himself from loneliness, he wrote a scrap of inspirational verse (which he saved—as he saved everything he wrote—and which may now be found among his papers at Harvard a few hundred yards from the room in which he composed it):

> A mollycoddle is not a man
> And never a man he'll be
> Till Eli wins from Harvard's crew
> Another victory.[13]

Many of his classmates had attended the larger preparatory schools—Exeter, Andover, Groton, St. Mark's—and had known each other for years. John was an outsider, whose family's position in Portland society—or what remained of it, since his father had become more or less an outcast and his grandmother was busily spending the last of the Green inheritance—meant little to the scions of eastern wealth. His first-year courses included English literature, French, German, Latin, history, and philosophy, and he found nothing inspiring in them. Thinking that perhaps an athletic career would provide popularity or at least acceptance, he went out for the freshman crew, even slipped into the boathouse nights, weekends, and during vacations to practice on the rowing machines. But it all went for nothing; he was "the last man kicked off the squad before they went to New London." His only friend during those first months at Harvard was a shy, rather melancholy Jewish classmate, whose name is unknown, but who was obviously not able to assist him in winning social acceptance. Reed was shrewd enough to see that settling for such a friendship would exclude him from the more glamorous circles he hoped to impress. Quite callously, he decided to cool off his association with the Jewish boy because "it seemed I would never be a part of the rich splendor of college life with him around." Later he was able to write of this classmate, "Since then he has forgiven it, and done wonderful things for me, and we are friends." [14]

Even without that encumbrance, Reed could not make headway against the prevailing tendency of his classmates to exclude those suspected of being "muckers." A westerner without much money, without direct social connections, was expected to stay in his place and wait to be sought out if he proved himself worthy of inclusion in the pipe-smoking, beer-drinking bull sessions and other extra-curricular activities. He recalled that he "used to *pray* to be liked, to have friends, to be popular with the crowd."

In those lonely months Reed, perhaps for the first time, became aware of the cleavage between classes, an awareness that could only be deepened in an institution which was both the citadel of social conformity and the seedbed of intellectual dissent. It was the "college aristocrats," with their haughty manner, their cool assumption that they were born deserving all the best things in life, who made him conscious of a caste system, the upper reaches of which would always be closed to him. The thought that he could be considered inferior, unworthy of their attention no matter what he did, came as a numbing shock to him. Gradually he acquired friends, many of them, but, he wrote, "I was never popular with the aristocrats; I was never elected to any clubs but one. . . ."

The "cold cruel stupidity" of the gilded youth living in the private "Gold Coast" dormitories along Mt. Auburn Street repelled him, he said, but later "I began to pity them for their lack of imagination, the narrowness of their glittering lives—clubs, athletics, society." Some, he noted, came to Harvard with fifteen-thousand-dollar annual allowances, automobiles, and servants.

If the socialites would not have him, perhaps the literati would. He began writing for the *Lampoon* and the *Monthly*, and making friends among the more literary-minded. In Reed's Class of 1910 and those just preceding and just following it, there was a rich, an unprecedented vein of literary and journalistic talent. Among those at Harvard with Reed were T. S. Eliot, Alan Seeger, Conrad Aiken, Heywood Broun, H. V. Kaltenborn, Willard Huntington

Wright (who, as S. S. Van Dine, wrote the Philo Vance detective novels but who was also, under his own name, a first-rate critic and editor), John Hall Wheelock, Hermann Hagedorn, Van Wyck Brooks, Lucien Price, and Walter Lippmann; and among those who would become prominent in the theater were Lee Simonson, Kenneth MacGowan, and Robert Edmond Jones.

In his second year he was elected an editor of both magazines, but was passed over in the competition for a place on the staff of the Harvard daily, the *Crimson*. He had begun making friends, but they were largely outsiders like himself. None of the clubs tapped him for membership. His peers found him amusing but, apparently, a little exhausting. It was not lack of social background that excluded him, or even the handicap of a limited allowance, since his brother was later admitted to the same clubs that refused membership to him. There is a clue to his lack of acceptance, his lack of the quality the British call "clubable," in the recollections of Edward E. Hunt, his classmate and close friend, who later wrote: "There was something Elizabethan in his huge vitality. . . . And through everything he did there ran a strain of the grotesque which turned the most serious event into laughter. The college authorities were compelled by his pranks to revive the archaic punishment of rustication, a kind of academic jail sentence, the first of his innumerable incarcerations. . . ."[15]

To his more serious classmate Walter Lippmann, even then aloof, sardonic, and intensely intellectual, it was Reed's exuberance that caused him to be frozen out of the more exclusive areas of college life. "He came from Oregon, showed his feelings in public, and said what he thought to the club men who didn't like to hear it." The fact that he was occasionally "rusticated" would not have dismayed most of the club men, but Reed seemed to court the displeasure of the authorities, and that betrayed a lack of sophistication, an inveterate boyishness, to cool young men wary of the Katzenjammer tendency. "Even as an undergraduate he betrayed what many people believed to be the central passion of his life," Lippmann noted, "an inordinate desire to be arrested."[16]

Reed wanted to conform and "belong," but the rebelliousness

ingrained in his character apparently impelled him to mock and jeer at critical moments. Perhaps it was owing to his ailing childhood; he simply had not had a chance to work the Peck's Bad Boy out of his system. Even after he left school, he reveled in recalling his defiant behavior. "I remember his telling me with glee how he sassed the dean," wrote Julian Street, "and if his account of the interview was accurate—his stories never lost anything in the telling—it is amazing that he got his diploma." [17]

The sophomore year was critical for anyone hoping for a Harvard career of social as well as academic distinction. It was during that second year that the more promising students were drawn into the elite. Reed, unlike many of his classmates who had no interest in how the social-selection system worked, knew exactly how the elite was recruited. "In sophomore year," he wrote, "the Institute of 1770 selects one hundred men from the class, presumably fit social material, who thereafter regard themselves as the socially elect. The waiting clubs, which are final to one another (that is to say, a man can belong to only one waiting club) elect a few more, and further refine the original hundred. This group of what is supposed to be the best men in the class comprises the material with which the final clubs fill their ranks in junior and senior years." [18]

When he realized that he had been rejected by the socially elect, Reed threw himself into other extracurricular activities. Three new clubs had been formed: the Dramatic Club, the Cosmopolitan Club, and the Socialist Club. The last of these had been organized to study social and economic problems, and it had elected Walter Lippmann as its president. Reed was not a member but often attended its meetings in his senior year. There, where resolutions were earnestly discussed and adopted, Reed first became aware, he said, that there was a desperately deprived and turbulent world outside the Harvard Yard. Admittedly the club's agonizing over social conditions had little effect on them or even on the carefree lives of most of the students, and probably, Reed said, "the club-men and the athletes, who represented us to the outside world, never even heard of it. But it made me, and many others, realize that there was something going on in the dull outside world more thrilling than college activities, and turned our attention to the writings of men like H. G. Wells and Graham Wallas, wrenching us away from the Oscar Wildian dilettantism which had possessed undergraduate litterateurs for generations." [19]

The Cosmopolitan Club and the Dramatic Club, however, absorbed more of his time and attention than did the Socialists, whose hard-breathing earnestness appealed to serious-minded John but was a little tedious to his alter ego, fun-loving Jack. The Cosmopolitans discussed world affairs, with students from many lands participating. Even more to his personal taste was the Dramatic Club, which he helped to organize along with Edward Sheldon, later a celebrated playwright, and a burly young man named Hans von Kaltenborn-Stachau, better known in later years as H. V. Kaltenborn. The club was an offshoot of Professor George Pierce Baker's course in writing for the theater, and mainly produced plays written by undergraduates. Sheldon was its first president, Kaltenborn its business manager, and Reed the latter's assistant. Owen Davis, a prolific writer of plays for the commercial theater in later years, was also a member, as was Lee Simonson, who designed the sets.

A fairly close friendship developed between Reed and Kaltenborn. The latter, the son of a Hessian baron who had migrated to Wisconsin, was nine years older than Reed and most of his classmates. Twenty-eight at the time he entered Harvard, Kaltenborn had served as a top sergeant with the Fourth Wisconsin Volunteers during the Spanish-American War, and part of his fascination for Reed was the fact that he had traveled throughout France and Germany and worked as a reporter in Brooklyn before deciding to enroll at Harvard.

"Both he and I," Kaltenborn wrote concerning Reed in his autobiography, "had dramatic aspirations but our fellow club members seemed to believe we would do better off stage than on. We worked hard and actually made money for the club, although I had to challenge author Owen Davis to a fight when he insisted on an expensive sunset backdrop for the final act."

Kaltenborn, later the editor of the Brooklyn *Eagle* and still later a world-famous radio commentator and correspondent, remembered Reed forty years after with affection. "He was not a fiery left-winger in those days. He was a nonconformist. He and I had planned to spend one brief vacation period together, walking through New England. This fell through when he was suspended or was 'rusticated,' as it was then called, for a brief period because of some minor infraction of university rules. He was extremely likable, good-humored, and attractive. He was possessed of great mental and physical vigor. Had he bothered to study he would have been a brilliant student. But he seemed rather bored by the intellectual discipline of college . . . he hated authoritarianism of any kind. . . ." [20]

Perhaps the club most to Reed's liking, and with an unruly atmosphere that suited his personality was the Western Club. Emulating his father's long reign over the luncheon table of the Arlington Club in Portland, Reed not only organized it, but also saw to it that he became its president. The Western Club, designed to shelter youths from the western states who, like Reed, found it hard going among Ivy League traditions, was distinguished on the campus mostly for its spirit of mischief and practical-joking. Not infrequently, bits of food were hurled around the table. When Walter Lippmann made a sedate appearance at the club as Jack's guest, his host leaped up and announced him: "Gentlemen, the future President of the United States!"

His chief collaborator in the Western Club was a small, mild-mannered youth from Mason City, Iowa, named Joe Adams, whom Reed led astray more than once. Their most serious offense against college regulations was going to Bermuda during the spring vacation in their junior year. They went broke, missed the boat home, and raised the fare back to Boston largely through Adams' talents as a piano player, which were displayed in a dive on the water front. On their return to Harvard they were sent to Concord to "rusticate" under the direction of a local schoolmaster for the rest of the semester. While serving out their sentence in Concord, they frequently sent bulletins on their experiences in the hitherto quiet village to the membership of the Western Club. One night they conducted a violent campaign against a moth miller fluttering around their room and disturbing their sleep. The result, as Reed informed the Western Club, was that "A large moth was severely injured about the neck and ears. Two old ladies who room below us and are Seventh Day Adventists thought that Christ had come again, and prayed violently all night. The hotel cat was so horrified by the tumult that the next morning she was found to have given birth to a litter of pups in the cash register." [21]

The two endeavors, aside from frolicsome defiance of the college's regulations, at which Reed shone were water polo—he was captain of the team—and as an exceptionally inspiring and frenetic cheerleader. To Walter Lippmann his dramatic appearances in front of the cheering section at Harvard football games were the beginning of his fame. Reed, as Lippmann wrote in his essay on that self-generating legend, "proved himself to be the most inspired song and cheer leader that the football crowd had had for many days."

Appearing before a crowd of thousands seemed to loose in Reed something almost demonic, something that was to be displayed later in the most turbulent scenes of World War I America, something between charisma and unadorned rabble-rousing. "At first there was nothing to recommend him but his cheek," Lippmann recalled. "That was supreme. He would stand up alone before a few thousand undergraduates and demonstrate without a quiver of self-consciousness how a cheer should be given. If he didn't like the way his instructions were followed he cursed at the crowd, he bullied it, sneered at it. But he always captured it. It was a sensational triumph for Jack Reed but wasn't altogether good form at college. . . ." [22]

In his junior year Reed was elected to the post of "Ibis" on the staff of the *Lampoon* and to the editorial board of the *Monthly*, of which his classmate Edward E. Hunt was now editor-in-chief and Alan Seeger a fellow board member. Seeger and Reed were friendly but not intimate, though Hunt drew numerous parallels, in an essay published after their deaths, between the two romantics: "They came of old American stock; they were educated at a great

American university; they were men of mark and distinction; they did not die for America. They gave their lives for alien principles, alien traditions, alien purposes and alien lands." [23] But there was also a great divergence. Reed expressed his romanticism in the grinding mill of revolution; Seeger, in joining the French Foreign Legion and dying in battle against the Germans after writing "I Have a Rendezvous with Death."

With one exception Reed regarded his studies as humdrum, something to be endured. The one course he attended eagerly was English 12, in advanced composition, given by Professor Charles T. Copeland. A small, waspishly dignified man, "Copey," as he was known to several generations of Harvard men who distinguished themselves in various literary fields, had an unerring eye for talent. Few were admitted to his class, and those only after passing a special examination Copeland gave the applicants. During Reed's time as a student of writing, such men of later prominence as Maxwell Perkins, Hermann Hagedorn, Robert E. Rogers, Edward Sheldon, H. V. Kaltenborn, and Lee Simonson were sitting at Copey's feet. This was literally true at the Professor's famous Saturday evening get-togethers in his chambers at Hollis Hall, when he held forth in his armchair in front of the fire, with his student admirers gathered around him on the floor.

At first Copeland, having heard that Reed was a contentious type given to arguing with his teachers and talking back to the dean, refused to admit him to English 12. He finally yielded, however, after Reed kept promising to behave himself and pleading for admittance. The Professor did not regret the decision; nor did Reed, who would credit Copey with stimulating him to "find color and strength and beauty in books and in the world, and to express it again."

Copeland insisted that his students express themselves with vigor and force, that they appreciate and emulate the sinewy quality that was the glory of American prose. Kaltenborn, who served as his secretary, later wrote, "In selecting men for his English 12, Copey sought the well-rounded man rather than the industrious grind. I once asked him why he had admitted a certain man whose intellectual virtues were not readily apparent to me. 'Oh, he just looked so healthy,' Copey replied. His judgment was far more perceptive than mine and that healthy individual later proved to be an exceptional student." [24]

During his senior year Reed felt confident enough of the Professor's amiability toward him to write a poem teasing Copey about his obdurate bachelorhood and publish it in the *Lampoon*:

> Chamber'd Nautilus of Hollis
>> When you'd play the lover's part,
> Do you find sufficient solace
>> For your heart?
>
> Don't your acolytes distress you,
>> In their circle Johnsonese?
> Vying which shall cry "God bless you!"
>> When you sneeze?
>
> Does your fancy scorn the Present
>> When your chorus leaves at last?
> Do you flirt with ladies pleasant
>> From the past? . . .
>
> Show some living maid your pity,
>> Make her happy past her hope;
> Here's health—the lovely, witty
>> Mrs. Cope! [25]

Years after he left Harvard, Reed wrote that there were two men "who give me confidence in myself, who make me want to work, and to do nothing unworthy." That was written in 1917, when he had become famous as a war correspondent and notorious as a radical agitator. The two men were Professor Copeland and Lincoln Steffens. Copeland always praised Reed's achievements as a writer but detested the "Bolsheviks" who, as he believed, seduced Reed from his true vocation.*

* Another member of the Class of 1910 who became notorious for his political activities, though of a violently opposed persuasion, was Ernst Hanfstaengl, known as "Putzi," who went to Germany and for a time was the piano-playing, court-jesting friend of Adolf Hitler in the early years of Hitler's rise to power.

No doubt one of Copeland's celebrated dictums that Reed took to heart was his prescription for young men tempted by a journalistic career: "Get in, get wise, get out."

Jack Reed got in, got wise, and got out—but in a direction that could only dismay his preceptor.

During his senior year Reed became involved in campus politics to an extent, and in a cause, that rather surprised his friends. The underclassmen who lived in the college dormitories put up their own slate of candidates for class offices opposed to the candidates of the "aristocrats" who lived in apartments on Mt. Auburn Street. By then Reed had proved himself somewhat more acceptable to the "aristocrats," who rewarded him by putting up his name as a candidate for Ivy Orator. Along with most of the other candidates of the Mt. Auburn Street oligarchy, Reed was defeated, and he wrote a bitter poem against the plebeians of the Yard who "broke the class spirit, while all the world wondered." The world, of course, wondered very little. If it did wonder, it was at Jack Reed for joining the college insiders. Reed was further rewarded for having deserted the downtrodden by election to the Hasty Pudding Club, which produced the annual musical comedy but was more an organization for the socially elect than the theatrically talented.[26]

Reed was not proud of having deserted the plebes for what turned out to be a social advantage, the only visible recognition during his college career from the gilded youth of Mt. Auburn Street. In his memoir, "Almost Thirty," he insisted that he was elected to the Hasty Pudding Club "largely because of a dearth of members who could write the lyrics for the annual show."

In his first brush with the class struggle, rudimentary as it was on the campus of an Ivy League college in 1910, Reed betrayed it. But that would never happen again.

3

A BULL-PUSHER
ABROAD

Late in June the Class of 1910 was graduated, exhorted, sent on
its separate ways to fame and obscurity. His parents came to Cam-
bridge to watch John Reed receive his degree with a pride that was
not quite equaled by any distinctions he had achieved as a scholar.
T. S. Eliot—incredibly known as "Sam" to his classmates—had
written the ode, Edward E. Hunt delivered the class poem, Frank
W. Sullivan was the Ivy Orator. John Reed was an ex-cheerleader,
an ex-editor of the *Lampoon* and the *Monthly* and, unofficially,
Peck's Bad Boy of the Class of 1910.

At twenty-two, he was one of those boy-men that America seems
to produce on an assembly line. And like so many recent American
writers—Jack London, Stephen Crane, Scott Fitzgerald, Thomas
Wolfe, Ernest Hemingway—he was a combination of explosive
vitality and sustained immaturity.

He was tall, broad-shouldered, and gave the over-all impression of being handsome. Taken in detail, his face was irregular, its features contradictory. Those who knew him often remarked on the difference between the upper and lower halves of his face. The upper half—his wavy brown hair parted in the middle, his forehead both broad and high, his lively and intense green-flecked brown eyes—was that of a poet. The lower half, with its slightly squashy nose, wide full mouth, and heavy chin, seemed a stranger to the upper half; not exactly coarse or brutal, but certainly sensual. Yet the total effect, illuminated by his quick intelligence and compelling personality, was attractive to men and women alike. A celebrated portrait of Reed by his classmate Robert Hallowell shows him in a fur-collared coat with a white scarf at his throat. He looks exactly like one of those knightly youths of the Dawn Patrol, with the haunted yet exalted look in their eyes, who fought in the skies over Western Europe during World War I.

Immediately on being graduated from Harvard he took up his pursuit of the unquiet life. In those days the thing to do for a college man with adventurous instincts was to work his way to Europe on a cattle boat. Reed planned to work his way to England, then, somehow, around the world. Perhaps he would be able to sell articles on his way. Over his protests, he was given a hundred dollars in cash and a letter of credit by his father.

He embarked from Boston Harbor aboard the S.S. *Bostonian* shortly before noon on July 9, 1910. He was always incident prone, but this voyage threatened from the start to be an overly rigorous test of his young manhood. As he summed it up in the autobiographical essay written seven years later, "I was arrested for murder, clapped in irons, and brought before an Admiralty Court at Manchester." [1] The truth was a little milder, and less melodramatic.

The trouble arose from his choice of a traveling companion, and fellow "bull-pusher," on the *Bostonian*. He had persuaded Waldo Peirce, a classmate and member of the Harvard football team, who came of a prominent down-East family and subsequently distinguished himself as a painter, to accompany him. The hefty Peirce's spirit was as irrepressible and adventurous as Reed's. He was going to Paris to study painting, but he could not see the virtue in sailing over there on a stinking cattle boat. He considered himself picturesque enough without such conscious indulgences in discomfort, hard work, and low company. He finally allowed himself to be persuaded, however, and went aboard the *Bostonian* with Reed.

With considerable dismay, Peirce took in the sights and smells of the cattle boat. Their quarters in the forecastle appeared to be verminous. Their fellow bull-pushers, except for several college men, were a hung-over and delinquent-looking group. The first meal they were given consisted of boiled beef and a soup with white worms floating on its greasy surface.

As the ship lifted anchor and headed for the Boston Light, Peirce took his friend aside and told him he was considering desertion. He asked Reed if it would be all right if he just slipped over the side, caught the fast Cunarder *Mauretania*, and awaited Reed in Paris. "Certainly not," Reed snorted.

A short time later Reed found Peirce's watch and wallet lying on his bunk in the forecastle. Peirce himself was missing. A search of the ship failed to turn him up. There was nothing for Reed to do but appear before the captain and tell him that his friend had jumped ship before the voyage was fairly started.

Reed was taken aback when the captain, eying the watch and wallet Reed displayed, suggested that he had murdered Peirce, robbed him of his possessions, and tossed the body overboard. Reed insisted that Peirce, when he realized what a predicament he had placed Reed in, would be waiting on the dock when they arrived in Liverpool. "God help you," replied the captain, "if he isn't." [2]

Reed was not immediately "clapped in irons," but was informed that he would be taken before a Board of Trade hearing in England when the *Bostonian* docked. He'd be in serious trouble if Peirce was still missing, and Peirce would be in almost equally dire circumstances if he did show up to clear Reed's name, because he had signed the ship's articles and, college boy or not, was technically a maritime deserter. Meanwhile, Reed would be permitted to work his passage.

In the unpublished account of that trip, Reed described the working and living conditions of the seagoing cowhands. There were six hundred and forty-eight steers aboard which required constant feeding, watering, and tending. Reed and a man named Walker were on the night watch from eight in the evening to four in the morning and also had certain duties to be taken care of during the day. "I had a hundred steers to water twice a day, and every steer drank at least five heavy buckets; then I hoisted hay until my joints cracked. At night with a little sea on, the cattle-pens became a roaring, strangling mob. Of every ten, there was room for only three to lie down; when four reposed at once, all the neck-ropes went taut—and then they'd have to be beaten to their feet, or a rope cut. Then one would get loose behind, and we'd tear around in a bunch of heels and horns until he was tied again." [3]

As class-conscious as any dowager, Reed took careful note of the caste system operating even in the microcosm of the *Bostonian*'s forecastle. The bull-pushers themselves, he recorded, were divided into three classes: "Gentlemen workers, who are common laborers working their passage, with a privilege of return on the same boat as steerage passengers (these get no pay); paid men (experienced cattle-tenders who get $25 and return passage); and foremen, who get $45 per trip and return passage." Reed's foreman was Tom Robbins, a tall tough Scot who had once served as one of Bob Fitzsimmons' sparring partners and was not a man to be defied. Otherwise, the forecastle was occupied by drunkards and misfits, "profanity mills" whose conversation consisted of a stream of blasphemy unleavened by originality. It stank of unwashed bodies and unwashed clothing.

Obviously the gentlemen-rankers aboard would have to make other arrangements for sleeping and eating. "We formed a University Club," Reed later recounted, "and erected a sleeping tent on the poopdeck." A pair of "middlewestern muckers from the University of Illinois" were allowed to join the University Club but "became such nuisances that we kicked them out. I told them to leave and never come back to our tent."

Reed and a delegation took their complaints about the wormy and rotten food to one of the ship's officers, informing him that "our own food was almost too bad to touch." He was unsympathetic toward the "gentlemen" when they suggested that they be fed as part of the officers' mess. "This was a surprise," Reed wrote later, "as other fellows who had been over on trips had told me of the exceeding graciousness of cattleboat officials." [4]

Surreptitiously Reed and his fellow members of the University Club, deciding that bribery would work better than appeals to the officers' better natures, came to an arrangement with the second cook. He would supply them with food from the officers' mess in exchange for money.

Meanwhile, Reed had made friends with the chief engineer, "a dry, serious-looking comedian," who permitted the members of the University Club to turn on the salt-water pumps every afternoon and take showers on deck. "That," Reed proudly noted, "is the exclusive privilege of the University Club." [5]

He also made friends with three Irishmen in the crew. One of them had been rolled in Providence before the *Bostonian* sailed, and Reed took up a collection among his friends for the man. That endeared him to the Irish contingent, which, having a low opinion of British justice, warned Reed that when the ship docked in Liverpool he would be railroaded for Waldo Peirce's murder and undoubtedly hung from a convenient yardarm in the Mersey. They suggested a remedy: when the *Bostonian* approached the Irish coast, he and they would slip overboard and swim for shore. They would hide him among trustworthy friends in Cork, they swore, and he would be safe from the dastardly English.

Reed laughed off their warnings, but when the ship approached Liverpool his concern mounted. A tug came out, and he strained his eyes hoping Peirce would be aboard it. He was not. The captain of the *Bostonian* was now convinced that Reed, for all his boyish manner, was probably a dangerous character. He ordered him confined to a small cabin and placed in leg irons.

The *Bostonian* proceeded through the locks, up the Ship Canal to Manchester while Reed brooded over his apparently desperate situation. What if Peirce simply did not show up? What if he had drowned in Boston Harbor while swimming for the shore?

Next morning the *Bostonian* docked at Manchester, and John Reed, murder suspect, was escorted from the brig. The leg irons, fortunately, were removed before he walked down the gangplank. "The procession formed," he later wrote. "First marched the captain; then myself, flanked by two enormous British bobbies; after me the three mates in order of precedence, the steward, the cook and petty dignitaries; behind them the crew, and beyond the cattlemen straggling up the rear. I expected to see the cattle bringing up the rear."

It had been a rather swift comedown, he might well have reflected. Only a month ago he had marched in cap and gown to receive his degree. Then he had gone out to seek those wider horizons the commencement speakers told him were awaiting him outside the university. How quickly those horizons had narrowed to a view of the gallows! How quickly a place in an academic procession had given way to an ignominious march under guard toward the mercies of British justice!

The ragtag procession halted in front of the Board of Trade building. He was taken to a somber room, in which it would be determined whether he should be held for trial on a charge of murder. No friendly faces were to be glimpsed as the proceedings began before "eleven stolid Britishers," whose chairman was an "enormous Scotch Presbyterian with a wooden leg."

A few moments later, while the facts were being recited by his captain, Reed glanced around and saw Peirce enter the chamber. The huge but somehow elfin Peirce, wrote Reed later, "leaned against the wall and regarded the proceedings with a bland and child-like smile." [6]

A moment later Reed interrupted the captain's droning voice to announce that Waldo Peirce, the presumed "murder victim," was alive and in the room. There followed an interlude of shouting, largely that of the *Bostonian*'s captain demanding that Peirce take Reed's place in the dock. Later Reed learned that Peirce had been waiting for the *Bostonian* on the dock at Liverpool, had even caught a glimpse of him on deck, but had decided he had better seek legal advice. The authorities might not be willing, after all, to write off the incident as a collegiate escapade. As Julian Street, a friend of both men, later pieced the story together, Peirce, while crossing on the *Mauretania*, "had told his story to an officer, who warned him that he was liable to punishment for desertion and advised him to avoid the cattleboat. Reed's predicament, however, forced him to come forward, and though the captain was at first inclined to make trouble, the young men succeeded in talking him out of the idea and went gaily on their way." [7]

Actually, the *Bostonian*'s captain insisted that Peirce should be held on charges of having deserted his ship, pointing out to the chairman of the Board of Trade that he had signed the ship's articles and therefore was subject to maritime law.

"Yes," retorted Peirce, whose session with the lawyer in Liverpool the day before had not been unavailing, "but you are liable for criminal negligence. I was seasick. I went aft to lean over the rail. I slipped, I cried for help, I fell overboard. You yourself were on the bridge at the time and paid no attention to me." [8]

The chairman swallowed the story and turned Peirce loose, but not before remarking that most Americans were a little crazy and not strictly accountable, by British standards, for their conduct.

Reed and Peirce strolled out of the Board of Trade building free men, the former to undertake a walking tour of England while Peirce waited for him in London. Then they would journey to Paris together. There were no hard feelings. Even for Reed the ordeal of being under suspicion of murder ended happily enough when, a year later, he wrote a slightly fictionalized account of the episode which, after being rewritten by Julian Street, was published by the *Saturday Evening Post* as a short story titled "Overboard."

Reed hiked through England to the Welsh border; then to Stratford, where he made the ritual visit to Shakespeare's tomb, to Kenilworth, Oxford, and finally to London, where he was reunited with Peirce. At the end of August they walked to Canterbury and then to Dover. Now the question was, for Reed, how to cross the Channel in the most colorful, legend-making way. Julian Street remarked in his post-mortem profile of Reed, "He greatly enjoyed the limelight and made it his business to keep his friends—who were widely scattered and assorted—well stocked with anecdotes of his latest exploits."

Peirce wasn't interested in that sort of thing. His only concern was to get to Paris without becoming involved in another joust with the law. He suggested that they simply board a Channel boat and cross to Calais without attracting any more attention to themselves. Reed insisted that they should smuggle themselves across the Channel on a fishing boat. Peirce would not hear of it. Finally they compromised by stowing away on the regular boat to Calais. They were caught and had to pay their fares anyway. Much irritated, Peirce announced they he would continue to Paris alone while Reed went on his misadventurous way.

During his rambles around the French countryside, as he later told the story to Julian Street, Reed came upon a château beyond a low wall and rolling acres of lawn. It was late afternoon, he was weary, and a haystack on the grounds looked inviting. He invaded the property and flung himself on the haystack. Shortly after lighting a cigarette, he found himself confronted by a manservant in livery who had come out from the château. The servant told Reed that the chatelaine, a Mrs. Vanderbilt, had been watching from the window and was alarmed when she noticed someone smoking in her haystack. The servant added, "You'd better be on your way."

Reed, as he told it, did not choose to be given the bum's rush. "Did you say Mrs. Vanderbilt?" he asked the servant. "Mrs. Alfred Vanderbilt?"

The servant nodded.

Surely, said Reed in his haughtiest tone, Mrs. Vanderbilt would not object to John Silas Reed spending the night in her haystack.

The servant, taking it that he was a friend of the family, asked whether there was anything he could do to make Monsieur Reed more comfortable.

"Not at present, thank you," Reed loftily replied. "However, you may call me at half past six in the morning. I will breakfast at seven."

Apparently his impudence amused Mrs. Vanderbilt. The next morning he was awakened by the servant, who bore a silver tray with Reed's breakfast on it.

In Paris, he rejoined Peirce for a few days and was reunited with several of his classmates, including Joe Adams. Then he set out on the roads south to continue his walking tour to Spain. According to the story of his adventures that he told to Julian Street, he contributed mightily to the American image in France. "Struck by the indifference of the French to vagaries of costume, he arrayed himself in mismated stockings, one red, the other black, knickerbockers, and an enormous cowboy hat, and paraded the boulevards. At night he would seek out tough little cafés frequented by apaches—cutthroats who at that period were much feared.

"Later he continued his travels afoot in the south of France, enjoying occasional meetings with the riffraff of the road. Twice he fell in with thieves and in one case traveled with a group of them for several days. Missing his watch one morning after having slept with them in an old barn, he said nothing of his loss, but guessed which one had taken the watch, and on the next night stole it back. This episode caused no ill will on either side, and they parted friends, without ever having mentioned it." [9]

Through southern France and into northern Spain, he wandered in his solitary way. Wearing the corduroy of the Iberian peasantry, he journeyed through San Sebastián, Tolosa, Burgos, Valladolid, Medina del Campo, Toledo, and on to Madrid. What Walter Lippmann called his "inordinate desire to be arrested" was appeased in Medina del Campo, though John's classmate exaggerated slightly, when he covered Reed's grand tour in his "Legendary John Reed" essay, in the sentence "He spent a brief vacation in Europe and experimented with the jails of England, France and Spain." Actually, Reed was detained briefly in Medina del Campo while waiting for a train. It seemed that minor Spanish royalty were expected to pass through the station, and the local police were arresting all suspicious characters. Reed, in his peasant costume, was suspected of being an anarchist—not too far from the truth, at that. He was released as soon as the authorities were shown proof that he was an American citizen.[10]

Returning to Paris by train, in the third-class coach, he took a room in a cheap hotel, slept late, and raised hell at night with Waldo Peirce and other companions. He wrote to his brother that he had concluded that hiking around Europe by himself was not for him. "It's no fun to bum your way alone in this beast of a continent, because if you haven't anybody to laugh with, there isn't a hell of a lot of humor in it." He more or less fell in love with a young woman of Montmartre whose mercenary instincts were not entirely visible to him. One night, in the best tradition of the Latin Quarter, he brought a cabful of flowers to her room and buried her under them on the bed. The romance ended abruptly one night when she interrupted a tender moment to inquire, "Tell me, *chéri*, how do you make your money?"

Perhaps to get the taste of that experience out of his mouth, he proceeded on one more walking trip, to the south of France, to Avignon, Tarascon, and Marseilles. The great port city of Marseilles fascinated him; he wandered the Canebière, "talking with all the motherly old prostitutes, and childish young prostitutes, and Lascar sailors," as he wrote to his father. He added:

"Marseilles is a much more *romantique* city than Paris, if you know what I mean. For instance, you see the sun go down over the Louvre, and you know it's going down over the English channel and the Hebrides. You see it set at Marseilles, and it goes to bed behind the Pillars of Hercules, with the nations tacking out to sea from Marseilles to fish in their red-sailed feluccas. In Paris, the Seine flows into the Manche, where the fast mail-boats tear across from Havre to Southampton; at Marseilles, the turquoise water leads your eyes gently out through the jungle of masts to the blue horizons—beyond them are Italy and Greece, Asia and Egypt, Algiers and Spain! The wind comes down from Germany at Paris— the mistral brings to Marseilles a sound of solemn bells from Avignon and guitars from Arles, and the smell of Provence. At Paris, Notre Dame and the Louvre are elegant, spic-and-span; at

Marseilles, there is a Greek inscription on the walls of the Chateau St. Jean, at the entrance of the Old Port, which the waves of the Phoenician Sea have worn thin for centuries and centuries. Paris is fine and insidious and chic—Marseilles is bluff and masculine." [11]

Still under the spell of Provence, presumably, he impulsively fell in love again. He had gone over to Toulon to meet Waldo Peirce and other friends. In the party as they walked along the coast were two sisters, Madeleine and Marguerite Filon. At Monte Carlo, Reed proposed to Mademoiselle Madeleine, and was immediately accepted. A few days later he sailed for America, to make his fortune, as he told his friends, and marry Madeleine Filon.

The news was greeted dismally at home. He had returned to Portland to announce his engagement, and his parents were far from overjoyed at the prospect of his marrying a French girl they had never met.

His high spirits were also dashed by the discovery that his parents were pressed for money. He had always been encouraged to think of himself as a son of comfortable means if not of wealth. Now he learned that his father, having been defeated in his campaign for a seat in Congress, was finding it hard going in reviving his insurance business. C. J. had made a few admirers but many more enemies through his vigorous participation in the federal prosecution. The people who could afford to buy insurance were the ones who hated him the most.

Obviously his parents were not going to be able to help him establish himself as a writer and a husband, especially since his brother was still in college. He decided to make his fortune in New York, where anything was possible, even the dream of John Reed becoming a millionaire.

About the time John was resolving to mend his helter-skelter ways and make himself worthy of Mademoiselle Filon, Reed College was established in his hometown. It had no connection with John Reed's family, but was founded by bequests from Simeon G. Reed, a Portland pioneer, and his wife. Its first president was William T. Foster. On the coincidence of those two names, in the years that followed a myth sprang up that Reed College was a Communist-dominated institution. Coincidental though it was, it contributed toward the feeling of Portlanders that it would have been better if John Reed had been born elsewhere.

"That neither John Reed nor any of his family had any connection by blood or act with Reed College mattered not at all," as the late Portland-based historian Stewart Holbrook has written. "The myth was born, and in time became so adamant that there are Oregonians who still believe that John Reed founded and supported Reed College for the express purpose of training young commissars. Lesser canards have ruined institutions. . . . The John Reed myth got the stoutest kind of support from the fact that an obscure labor leader named William Z. Foster had just headed a tremendous and violent strike, and had thus become a national front-page menace. Well, wasn't he the same William Foster who had trained young communists at Reed College, of which he was president?" William Z. Foster later became head of the American Communist Party. "Nobody," added Holbrook, "connected with Reed College at that period, or since, has ever doubted the sinister effect of the John Reed and William Z. Foster myth. From it stemmed a scandalous trinity of 'communism, atheism and free love' which was so firmly attached to Reed College that a quarter of a century has not wholly dissipated the libel. . . ." [12]

John Reed would never be a home-town hero.

4

A ROOM ON
WASHINGTON SQUARE

On arriving in New York, John Reed gravitated to Greenwich Village as swiftly and inevitably as a steel filing attracted to a magnet. His first move on arrival was to join the Harvard Club, his second to look up the old family friend Lincoln Steffens, and his third to establish himself in the Village, then beginning its most idyllic and romantic period. For a young man contemplating marriage and hoping to make his fortune, however, it was hardly the place to make a start. It was, in fact, an excellent place to forget about taking up the burdens of supporting a wife and family.

That, undoubtedly, was what his father had in mind when he wrote Steffens asking the middle-aged editor and ultraliberal crusader to keep an eye on his son. Steffens believed that C. J.'s prescriptions for his son's happiness were among the wisest and most generous words of parental solicitude ever uttered, but there may have been a concealed motive behind them: the unvoiced hope that Jack would forget about Mademoiselle Filon. The senior Reed wrote Steffens: "Get him a job, let him see everything, but don't let him be anything for a while. Don't let him get a conviction right away or a business or a career, like me. Let him play." [1]

Steffens took his roles as surrogate father to Jack Reed and as a recruiting agent for American social reform with the utmost seriousness. Many a promising young man was guided on the path leftward by Lincoln Steffens, acting in his capacity as dean of the muckrakers and a figure much admired by young intellectuals, writers, and journalists, becoming to American liberalism what Bertrand Russell was to become to the British protest from the left, but none of them blazed up under his inspiration so quickly and hotly as young Jack Reed. Steffens, as Reed wrote a half-dozen years later, was "full of understanding, with the breath of the world clinging to him." Steffens insisted, "You can do anything you want to" and, Reed affirmed, "I believed him." [2]

Despite the fact that they were separated by a generation, there was a strong attraction between Reed and Steffens, based largely on the fact that both were romantics to the marrow. Steffens, a neat little man with bangs combed carefully over his high forehead, throbbed with enthusiasm for his personal creed, which he described as Christian anarchism. He may well have been the only Christian anarchist in the country. To Max Eastman, later as close to Reed as Steffens was, he was one of the "Sentimental Rebels," an obscurantist brimming with vague and naïve hopes for social and economic justice. "Steffens," Eastman wrote, "learned to be happy without hard thinking by developing a kittenish delight in paradox. If he could find a pause in which to remark that 'the good men are worse than the bad,' or that 'enough organization will disorganize anything,' or some such sly jab at rationality, he would feel that he had arrived at the end and summit of the life of reason." He often yearned to admonish Steffens, "Steff, let's lay aside our cleverness for once and try to think things through!" Steffens was a brilliant journalist, Eastman conceded, but seemed to him "a sprightly and rather self-pleased cork bobbing about on currents of which it had no understanding and upon which it had no effect." It was only Steffens' kindness and his honest search for the truth, Eastman said, that impelled Eastman and others of a more vigorous revolutionary school to "join him in the conspiracy to coddle his frail and rather childlike vanity." [3]

Steffens used his influence to obtain for Reed an assistant editor's post on the staff of the *American Magazine*, which Steffens had recently left and which now was the literary home of many of the old muckrakers. The more senior members of the staff included Ida M. Tarbell, Albert Jay Nock, Ray Stannard Baker, and William Allen White. Reed's duties consisted mostly of weeding out unsolicited manuscripts, reading proof, helping with the make-up, and contributing to the newly established "Department of Interesting People." The first profile he wrote for "Interesting People" was one of Professor Copeland. Copey was fussy about his personal publicity and kept wiring directions to his former student on how he was to be presented, particularly in the choice of photographs. "Stress doubtless on function as teacher not on so-called wit and humor," the Professor telegraphed Reed. "Don't use snapshot. . . . No friend of mine would use snapshot." He sent along a recent studio photograph of himself and then complained because Reed hadn't assured him it would be used with the article. "Why haven't you acknowledged photo sent Harvard Club . . . Never man so benevolent and so churlish. You have put a bankrupt to the expense of two night letters. Now assure him you have the cabinet [photograph] to be enlarged if you like and that you have destroyed snapshot and negative." Copeland was so pleased with the result that he invited Reed to come to his Hollis Hall rooms and share a glass of yellow chartreuse and a biscuit with him. "If you cannot come then," he added, "when are you coming to dine with me? We could dine that evening at the dreary old Union and talk of several things that concern us both. Don't let anybody put the idea of the sailing ship and the Horn out of your mind. Think of Conrad!" [4]

Reed had been considering an adventure before the mast, possibly in emulation of Jack London, who was setting out on a voyage around the Horn aboard a four-masted bark with all the publicity that usually accompanied his voyages. Within a few months he had forgotten all about making a million and plunging into marriage. During the spring of 1911 he found New York so enchanting to him as an unfettered bachelor that marriage, in fact, was unthinkable. And in the bridal month of June, much to the relief of his parents and the approval of Lincoln Steffens, he broke off his engagement to Madeleine Filon. He had even found it irksome, he said, to have to write his fiancée and "be passionate every other day."

He had moved into romantically shabby rooms at 42 Washington Square, which he shared with three friends from Harvard—Robert Andrews, Robert E. Rogers, and Alan Osgood—and which was a stopping-off place for other classmates, including Joe Adams and Alan Seeger, who was an unpaying and dreamy-eyed guest until he sailed off to Paris and his rendezvous with the Foreign Legion. Reed's room was in the back and gave him an almost Parisian view of the chimney pots and eccentric rooftops of the Village. Days he worked at the *American*, and nights he roved the city soaking up impressions of its crowded streets, its swarming tenements, its overwhelming diversity. "Within a block of my house," he related in his autobiographical essay, "was all the adventure in the world; within a mile was every foreign country. . . . I know Chinatown, and Little Italy, and the quarter of the Syrians; the marionette theater, Sharkey's and McSorley's saloons, the Bowery lodging houses and the places where the tramps gather in the winter; the Haymarket, the German Village, and all the dives of the Tenderloin." [5] He talked with whores who walked the streets of "Satan's Circus," the section west of Sixth Avenue in the Thirties, with drunken sailors in the bars along South Street, with pushcart merchants in the narrow streets of the lower East Side, with gangsters at the Five Points.

The city intoxicated him, sent him reeling back to the giddiness of his adolescence when he saw visions of the Holy Grail over

Morristown's football field, and gave him sensations that he could only convey in exclamatory verse:

> This spawning filth, these monuments uncouth
> Are but her wild, ungovernable youth.
> But the skyscrapers, dwarfing earthly things—
> Ah, that is how she sings!
> Wake to the vision shining in the sun!
> Earth's ancient, conquering races rolled in one,
> A world beginning,—and yet nothing done.[6]

But the gay center of Jack Reed's life was the apartment at 42 Washington Square, and his roommates were his closest associates of the time. Lincoln Steffens, distraught at the recent death of his wife, decided to move into the building simply to warm himself and, at forty-four, to recover some of his own youthful enthusiasm amid the high spirits of Reed and his companions in the new Bohemia. The Village, with its maze of narrow streets radiating from Washington Square and lower Fifth Avenue, was flowering with a new generation of aspiring talent; only a few doors away from Jack's apartment, at No. 61 Washington Square South, was the House of Genius, which symbolized an earlier Village and at times had sheltered O. Henry, Willa Cather, Theodore Dreiser, Frank Norris, and Stephen Crane.

Steffens never regretted moving into the apartment under Jack's; it revived him, as he testified in his autobiography twenty years later. "I used to go early to bed and to sleep, but I liked it when Jack, a big, growing, happy being, would slam into my room and wake me up to tell me about the 'most wonderful thing in the world' that he had seen, been, or done that night. Girls, plays, bums, I.W.W.'s, strikers—each experience was vivid in him, a story, which he often wrote; every person, every idea; Bill Haywood, some prostitute down and out on a park bench, a vaudeville dancer; socialism; the I.W.W. program—all were on a live level with him. Everything was the most wonderful thing in the world. Jack and his crazy young friends were indeed the most wonderful thing in the world." [7]

By Christmas Eve of 1911, Steffens was still delighted, wearing though their enthusiasms and antic humors could be, with Jack and his apartment-mates. He had just taken the young man out to dinner and listened, over a bottle of wine, to a poem Jack had written. Jack and his friends were "all my friends; and I theirs," he wrote Laura Steffens, his sister. "In one way or another I've served them all, love-scrapes, jobs, and money troubles. It's the way I have of settling old scores, not on my original creditors, but on the next generation." He even took the credit for the breaking off of Jack's engagement. "I got Jack clear; by insisting only that he not marry unless he loved the girl. He didn't really love her. So it was called off and no harm done." [8]

Many of Reed's discussions with the older man naturally concerned their mutual conviction that before America could realize her glorious destiny the social order would have to be shaken up and rearranged. Steffens encouraged him to roam the city and see for himself the abyss that separated the rich and privileged on Fifth Avenue and the crowded masses of sweatshop workers in lower Manhattan and the red-brick jungles of the West Side. He also introduced Reed to radicals and reformers of all kinds, and "all the hair-splitting Utopians." But the postgraduate course that taught him the most, Reed affirmed, was his solitary walks through the city. His sympathy for the underdog, which had been growing steadily through the years, was quickened more by what he saw on the streets and heard in alcoholic confessionals, on park benches or in cheap saloons, than by all the theorizing and haranguing of the radical intellectuals.

"On the whole," he recalled as a mature revolutionary of "almost thirty," "ideas did not mean much to me. I had to see. In my rambles about the city I couldn't help but observe the ugliness of poverty and all its train of evils, the cruel inequality between the rich people who had too many motor cars and the poor people who didn't have enough to eat. It didn't come to me from books that the workers produced all the wealth of the world, which went to those who did not earn it." [9]

Others who came to know him during his first year in New York were several degrees cooler toward his ebullient personality than was Lincoln Steffens. Already he was becoming the "wonder boy" of the Village, but men a few years older than he, who had moved uptown and away from their own scenes of youthful discovery, considered him a trifle too juvenile, too eager to make an impression. Thomas Beer, the future biographer of Stephen Crane, met him at the Yale Club and thought him a little too eager to dominate the conversation. He was more impressed a short time later when he met Reed on Riverside Drive and there was no crowd around to be dazzled and played up to. Alone, he observed, Reed was less of a performer, less conscious of his self-conceived role of a Byron reborn. "I said that the Hudson looked cold as Puget Sound. So Jack Reed began to talk about the Northwest, and was not a playboy about it. We talked for a long time about Puget Sound and the smell of burning cedarbark in Portland. I told him about a Chinese junk in the bay of Seattle, and he told me about a blind man who grew roses in a backyard in Tacoma. He did all the talking, soon, standing with his hands in the pockets of a loose overcoat, staring at the river. He was no more a brilliant talker than he was a brilliant writer, but he talked about Tacoma, and the long Sound, mist, Swedes, ramshackle brothels strung up slopes. He said nothing profound, but he made beauty talking. Men do that when they talk about things they have loved much, and Americans often talk very well when they are not trying to be wise or funny." [10]

During that first year, Reed had to live off his beginner's salary at the *American,* because most of the sketches, stories, and poems he submitted to the *Saturday Evening Post, Collier's,* and other slick magazines were quickly rejected. He did manage to sell an editorial to *Collier's* on immigration policy, but *Smart Set* agreed to publish a short story only after considerable revision and delay. To help pad out his income, he was introduced to a well-known woman illustrator who needed someone to write the commentary under a series of drawings of famous Europeans. The artist took an instant dislike to Reed, considering him a rather conceited and overbearing young man. Perhaps to get rid of him, she suggested that Reed ad-lib an interview with an imaginary duchess who had just arrived in New York. Eagerly Reed met the challenge. He described how his calling card was dispatched to the duchess through the pneumatic tubes of the establishment at which she was staying, comparing the tubes to the intestines, and how it was "evacuated" at the other end in the duchess's apartment. Reed's extended metaphor, and the relish with which it was conveyed, appalled the lady. She expressed herself frankly on the subject of indelicacy. Reed replied with equal tartness, and they agreed that collaboration was impossible.[11]

Julian Street met him shortly after he came to New York, when he agreed to rework Reed's account of his cattle-boat adventure, which they sold to the *Saturday Evening Post*. On first acquaintance Reed seemed "perverse and disputatious," with a mind "crammed with ideas" and shrewd green eyes "which took in everything." A "little devil armed with a sharp lance" was "riding always on his tongue." In his eagerness to soak up experience, Reed "went after it with the scattering zest of a big, shaggy puppy hunting new objects on which to try his teeth." [12]

Reed quickly absorbed the anarchist attitudes toward authority in all forms, Street observed. One night Reed showed up at Street's house with a face bruised from an encounter with a couple of thugs. "I had less than a dollar in my pocket, but they didn't get it," Reed announced. Street suggested that he report the incident to the police, but Reed indignantly refused. In time, Street came to understand the younger man better. "Lawlessness fascinated him, and if he was consistent in one thing it was his sympathy for the under dog. He was for the under dog even if it was a mad dog. He was for it even when it bit him. Footpads were of the downtrodden masses, so he could forgive them for knocking him on the head; the police, on the other hand, represented law, order and vested authority, to all of which he had an instinctive aversion."

Jack, he said, also took to the traditional Bohemian attitudes of Greenwich Village with alacrity. He conceived of the Village as "another Latin Quarter . . . in which it was correct to wear long hair, be dunned by one's landlady, owe bills at little restaurants, and generally jeer at the conventions and the dull folk who heeded them." It was the old story, in fact, of the young nonconformist doggedly conforming to nonconformism.

Since it was considered romantic and proper for a poet to miss a few meals, Jack "sometimes did a little amateur starving," as Street put it. His strongest trait, it appeared to the slightly older writer, was self-dramatization.

A woman friend who was in the hospital for several weeks told of Jack's visit to her. On that occasion his hunger was genuine enough. "The nurse brought in a tray on which were a squab and other delicacies," she related. "I couldn't eat, and I noticed that Jack kept eying the tray. 'Aren't you going to eat that dinner?' he asked, and when I told him I couldn't he drew up his chair and made a clean sweep of it. I remarked that he seemed hungry. You know the way he used to wriggle, like a big puppy, expressing his joy. He did that and said: 'I was. I've had nothing but a cup of coffee since last night.' While I remained in the hospital he came and ate my dinner every evening until my appetite returned, and after that we shared it." [13]

Within his first year at 42 Washington Square, by his tireless enthusiasm, by exhibiting his personality on all possible occasions and his talent in whatever market place offered an opportunity, he became a Village celebrity. Then, quite quickly, he began attaining recognition uptown, principally in the magazine offices. *Collier's*, the *Saturday Evening Post*, *Forum*, the *Century*, and *Metropolitan Magazine* began showing an interest in him and publishing his short stories and articles. He had the quick facility for journalism, for comment on the topical, which is always marketable.

Downtown he attracted attention to himself by always appearing in top form and at the top of his voice, joking, telling stories, "perpetually *en rose*," in whatever company he found himself, whether it was a studio party in the Village, a beer-drinking contest at McSorley's Old Ale House, or one of the impromptu forums at which more serious problems were discussed. He couldn't bear going unnoticed. His classmate Van Wyck Brooks noted that Reed was "an actor in his way," and included him as an exemplar of what he called "The Confident Years." Certainly Reed brimmed with self-confidence; he was always the cheerleader, whether it was before the Harvard stands at a football game, in a gathering of would-be revolutionaries, on a soapbox before a throng of desperate workingmen on strike, or at the downfall of an empire. In a few months, Brooks observed, Reed "had become the wonder-boy of Greenwich Village, the Liberal Club, McSorley's saloon and Polly's [a restaurant operated by Polly Holladay, an anarchist, and much favored by the Village]. The Jo Hancock of Max Eastman's *Venture,* 'young and irrepressibly in love with life,' an exuberant satirical poet and a writer of stories about upper-class Pharisees and hypocrites and 'Haymarket girls,' he was one of many who were proving the truth of Aubrey Beardsley's saying that the present, in literature and art, was the day of the harlot." [14]

Reed made himself a personage among the Village's many other striking personalities—most of them much more notorious, famous, talented, or exhibitionistic than he was. The year 1912 was the Village's magic year, as its historians (notably Allen Churchill, in *The Improper Bohemians*) have pointed out. In the year that saw Woodrow Wilson's election to the Presidency—and in which Eugene Debs received a million votes as the Socialist candidate for the same office—there was great intellectual ferment and unrest. The younger generation, for whom the Villagers acted as self-appointed standard-bearers, had "awakened to the fact," as Joseph Wood Krutch epitomized it, "that both the ends which its fathers proposed to themselves and the emotions from which they drew their strength seemed irrelevant and remote." Emma Goldman, the anarchist who made the middle class believe that the devil, after all, might be a woman, was publishing her magazine *Mother Earth* in the Village and demanding equal sex rights for women. Her own lover was Alexander Berkman, the man who had shot at and wounded the steel magnate Henry Clay Frick as a gesture of disapproval during the Homestead strike. Isadora Duncan, the high priestess of the dance, was also proclaiming sexual freedom

and acting vigorously on her own proclamations. Gertrude Vanderbilt Whitney, whose husband was worth two hundred million
dollars, had established herself as a sculptor in a studio on Mac-
Dougal Alley. J. G. Phelps Stokes and William English Walling
were millionaires to their brokers and Socialists to their friends
and neighbors in the Village. Max Eastman, Harry Kemp, Big
Bill Haywood, Frank Harris (the odd little Englishman who
would bellow on making an entrance, "I am Frank Harris, the son
of man—and the son of God!"), Carlo Tresca, and many other
men of talent and/or intellect had appeared on the scene.

Yet Jack Reed made himself the golden boy of the Village, and
not only through an instinct for self-dramatization and a genius
for publicizing himself. He caught the Village's spirit, embodied
it as Edna St. Vincent Millay was to do a few years later, and
captured that spirit in verse that still vibrates with the hopes and
attitudes of the generation which filled the trenches of World
War I.

He wrote the verse subsequently published as *The Day in Bohemia, or Life Among the Artists* during the summer of 1912. It
was composed during the several months following his father's
death. C. J. died suddenly on July 1, 1912, worn out by his struggle to make a living and send both of his sons through Harvard.
He died shortly after returning to Portland from attending the
graduation of his younger son, Harry. As his older son wrote in a
brief and loving memorial, he died "with a proud shield of Honor
at his side" and was buried with civic honors bestowed by men
who, as Jack knew, were not at all convulsed by grief over his passing.

To please his mother, Jack remained home that summer and
into the fall, though it was hard to stay away from New York and
the glittering future he foresaw for himself. He was comforted in
exile by a letter from Lincoln Steffens, who said he could not express his grief over the senior Reed's death, and added, "I am with
you these days . . . and if I can be of any use, Jack, in any way,—
that you know, too." [15]

To ease his own sorrow and occupy the time Reed wrote reams

of verse. One poem, titled "Sangar," celebrated Lincoln Steffens' activities during the trial of J. B. McNamara and others charged with dynamiting the Los Angeles *Times* building and causing the deaths of twenty-one persons. Steffens claimed that his personal pleas to the ruling powers of Los Angeles resulted in a compromise by which the state agreed not to demand the death penalty if McNamara and his codefendants pleaded guilty. He had arranged this, Steffens said, by convincing the local power structure that "the doctrine of forgiveness instead of punishment for the sinner is sound." McNamara and his fellow conspirators had dynamited the bitterly antiunion *Times* building as part of their campaign for recognition of the Structural Iron Workers Union and its bargaining rights.

Just after finishing "Sangar," Jack wrote to Harriet Monroe, the editor of the newly established *Poetry* magazine in Chicago, telling her about the poem and the trials of a poet battling his way out of the swamps of commercialism. "There are many of us who have published in the magazines," he wrote Miss Monroe on September 11, 1912, "and who, without any feeling that a materialistic public refuses us recognition, still feel that the magazines are degrading the Short Story, for which they were originally responsible. I am myself on the staff of a magazine, and have often heard the editors say that poetry is a declining art. . . . I have found that among men of whatever class, if they are deeply stirred by emotion, poetry appeals; as indeed, all the arts appeal. The apathetic, mawkishly religious middle class are our enemies. A labor-leader, for example, who has been indicted for complicity in the dynamite plots, read aloud to me more naturally and beautifully than I have ever heard a verse read. And I think that wherever men are deeply stirred, all their living becomes attuned to the unheard systole and diastole of their pulses. Art must cease, I think, to be for the aesthetic enjoyment of a few highly sensitive minds. It must go back to its original sources." [16]

It was the first of Reed's manifestoes against the "mawkishly religious middle class," firm evidence that he was well started along the revolutionary road.

"Sangar" itself won him praise, when it was published in *Poetry*, from Edwin Arlington Robinson, Sara Teasdale, Louis Unter-meyer, and others whose opinions were respected. But not from its subject, Lincoln Steffens, to whom it was dedicated. Steffens was "Sangar," the peacemaker who had "borne the brunt" and was slain for his efforts. Reed pictured him as ascending to an allegori-cal heaven and being welcomed there:

> Oh, there was joy in Heaven when Sangar came.
> Sweet Mary wept, and bathed and bound his wounds,
> And God the Father healed him of despair,
> And Jesus gripped his hand, and laughed and laughed.

Apparently it was the line referring to Christ laughing that con-vinced Steffens that Reed was making satirical fun of his efforts to effect a compromise in the McNamara case. On returning to New York from Los Angeles, Steffens learned that the intelligentsia despised him for it, for "betraying the class struggle with a sancti-monious imitation of Christ," as Max Eastman put it. "We talked of him as an old-maidish fuss-budget who ought to be teaching a Sunday-school class."

And it was Reed's poem, Steffens believed, that expressed the derision of the people whose opinion mattered the most to him. "When I got back to New York, I felt defeated, disgraced some-how, and helpless. . . . Jack Reed, 'my own boy,' wrote a fierce poem, 'Sangar,' denouncing me. . . . At a gathering of writers, artists, radicals, they all hated me."

Jack was appalled at Steffens' reaction to his earnest tribute, but finally managed to persuade the older man that he had not been poking fun at him.

During the months in Portland he also composed the verses for *The Day in Bohemia*, which was privately printed in a paperback volume. It encapsulated his life at 42 Washington Square, and in compelling rhythm described his friends and the hectic gaiety of their nights in the studios, saloons, cafés, garrets, and cellars of the Village. He told of the view from his window, with its Italian tenements and their lines of varicolored laundry "like battle-riven pennants fluttering" in the air, and of the room itself:

> The dust it flies in at the window,
>> The smells they come in at the door,
> Our trousers lie meek where we threw them last week
>> Bestrewing the maculate floor.

> The gas isn't all that it should be,
>> It flickers—and yet I declare
> There's pleasure or near it for young men of spirit
>> At Forty-two Washington Square!

The self-satisfied burghers in their overstuffed apartments to the north might think they were leading lives of squalor and despair down in the Village, but they were wrong.

> Yet we are free who live in Washington Square,
>> We dare to think as Uptown wouldn't dare,
> Blazing our nights with arguments uproarious;
>> What care we for a dull old world censorious
> When each is sure he will fashion something glorious?

He would concede that "life among the artists" knew its moments of discomfort and inconvenience, but the Village's atmosphere of freedom more than made up for them.

> In winter the water is frigid,
> In summer the water is hot;
> And we're forming a club for controlling the tub
> For there's only one bath to the lot.
> You shave in unlathering Croton,
> If there's water at all, which is rare—
> But the life isn't bad for a talented lad
> At Forty-two Washington Square!

> . . . nobody questions your morals,
> And nobody asks for the rent—
> There's no one to pry if we're tight, you and I,
> Or demand how our evenings are spent.

The furniture's ancient but plenty,
The linen is spotless and fair,
O life is a joy to a broth of a boy
At Forty-two Washington Square!

In his journey-in-verse around the Village, Reed also pilloried a number of familiar types whom he did not consider worthy of sharing in the joys of Bohemia. One was the artist he called Umbillicus, who spent eleven years in Europe studying the great masters.

At last he knew so much, he was so deft,
That neither vision, fire, nor self was left.

He also launched satiric shafts at nonproducing poets, girls whose role in life was "simply to inspire," rich men playing at being patrons of the arts, and female cranks who "talk about talking and think about thinking, / And swallow each other without even blinking," but for the most part his *Day in Bohemia* was a joyous, rollicking, and touchingly innocent celebration of life in Greenwich Village. As much as anything else, it made him a celebrity, the poet laureate of the new Bohemia, when he returned to New York.

And the self-made legend was continually refurbished by his Puckish behavior, his antic sense of humor, his tilting with convention, his boyish winsomeness, which was soon to be obscured, but never entirely disappeared, as he became more deeply involved in the revolutionary movement. The idea of turning society upside down was taking a firmer grip, but if he had anything to say it would be done with style, with bravura. He proposed to mount the barricades with a song on his lips, and manifestoes written in rhyme. His style was more that of a Villon than a D'Annunzio. The tousled poet-rebel was his chosen role in life, and he would play it to perfection.

Even his fecklessness could be turned to account, and made charmingly picturesque anecdotes, told about him wherever Villagers gathered. One night he went to a party in the upper reaches of Manhattan. His hostess appointed him to take a girl home who lived far downtown. He did not feel obliged to announce that he was almost broke. The sensible thing would have been to walk to the nearest bus stop or subway station, but Jack had his own way of doing things, of turning the ordinary into the spectacular. He called a cab, climbed in with the girl, and told the driver to take him "seventy-six cents' worth downtown." To the girl he explained, "That's all I've got, so we'll have to walk the rest of the way." Seventy-six cents' worth of the way downtown, the cab stopped, and Jack and the girl continued on foot—for forty blocks.[17]

He even charmed the dignified and strait-laced Ida Tarbell, who was his colleague on the staff of the *American*. Occasionally she invited him to spend the weekend at her summer home in Redding Ridge, Connecticut, although she was never quite sure in what guise—or condition—he would appear. On one occasion, striking dismay in his hostess and her staidly respectable guests, it was as a hobo. Jack had set out for Redding Ridge with enough money for his railroad fare, but on his way to Grand Central he caught sight of a bright-orange tie in the window of a Fifth Avenue haberdashery. He jumped off the bus, spent all his money on the tie, and hopped a freight instead of riding the cushions. When he arrived at Miss Tarbell's home just before dinner, his face and hands were blackened by soot, his coat was torn, and his trousers were out at the seat, but his tie was gorgeous. Dinner was delayed while Jack took a bath and one of Miss Tarbell's friends cleaned and mended his clothing. That evening, unabashed, he dominated the conversation by recalling in detail his conversation with a tramp-philosopher he had met while riding the rods.

The next morning while walking around Miss Tarbell's property he discovered a magnificent slope wooded with oak and pine which he declared would make a splendid natural amphitheater. Overflowing with enthusiasm, he led Miss Tarbell out to the slope and exclaimed, "It's a perfect situation for a Greek theater. I've never seen anything to equal it!" He showed her how the trees could be trimmed on the curving hillside, where the stage would be placed on the level ground below. Miss Tarbell pointed out that the property did not belong to her, but was part of a neighbor's estate. No matter. Jack spent the rest of the day rushing around, drawing sketches, interviewing the neighbor and finding out how much he wanted for the piece of land on which the theater would be located. Where was the money coming from? He would raise it among his "rich friends," Jack assured Miss Tarbell.

The following morning he roared off to New York declaring they would be hearing from him, with the money pledged, in a few days. Miss Tarbell never heard another word of the project. Years later, however, she met a wealthy woman who told her that Jack had approached her for a pledge of assistance. "He described the possibilities so charmingly that I seriously considered putting money into it. But he went away and I never heard from him again. I've always wondered what happened. Did he ever build the theater?"

Not in the physical sense, Miss Tarbell had to reply. But, as she later confided, she knew that in Jack's imagination the theater had been constructed and great dramas were being enacted on its stage, the whole thing created more beautifully in his mind than any marble-columned structure raised on the hillside. And then, after it had become real to him for a few days or a week, he had wiped it from his mind and gone leaping and bounding after some other great project.

Dreamer though he was, he could buckle down to a specific task and see it through. Shortly after he returned from Portland he had joined the Dutch Treat Club, an organization of writers, editors, artists, and musicians who put on an annual show. Julian Street was a member and urged him to join; so were such successful men as Irvin S. Cobb, James Montgomery Flagg, Charles Hanson Towne, Will Irwin, Charles Dana Gibson, and Owen Johnson. He was asked to write the lyrics for a show to be called "Everymagazine" and presented at the annual dinner at Delmonico's in the winter of 1912-1913. It was acclaimed one of the cleverest ever presented by the club. His lyrics jabbed artfully at all the pretensions of the magazine business and the people involved in it. There was his ode to the artist, which began:

> The artist never pros-ti-tutes
> His ge-ni-us, you bet your boots!

And there were his sallies at the slick-paper magazines, delivered by an old lady in bombazine seated in a rocker with her knitting needles clicking, who represented the literary monthlies:

> You are mistresses of Mammon;
>   I'm a literary virgin—
> All the warmness of a salmon,
>   All the passion of a sturgeon.
> I'm aristocratic, very,
> I'm a live obituary
> Of the giants literary
>   Who have given up the ghost.
> In illuminating snatches
>   Since the spring of Sixty-one
> I've been publishing dispatches
>   From the battle of Bull Run.

William Randolph Hearst's money-grubbing *Cosmopolitan* was ticked off as "refreshment for the tired business man":

> Every month I'm full of spice
> And naughty Robert Chambers makes it nice.
> Some lingerie, a glimpse of stocking,
> Lips unlocking, nothing shocking . . .

The curtain rang down to hearty applause, and several of the members told Jack he ought to consider writing for Broadway. Certainly, his fellow clubmen observed, he did not lack a sense of opportunism. Emboldened by the liquor he had consumed, Jack went around the tables peddling copies of *The Day in Bohemia*.

By now he believed that he could achieve success on his own terms. The acclaim given his Dutch Treat show indicated that he could write for the commercial theater and the slick magazines; he could keep one foot in the Village, the other in the market place uptown. He had already decided that he could not be content merely with making money. He also had to be a poet and revolutionary. The well-fed but anxious-eyed men who were fellow members of the Dutch Treat Club were only an articulate sector of the *bourgeoisie*, eternally chattering about royalties, box-office returns, and subsidiary rights. The big money was fine, but it did not warm you like the talk of your friends in the Village. The nation was being shaken by a series of strikes, and the cause of the workingman was their cause. Even while he was making a splash with the moneyed writers and editors uptown, he was studying the causes of the strikes. His investigations, he wrote later, "brought home to me hard the knowledge that the manufacturers get all they can out of labor, pay as little as they must, and permit the existence of great masses of the miserable unemployed in order to keep wages down; that the forces of the States are on the side of property, against the propertyless." [18]

It was also vividly apparent that if he wanted to be a commercial success he would have to write the sort of pap he detested. The slick magazines would take a sugar-spun love story or a clean-cut tale of adventure, but anything that approached the realistic quality of the life he observed in the streets of New York was quickly rejected. A case in point was a short story he had written shortly before being summoned to Portland. Titled "Where the Heart Is," it was about a girl who was employed at the Haymarket, the big Tenderloin dance hall on Sixth Avenue. Martha was a dime-a-dance girl, with prostitution as an amiable side line. She also had vague cultural aspirations. Taking her meager savings, she went on a sight-seeing tour of Europe, met a wealthy Portuguese, and was taken to Brazil as his mistress. Her luxurious life did not satisfy her, and she was homesick for Sixth Avenue. So she returned to dancing with the hooligans at the Haymarket.

The script made the rounds of the mass-circulation magazines and was turned down by the men who had praised the cleverness of his lyrics for "Everymagazine." Even his own journal, the *American*, rejected it. He had to be more careful in his choice of subject matter, he was told; then he could join the ranks of such money-makers as Jack London, Robert W. Chambers, and George Barr McCutcheon. Become a hack, in other words. He knew he could do it, but it would not be worth the effort.

Finally one day he called the editor of the *Masses*, which had recently been rejuvenated. It had been founded in 1911 as a Socialist monthly. A year later it was foundering, and the proposal was made to merge it with a woman's-suffrage periodical. Instead, its backers, including the millionaire William English Walling, Mary Heaton Vorse, Horatio Winslow, Art Young, Ellis O. Jones, and Eugene Wood, decided in the fall of 1912 to shake it up under a new editorship and make it a more aggressive journal of social and economic reform. Max Eastman, a tall handsome young man who had been teaching at Columbia, was invited to undertake the job. For a score of years after that, converting from mild Socialism to advocacy of upheaval in every sector of American life, and finally to Communism, it became the nightmare in newsprint of all who hoped to keep things as they were.

Shortly after he took over the editorship of the *Masses*, Max Eastman has recounted, he received a phone call one morning from someone who announced: "I am a person named John Reed. I work on the *American Magazine*, and I've got a story they won't print. I'd like to offer it to the *Masses*."

Send it along, Eastman told his caller.

"No," Reed replied, "I'm right here on 11th Street and I'll bring it over. I want to see you."

Eastman reluctantly agreed, and a few minutes later he was meeting a man whom he would grow to love and admire. His first impressions of Reed, however, were not favorable. "He had a knobby and too filled-out face that reminded me, both in form and color, of a potato. He was dressed in a smooth, brown suit with round pants' legs and a turned-over starched collar, and seemed rather small and rather distracted. He stood or moved about the room all through his visit and kept looking in every direction except that in which he was addressing his words." Eastman later wrote that he was "hopelessly embarrassed" by Reed and wanted nothing more than to get rid of him.[19]

As soon as he read "Where the Heart Is," however, Eastman knew that his first impression of Reed had been mistaken. He had suspected on taking over the editorship that a magazine like the

Masses, which published material that the big magazines would not touch, "would probably be filled for the most part with claptrap." The "unlabored grace" of Reed's story convinced him that the *Masses* could be made into something worth while, that "there really was a creative literature stifled by commercial journalism" waiting for an outlet. He published "Where the Heart Is" in the January, 1913, issue, urged Reed to submit contributions every month, and placed Reed's name on the masthead as a contributing editor.

At a subsequent meeting, Eastman recalled, Reed was "dressed now in a soft collar and a tweed suit that made him seem as big as he was, and as kindly and sagacious." [20]

Always quick to move in on an opportunity, Reed had brought with him a statement that he proposed the *Masses* publish below its masthead in every issue. It declared that the periodical would publish "exactly what we please." Readers would not be conciliated. "The broad purpose of *The Masses* is a social one: to everlastingly attack old systems, old morals, old prejudices. . . . We intend to be arrogant, impertinent, in bad taste, but not vulgar. We will be bound by no one creed or theory of social reform, but will express them all, provided they be radical." He also proposed that the *Masses* lunge at the specters that haunted middle-class minds "with a rapier rather than a broad-axe, with frankness rather than innuendo."

Eastman picked up a few of Reed's phrases, but composed his own manifesto. Jack was not affronted. From then on, with the *Masses* as his base, he marched steadily toward the goal of becoming an active revolutionary.

5

MAN-EATING
MABEL

In the early months of 1913 the talk of the Village was the salon established at 23 Fifth Avenue by Mabel Dodge, better known in later years as Mabel Dodge Luhan, friend and patroness of genius, who would shelter D. H. Lawrence at Taos and write a four-volume autobiography remarkable for its candid recollection of four husbands and a steady procession of lovers. She and her second husband, Edwin Dodge, a Bostonian whose independent income matched her own, had returned from Italy late in 1912 so that her son by her first marriage could attend an American school. At her first glimpse of the New York sky line in ten years, she was overcome by grief at the prospect of repatriation, and in a trembling voice told her ten-year-old son, "Remember it is ugly in America. We have left everything worthwhile behind us. America is all machinery and money making and factories—it is ugly, ugly, ugly." [1]

With characteristic energy she set about making her own corner of the homeland as beautiful and interesting as possible. The Dodges moved into a high-ceilinged and spacious apartment at 23 Fifth Avenue, a four-story brownstone which soon became the center of Village intellectual life and sexual intrigue. She painted all her woodwork white, ordered the walls papered white, furnished her drawing room with French chairs and chaise longues, and hoisted a white porcelain chandelier lighted by candles to the ceiling.[2] Finally she was satisfied with her setting, but where were the people who would amuse her and satisfy the cravings of her restless mind? Edwin Dodge suggested that she establish a salon to distract herself. "It was ironic," she wrote, "that Edwin, in his effort to help me, launched the boat that sailed away and left him behind."

The skipper of that frail, unseaworthy craft was John Reed.

Early in 1913 he kept hearing of "Mabel Dodge's Evenings," usually Wednesday nights, at which she received the brightest and most talented people in the city. Her salon had become what Bertram D. Wolfe called "a unifier of Village life . . . she had a rare gift for bringing together the atomized particles of our centralized culture."

It would have been easy enough for someone as well known as Reed to wangle an invitation. Perhaps he was put off by what he had heard of her. She seemed to be merely another wealthy lion hunter and sensation seeker. Max Eastman's description of her was not flattering. He attended a peyote party (Mabel had anticipated the LSD craze by almost half a century) at the Dodge apartment, and as he recalled, "We all sat down at about ten in the evening and began to chew on these nauseatingly bitter buttons. . . . Mabel, to whose audacity the adventure was due, became prudent when it got started and slipped the buttons under her big skirt instead of eating them."

Mrs. Dodge's attraction, Eastman felt, was something of a psychological mystery. "She has neither wit nor beauty, nor is she vivacious or lively minded or entertaining . . . for the most part she sits like a lump and says nothing. She seems never to have learned the art of social intercourse—a rather dumb and stumpy little girl, you would say . . . but before long you would be around there again trying to talk to this little girl again. For there is something going on, or going around, in Mabel's head or bosom, something that creates a magnetic field in which people become polarized and pulled in and made to behave very queerly. . . . Many famous salons have been established by women of wit or beauty; Mabel's was the only one established by pure will power." [3]

Other writers who knew her also commented on Mrs. Dodge's "sphinx-like" quality. Carl Van Vechten, one of the first persons she invited to her Fifth Avenue apartment, said her face was "a perfect mask." Those who were fascinated, or repelled, by her curious immobility, facial and otherwise, would have to wait for publication of her four-volume *Intimate Memories,* in which so many of them were preserved like butterflies under glass, for an explanation. The poker-faced quality, she explained, went back to her childhood in Buffalo, where she was born in 1879 as Mabel Ganson. Her wealthy parents were mismated and given to violent quarrels and scenes, which their daughter learned to endure with a stoic and expressionless face.

She was still doing her best to live down that unhappy childhood. In Florence she and Edwin Dodge had bought the Villa Curonia and turned it into one of the show places of an ancient city in which the palatial was commonplace. They had made themselves figures of consequence in international society. Gertrude Stein, one of their guests, was so overwhelmed by the lavishness of her surroundings and—more apparent to her than to mere men—the magnetism of her hostess that she memorialized her visit in "A Portrait of Mabel Dodge and the Villa Curonia."

Mrs. Dodge was determined to make an equal success of her enforced stay in New York. Society of the purely social type did not interest her any longer; it lacked vitality, and, in any case, she was too unconventional for the remnants of the Four Hundred. She was unaware, Lincoln Steffens observed, that society "could and did cut her." [4] The people who interested her were the wildly various guests at her Wednesday Evenings, "from Walter Lipp-

mann, representing the drift toward respectability," as Max East-
man phrased it, "to Alexander Berkman, representing revolt *in
excelsis.*" Jo Davidson, Lincoln Steffens, Hutchins Hapgood,
Emma Goldman, Helen Westley (later a founder of the Theatre
Guild), Frank Harris, Margaret Sanger, Lee Simonson, Marsden
Hartley, Amy Lowell, Edwin Arlington Robinson, Harry Kemp,
Alan Seeger, and George Sylvester Viereck all trooped up the stairs
to her home to sample her pinch-bottle Scotch, Virginia ham,
Gorgonzola sandwiches, and imported cigarettes. Many may have
come for the food and drink, served by a butler, but most agreed
with Steffens that hers was the "only successful salon I have ever
seen in America."

She and Reed, as the two showiest celebrities in the Village,
were bound to meet sooner or later. The delay in that surcharged
event probably was occasioned by the fact that during the early
months of 1913 he was working on a three-act play and on a novel
in addition to his daytime duties on the staff of the *American*.
Their paths finally crossed one night late in the spring, though
not at one of the Evenings at which she presided to elegant advantage swathed in white chiffon against a setting of lilies and
larkspurs.

At the time, according to Mabel's later recollection, Jack had
been "living for some months with a lovely girl named Rose, a
schoolteacher, fair and smooth and affectionate, and their life together had been of an intermittent nocturnal kind."

Mabel herself was feeling the first pangs of dissatisfaction with
Edwin Dodge, to whom she had been married for nine years.
Dodge was a decent fellow, but lacked the primitive force, the restless intellect, which she sought in a man. Too seldom, she had
noticed, were those qualities wedded. Above all, she required a
man with a sexual potency to match her own. When she met
Reed, she said, she was "like a Leyden jar, brimful to the edge,
charged with a high, electrical force." [5]

This bolt of electricity, though concealed in a face with irregular
features and narrow dark eyes and in a body that lacked the fleshy
curves then fashionable, struck Jack Reed on a spring evening

when he was visiting the flat shared by Big Bill Haywood, the old lion of the I.W.W. movement, and his current mistress, who was also a schoolteacher.

Mrs. Dodge appeared there with Mr. and Mrs. Hutchins Hapgood, who had dined with her at 23 Fifth Avenue. Hapgood, a philosophical anarchist and a columnist on the New York *Globe*, explained the Haywood ménage to Mrs. Dodge on their way across Washington Square. The schoolteacher, he said, was a "young woman whom our present system obliges to live what might be called a double life. . . . In the daytime she teaches in a public high school where she leads the youth of our country to respect the flag and honor our government, and at night she sleeps with Big Bill Haywood. . . . Many of our brave young women are adapting themselves in this way of life, and thus doing their share towards a final disintegration of the community." [6] He spoke with a grave approval of cohabitation as a means of undermining the government.

They found Haywood and his schoolteacher living in rooms furnished only with a few chairs and a bed and lit only by candles. There were a number of other people present, most of them sprawled on the floor around Haywood. The veteran agitator, big and flabby and exhausted, was explaining in a monotone how hopeless was the condition of the several thousand workers in the Paterson, New Jersey, silk mills who were on strike. His one good eye occasionally glowing with something of the fire of his youth, Haywood told of how difficult it was to arouse public opinion on the side of the strikers. Most newspapers were arrayed against the strike, and now the New York papers were largely ignoring it.

"God!" Haywood said, leaning forward on his chair, "I wish I could show them a picture of the funeral of Modestino, who was shot by a cop. Every one of the silk mill hands followed his coffin to the grave and dropped a red flower on it. They cut their geraniums from the pot in the window—and those who hadn't any made a little flower of red tissue paper. . . . The grave looked like a mound of blood."

"Can't you get any reports of it into the papers by hook or crook?" someone asked.

"Not a damned word," Haywood replied.

Mabel Dodge had listened in her accustomed trance. Suddenly, as often happened, she came out of it and offered one of her catalytic remarks: "Why don't you bring the strike to New York and *show* it to the workers? Why don't you hire a great hall and re-enact the strike over here? Show the whole thing: the closed mills, the gunmen, the murder of the striker, the funeral. And have the strike leaders make their speeches at the grave as you did in Paterson—you and Elizabeth Gurley Flynn and Carlo Tresca."

"Well, by God!" Haywood said. "There's an idea." But, he wanted to know, where would the re-enactment be staged?

"Madison Square Garden!" Mabel Dodge exclaimed. "Why not?"

She noticed that a young man who had been sprawled on the floor rose to his feet beside her. She was immediately taken by his tousled brown hair, his greenish eyes flashing in the candlelight, his thrusting jaw, and the slight hollows in his temples—the pictorial epitome, she thought, of the activist-poet.

"I'll *do* it," the young man announced.

Mrs. Dodge heard someone else say, "If anybody can do it, you can, Jack."

"My name is Reed," he told her. "That's a *great* idea." [7]

In that moment, on a characteristic impulse, Jack Reed changed the direction of his life and propelled himself into his most turbulent love affair.

The Paterson silk strike was one of the *causes célèbres* of the American labor movement. Almost from the time it was established in America, the silk industry had been torn by labor disputes, all of them eminently justified. It began operating on an industrial scale after John Ryle devised a method of spooling silk instead of skeining it. Paterson, known as the "Lyons of America," had long been a textile center. In 1794 protesting calico-printers were locked out by their employers. Working hours were often sixteen hours a day; even the women and children were summoned to their spinning machines at 4:30 A.M. and whipped by the foremen if they faltered late in the day. In 1828 and 1835 there were violent strikes for better working conditions. By 1870 Paterson had converted to silk weaving, and half the silk fabric produced in the United States was manufactured there. Most of the millworkers were imported from abroad, in the hope that they would be easier to control, at long hours (twelve at this time) and low pay, but by the turn of the century they, too, were organized by outsiders. There was a strike in 1902, the same year a retributive fire swept through the city's mills and hovels, but the employers prevailed as usual.

In 1912 the Industrial Workers of the World, led by Haywood, moved into Paterson with the determination to overcome more than a century of injustice and cruelty. For five months the I.W.W. organizers campaigned for an end to the plural loom system which forced weavers to tend more than one loom and maintain a killing pace. Finally there was a mass walkout. Against the workers and the Wobblies, as the I.W.W. agitators were known, was arrayed a large and brutally efficient police force. The weapons at hand for workingmen to adjust their grievances with their employers were few and ineffective, if they were confined to nonviolence and obedience to the law. The legal picket line was many years in the future. It took another twenty-odd years, in fact, for the establishment of an industrial commission and just treatment of these workers.[8]

Jack Reed plunged into the Paterson situation with his usual headlong enthusiasm. At five o'clock in the morning, after the session in Haywood's flat broke up, he hastened to the station and caught a train for Paterson. It was the morning of April 28, one of the more significant days of Reed's brief years. When he arrived in Paterson a light rain was falling, and the streets were empty. He found three or four men huddled on the porch of one of the company houses near the mills, and went over to join them.

The strikers told him how their most elemental rights as citizens had been denied them by the local police power, acting always on behalf of the employers. They were not allowed to congregate on the streets, and to hold their mass rallies on Sundays they had to march to the nearby village of Haledon, whose mayor was a Socialist, where they stood in a meadow and were addressed by Haywood and the other strike leaders from the balcony of a house.

While they were talking on the porch, a phalanx of police, about twenty of them, tapping night sticks in the palms of their hands, appeared at the head of the street to clear it of the men loitering in small groups. Despite the Constitution, the right of assembly had been suspended in Paterson. The police plucked one striker out of a group that had gathered under the canopy of a saloon.

A detective bustled up to the porch on which Reed was standing and told him to "move on." Reed protested.

"You get the hell off this street," the detective roared.

"If I'm breaking any law," Reed replied, "arrest me."

He was instantly obliged, marched off to the Paterson jail, and crammed into a cell four feet by seven with eight other men, all strikers who had been slow to disperse on police orders. None of them had been given food or water for twenty-four hours.[9]

Within a few hours Reed was converted from a parlor radical to an active one ready to lay life and liberty on the line. Even in his wrath, however, he held onto his irrepressible humor.

A few hours after his arrest he was brought into court before Recorder Carroll, whom Reed later described as having "the intelligent, cruel, merciless face of the ordinary police court magistrate."

Recorder Carroll asked him what his profession was.

"Poet," replied Reed, with his boyish grin.

"Twenty days," snapped the magistrate.

Reed was hauled off to the Passaic County Jail, and by that evening the story broke in the New York papers that a "Harvard poet" had been thrown into jail along with fifty silk strikers. Among them were Haywood himself and Carlo Tresca, the old revolutionaries, who gave the young recruit a short course in the dynamics of labor agitation as they paced around the exercise yard. Friends came from New York offering to pay his fine, but Reed asked that they give him food and cigarettes instead. He was appalled by conditions in the jail, and later wrote that it was "a place that takes in weak men and turns them out weaker"; the food was worse than that served to the crew on the cattle boat—stale bread and soup consisting of rotten meat, decayed vegetables, and dead vermin. The only diversion was holding cockroach races.[10]

After four days, he consented to be bailed out. On his release he found that the New York papers had played up the story of his confinement, and the Paterson silk strike was finally getting extensive coverage. A Paterson police captain complained that jailing one lousy poet had attracted more journalistic attention than the hundreds of strikers they had thrown behind bars.

Reed rode back to New York with his Harvard classmate Edward E. Hunt, who had bailed him out, and immediately plunged into a frenzy of activity on behalf of the Paterson strikers. At white heat he wrote an account of what he had witnessed and experienced in the streets and jail cells of the mill town. Titled "War in Paterson," the article appeared in the June, 1913, *Masses*. It began in the exhortatory style that was to mark so much of his reportage.

There's war in Paterson! But it's a curious kind of war. All the violence is the work of one side—the Mill Owners. Their servants, the police, club unresisting men and women and ride down law-abiding crowds on horseback. Their paid mercenaries, the armed detectives, shoot and kill innocent people. Their newspapers, the Paterson *Press* and the Paterson *Call*, publish incendiary and crime-inciting appeals to mob-violence against the strike-leaders. Their tool, Recorder Carroll, deals out heavy sentences to peaceful pickets that the police-net gathers up. They control absolutely the Police, the Press, the Courts.

Opposing them are about twenty-five thousand striking silk workers, of whom perhaps ten thousand are active. Let me tell you what I saw in Paterson and then you will say which side of this struggle is "anarchistic" and "contrary to American ideals." [11]

Once he had that on paper, he hurried over to 23 Fifth Avenue and Mabel Dodge. "Reed blew in one day," she recalled, "pale and excited, and ready to start immediately upon the Pageant!" It was weeks before Hutchins Hapgood and Carl Van Vechten, who had formed the habit of dropping in at the Dodge apartment every afternoon for tea, saw her again. She and Reed were feverishly working on the pageant they and others would present for the moral and financial benefit of the Paterson strikers.[12] The old Madison Square Garden, on Twenty-sixth Street, was rented for one night, June 7. Meanwhile, the pageant itself had to be blocked out on paper and rehearsed. Reed himself wrote the scenario and trained the choir of Paterson men, women, and children who would sing strike songs, which he also composed. (One, to which some of his fellow Harvard men strenuously objected, was set to the music of a Harvard song.) He also called in his former classmate Robert Edmond Jones to design the setting and staging of the pageant. The strikers' funeral procession, in a re-enactment of the Modestino burial, were to march slowly through the audience and onto the stage, where Jones created a background of a huge and menacing mill towering over all. John Sloan, the artist of New York's underside, painted the scenery. The conferences were held in the home of Margaret Sanger.

In the month of planning, rehearsing, and publicizing that preceded the pageant, a sizable anticipation was whipped up in the city. It caught the public's imagination, at least that sector not automatically committed to the antiunion side of any labor dispute. For the first time the victims of social and economic injustice would relive their experiences on stage in a direct appeal for sympathy. It was an agitprop device the Communists would adapt in later years, though without the theatrical expertise and the emotional background of the pageant devised by Reed and his associates.

His more conservative friends in the uptown clubs and magazine offices were not at all amused by Jack's flaming enthusiasm for the strikers' cause. Julian Street recalled that a friend asked Reed, when they met in a club, "What makes you do that sort of thing, Jack? Why don't you stick to your work and your own sort of people?"

"I would rather eat with a bunch of murderers any time," he shouted, jumping up from the table, "than with this crowd in here. They're a lot more interesting."

His friend, Street recalled, "remarked with a smile that he [Reed] was sophomoric, but would some day grow up and get over it. Most of us believed that, but we misjudged our man. Radicalism was running like a poison through his system and was not to be thrown off. True, there were times when he emerged as his old charming self, but his consuming egotism grew continually more apparent, and . . . he could not long enjoy conversation that took no account of his beliefs." [13] Street wrote this for the *Saturday Evening Post* of 1930.

Something else besides "radicalism" was coursing through Reed at the time: the curious but undeniable attraction of Mabel Dodge. Domineering, possessive, with no physical beauty apparent to those who were unsmitten, she soon became an obsession with Reed. It was not a one-sided attraction. "I knew I was enabling Reed to do what he was doing," Mrs. Dodge wrote later. "I knew he couldn't do it without me. I felt that I was behind, pouring out all the power in the universe through myself to him."

Day and night they worked together, with John Sloan and his wife, Robert Edmond Jones, the novelist Ernest Poole, Edward Hunt, and Walter Lippmann. It was soon apparent to the others that a more intimate collaboration was going on between Reed and Mrs. Dodge: languishing glances from Mabel, sighs from Jack, long interludes when they had eyes only for each other.

The day came, Mabel recorded, when "we loved each other," but, denying the flesh, they realized that the pageant must come first. "That it was no time for lovemaking was accepted without words between us." Then, too, there were the complications in their separate lives: Jack's schoolteacher and Mabel's Edwin.

One obstacle, Mabel said, was removed when Jack went to Rose, the bed companion of his Village nights, and told her, "I don't love you, Rose, I love Mabel Dodge. When the Pageant is finished I'm going to Europe with her." Rose "buried her face in her hands" and began weeping, as Mabel remembered Jack's account of what happened. "I'm very unhappy," Rose told Jack. Then, remembering that she was a citizen of Bohemia, she looked up, smiled, and said, "Why, no, I'm not, either." [14]

The obstacle represented by Edwin Dodge would simply be brushed aside when the time came, and an amicable divorce arranged. Her son by her first marriage, John Evans, a pale and with-drawn little boy, was only eleven and would go with his mother.

The fact that Jack was twenty-five years old to Mabel's thirty-three apparently did not concern either one.

At the moment they were too busy with the pageant. For three weeks before June 7, Jack got by with only a few hours of sleep a night. He rushed around town from the offices of the *American*, where he was still nominally employed, to Paterson, where he re-hearsed the strikers and their families in the songs they would sing—the "Marseillaise" and "Solidarity Forever" and his own compositions—and to Madison Square Garden, where the set was being constructed and other rehearsals were held. He also button-holed men who could, if they would, publicize the pageant. Franklin P. Adams, a columnist for the *World*, recorded in his archly archaic style that Reed had been pounding I.W.W. prop-aganda into him, and that "he told me the Industrial Workers of the World are sorely misjudged and that the tayles in the publick prints of their blood-thirstiness are lies told by the scriveners. And out of it all I wish I did know how to appraise what is true and what is false, but I am too ignorant, and ill-fitted to judge truly."

There was, too, a backwash of public opinion whipped up by the authorities and the press. Sheriff Julius Harburger wanted to forbid the singing of the "Marseillaise." The newspapers, or most of them, informed their readers that the pageant would benefit a mob of bomb-throwing anarchists and foreign-born rabble who didn't appreciate the blessings of liberty.

The sheer logistical effort required to get hundreds of underre-hearsed people, many of whom did not speak English or understood it imperfectly, on and off stage at the proper time was driving Jack to distraction. According to Mabel, he almost cracked up a few days before the pageant was presented. He came to her apartment, slumped into a chair, and muttered, "I can't do it. . . . I just can't push it through."

Mabel, regarding herself as his inspiration and source of strength, shouted at him, "Don't talk like a fool! You coward! Get up out of that chair and stop wasting your time here!" [15]

He plodded back to Madison Square Garden and carried on. When the great night came, the streets around the Garden were thronged, and extra police details had to be summoned to handle the crowd. Fifteen thousand filed into the arena. The cheaper seats were quickly filled, but the rows of one- and two-dollar seats were almost vacant. It was hastily decided to admit anyone who would pay a quarter. In addition, hundreds of I.W.W. members flashed their red cards and came in free.

Outside the arena the police grappled with a new problem. At a prearranged signal, a switch had been thrown, and a sign ten feet high, in red light bulbs, emblazoned itself against the sky line from the top of the Madison Square Garden Tower. "I.W.W.," it read. The height of provocation, it may have been Reed's inspiration or that of one of his collaborators. The police charged into the Garden, coursed through its cellars, and searched every nook for the hidden switch. "By then," as Mabel Dodge wrote, "it was too late to get the heavy municipal machinery in motion to have the Seditious Blaze turned off. By the time the red tape was unwound, the show was over!"

People who saw the Paterson Pageant still remember it as a tremendous emotional experience. It was staged with great skill, but the dramatic impact came from the strikers and their families who re-enacted the events depicted without self-consciousness. Even Bill Haywood, Carlo Tresca, and the other professionals, though intoxicated by the size and receptiveness of their audience, managed to restrain themselves as they portrayed their own roles in the drama, which the program notes defined as "the conflict between two social forces."

The scenario, as composed by Jack Reed, still conveys some of the feeling that charged the occasion:

Episode 1: The Mills Alive—The People Dead. Going to work in the gray dawn. Shambling along the street half asleep. Knots and groups forming. The beginning of the strike.

Episode 2: The Mills Dead—The People Alive. The gathering of the people before the mills. The picket line. The Scab passes. Coming of the police. "Boo!" Clubbing and brutality. Arrest of forty pickets. "Boo!"

Episode 3: The forty strikers brought before the judge. The policeman's story. Strikers attempt to answer. "Tell it to the next fellow. Held for the Grand Jury on a charge of Unlawful Assembly; five hundred dollars bail." Strikers: "Fill up de jail. We take no bail. To hell with the AFL. Hooray for the I.W.W."

Episode 4: The armory meeting. AFL try to break strike. They refuse to let IWW leaders speak. "Let's go home." The police.

Episode 5: A Sunday meeting in Haledon. Tresca just finishing speech in Italian. "Musica! Musica!" The Italian singers. The German singers. The two bands. The strike song.

Episode 6: The funeral of Valentino Modestino. The coffin borne past, while each striker drops a red carnation into it. The burial.

Episode 7: The departure of the children. The mothers hold up their babies to Miss [Elizabeth Gurley] Flynn. May Day. The strike mothers receive them.

Episode 8: A strike meeting at Helvetia Hall. Strikers with their backs to the audience addressed by Big Bill Haywood, who faces the audience. Also by Miss Flynn and Tresca. "Pass the eight-hour law." They raise their right hands and swear they will not go back to the mills until the strike is won.

Two thousand strikers, their wives and children, participated in the pageant; the silk-mill setting loomed menacingly and glowed from a sinister back-lighting; whistles shrieked and shots were fired and the heroic masses marched and sang, some in Italian and some in German accents. At times the recaptured emotions attained such a pitch that the audience roared. When the coffin of Valentino Modestino was carried up the center aisle of the arena, his widow, in a box seat, became hysterical with grief. Sheriff Harburger, watching from the rear with his cohorts, was muttering, "Just let anyone say one word of disrespect to the Flag, and I will stop the show so fast it will take their breath away." [16]

The sincerity of the participants was so moving that even the reporters representing the more conservative newspapers gave it their approval. Several papers sent their dramatic critics, who reported that a "new art form" had been discovered in the Garden. Those journalists who actually witnessed the pageant were so enthusiastic, in fact, that their editors felt that corrective measures were required in the editorial columns, which pointed out that, impressive though Reed's production was in theatrical terms, and despite whatever justification there might be for the strikers' grievances against their employers, the public must keep in mind that behind it all was that "seditious and destructive" organization, the Industrial Workers of the World. Hutchins Hapgood, of the *Globe*, was naturally enthusiastic and declared that the pageant and its reception indicated that "self-expression in industry and art among the masses may become a rich reality, spreading a human glow over the whole of humanity," from which "we shall all be gainers—in real life, in justice, in art, in love." [17] That prophecy was not justified by the events that followed.

For all the excitement it aroused, for all the sympathy temporarily engendered for the strikers, the Paterson Pageant was a limited success. It was a personal triumph for Jack Reed. It gave the strikers their moment in the limelight. It was a temporary thrill for those who witnessed the spectacle. But it did not help the cause. Three weeks after the pageant was staged, the grim financial statistics were announced. Total receipts were $7,645.45. Total expenses were $9,641.95.

Strike sympathizers apparently felt they had done their best by attending the pageant, and funds for the strikers sharply dwindled. The strike itself dragged on into July. Then one faction of the strike committee negotiated with the mill managements, and I.W.W. plans for a settlement to be imposed on the entire silk industry collapsed. The strike was over, and the workers went back to their looms under approximately the same working conditions that had prevailed before they made their desperate attempt to better themselves.[18]

By that time Jack Reed was basking in the Florentine sun, surrounded by smiling peasants, the luxury of the Villa Curonia, and the adoring attentions of Mrs. Mabel Ganson Evans Dodge. Jack had exhausted himself on behalf of the strikers, he felt, and deserved a respite far from the gray streets, black chimneys, and hollow-eyed faces of the New Jersey mill town.

A few days after the pageant had been presented, with the praises of the city and even a few echoes from the nation still ringing, Reed had boarded a luxury liner for Europe with Mabel, her son, the boy's nurse, and with Robert Edmond Jones as chaperon. They were all, except possibly the child and his nurse, in a high mood of self-congratulation. So far, Mabel and Jack had made love only in words; they were able to forget that each was an individual highly charged with egotism, each willful and self-centered and a touch narcissistic, and were sure that this was going to be one of the love affairs of the ages.

Bobby Jones confirmed it for Mabel, telling her, "I feel there is something wonderful and immortal between you and Jack, Mabel."

Jack, however, was less eager for immortality than for an amatory showdown on the high seas. Mabel had previously fended him off by reminding him that the Cause must claim all their energy and devotion. He was willing to take a romantic and poetic view of things, as Mabel demanded, but there was a limit to his patience.

One evening, when his importuning became feverish, she told him, "Oh, Reed, darling"—she always called him by his surname —"we are just at the Threshold and nothing is ever so wonderful as the Threshold of things, don't you know that?"

He did, of course, but at midnight he slipped a poem under her door, which ended: "But the speech of your body to my body will not be denied!" [19]

All during the voyage to France Mabel warded off his advances, probably as much because of her son's presence as her delight in anticipation.

In Paris, while the others continued on the journey to Italy and the villa at Florence, Jack and Mabel stopped off and checked into the Hôtel des Saints Pères. She was now prepared to allow him to cross the Threshold, letting Reed the Poet transform himself into Reed the Lover. He acquitted himself nobly, by her account, and proved himself one of the "movers and shakers," amatively speaking, she so admired. Even her first sexual experience, she reported to the readers of her autobiography, was "the amazing explosion of internal fireworks," but with Jack "I learned what a honeymoon should be." Jack, she indicated, had hitherto indulged only in the catch-as-catch-can sexual encounters of the young Bohemian and known only the favors of girls who regarded sex as a friendly or comradely gesture, and he was delighted by her lack of inhibition; it "seemed a marvel to him."

In the darkness, necessarily without pen and paper at hand, he even managed to ad-lib a bit of poetry, whispering, "I thought your fire was crimson, but you burn blue in the dark." [20]

Mabel's blue flame had barely flickered out in the Parisian night before she sensed the first doubts that their love was immortal. She was almost suffocatingly possessive—and Jack Reed was not the kind of man easily possessed by anything but his dream of accomplishing vast deeds. They were still in bed when someone beat lustily on the door. Jack, without so much as a tender word for his companion, leaped out of the covers and admitted someone with a booming voice. She heard the two men thumping each other on the back and roaring affectionate greetings. Mabel was entirely forgotten.

A few moments later Jack hastily dressed at the urging of his caller, who was Waldo Peirce, still studying in Paris, and ran off with his friend to stroll the boulevards. All day Mabel was left alone at the hotel, and, she recorded, "my heart began to break a little right then." [21] Was Jack, after all, that most hideous of American specimens—not nearly so prevalent on the Continent—a man's man? There was nothing worse in Mabel's book.

Even at the Villa Curonia, in the setting Mabel considered peerless for inspiring and nurturing love, the doubts persisted. The night after their arrival Jack descended from the dressing room upstairs on the silken ladder that less than a year ago had borne the weight of Edwin Dodge, and went toward the bed with the four golden lions on the posters—and the lioness in it—and "for the first time that place was the cradle of happy love for which it had been created. But was it? What is the matter with life that nothing is ever right, I wondered. Now nothing came between me and my desire in the short summer night, but I was not happy."

Jack, however, was unaware of her bemusement and was enraptured by the beauty all around him. "But it's old, Mabel," he kept saying, in reference to the villa. "It's beauty, but it's so *old*."

It constantly irked her that his attention strayed from her to other people and things. Her almost hysterical jealousy and smothering insistence that he focus all his attention on her only seemed to amuse, when it did not annoy, him. Friends gathered around the illicit lovers of the Villa Curonia: Muriel and Paul Draper, Gertrude Stein (whom Reed irritated with his Munchausen tales of his earlier visit to Europe), Carl Van Vechten, and Artur Rubinstein. Even though she had invited most of them, she was angered by the way Reed played up to them. "Reed was terribly interested in *people*. I lost him every hour to 'humans.' "

The febrile atmosphere of the villa and its assorted occupants was amusingly described by Muriel Draper as she recalled it many years later. "I cannot conceive of more conflicting psychological elements meeting under similar conditions without an explosion. . . . Almost everyone was in love or in hate. . . . The breakfast hour was comparatively serene, as we all had it in our rooms, or at least the rooms of our choice. As the morning grew to noon, different members of the household would begin wandering through the many large and small rooms that honeycombed the villa. Enemies of the night before could pass each other safely in the big rooms, but in a small room of many doors it was a precarious adventure. Friends would meet by assignation in what they had anticipated would be a deserted gallery and find themselves unwelcome intruders in a whispered confidence."

On that scene Jack Reed often appeared in the unusual guise of peacemaker, soothing hurt feelings and calming explosive temperaments. Bobby Jones and Carl Van Vechten, she recalled, quarreled loudly over Jones's execution of the drawing of a stage set for which she was posing. Jack, "alarmed by the loud voices in which the altercation between Carl and Bobby was by now pitched, would appear suddenly, standing nervously still but ready to move powerfully. 'Carl, stop it, or you'll cry!' he would shout. . . . Always I see Jack Reed stopping things to make room for life to be lived in. . . ." [22]

His hostess resented even his attempts to keep her guests from each other's throats. Mabel's jealousy was all-encompassing; she could not bear it when his attention strayed from her. She organized an automobile tour of the countryside and was annoyed by his enthusiasm for the architecture, which by now was old hat to her. "I hated to see him interested in Things. I wasn't, and didn't like to have him even *look* at churches and leave me out of his attention." In Venice she might just as well not have been at his side; he kept roaming the ancient city "unaware of me." Occasionally he would share his thoughts as she trudged along after him. " 'The things Men have done!' he murmured once or twice. 'But I wish that I could have been here at the *doing* of it or that they were doing it *now*,' he said. Past or present, I did not care what they had done. I was jealous of the way he said '*Men*.' "

Even his enthusiasm for the Villa Curonia, overlooking Florence and the Arno Valley, was irksome to his mistress. It was simply a bore to her that a ghost was said to float around the premises; and she could not join Jack in his goggle-eyed fascination when the local priest arrived, with his acolytes swinging censers and sprinkling holy water, to exorcise the local apparition. He went swimming daily in a pool at a nearby villa, set in an olive grove, which Michelangelo was supposed to have designed. At night he matched wits with the "smart, clever, hard Londoners, very *raffine* and effete," as he described them in a letter to Edward Hunt, and the equally glittering examples of "ultra-modern, ultra-civilized Continental, society" whom she kept inviting to the villa.[23] Despite her subsequent protests that she wanted him all to herself, she also wanted to show him off. An acquisition that would not arouse envy apparently would not have satisfied her. Before her captive audience she insisted on reading Jack's *The Day in Bo-*

hemia, which must have seemed a lot of naïve blathering to Continental sophisticates, and on recounting in detail how they had taken New York by storm with their presentation of the Paterson Pageant. The *rentiers*, remittance men, heiresses, and other remnants of the *belle époque*, living as they did off dividends and distant landholdings, could hardly have been enthralled by the whiff of revolution she brought into the flower-scented air of the Villa Curonia.

Mabel was not at all pleased when Jack and Robert Edmond Jones, who planned to go to Germany to study under Max Reinhardt, went off on a walking tour without her. A few days later he was brought back to her, ill with diphtheria. He had caught it, apparently, in his characteristic romantic manner. Along the way, he and Jones had come across an old cistern which was said to have been used by Leonardo da Vinci. Jack, of course, had to plunge in for a dip.

Jack was returned to Mabel seriously ill, and at first Mabel was secretly delighted. "So I had Reed, I thought, for my own—but that was a pleasure soon over. No sooner do we get them where we think we want them, than we find we do not want them so. A man completely at a disadvantage, disempowered, and delivered up to us, we find to be no man at all."

She diligently nursed him back to health, but inwardly resented her lady-with-a-lamp role. "Reed, sick in bed in the cool, brown and white, north bedroom, has left no impressions with me—nor even when we moved him up to Vallombrosa, where it was cool among the pine trees. I was bored then—and peaceful." [24]

After two and a half months of the Italian idyll, prolonged by his convalescence, Jack began to get restless for New York and the continuation of his career, whatever turn it might take. The Paterson cause had been defeated, but he could not forget the strikers who "blithely defied the lawless brutality of the city government" and "had gone to prison laughing and singing." It was too late to resume that cause, but there would be others. Besides, in the Village he was a hero; in Italy, merely another idle American living off the sweat of honest workingmen.

"I'm not a Socialist," he assured his mother in a letter home, "any more than I'm an Episcopalian—my business is to interpret and live life." [25]

In late September, accompanied by Mabel, he sailed for New York to get on with that process.

6

A FOLK HERO NAMED
PANCHO VILLA

In the fall of 1913 Mr. John Reed and Mrs. Mabel Dodge were
at home to the artists, reformers, and intellectuals who were attracted to the white-walled drawing room that served as her salon
at 23 Fifth Avenue. Edwin Dodge had moved out, of course, and
they lived together "quite openly," as Mabel said, without suffering any social discrimination. They shared the four-story brownstone with two old gentlemen who apparently were too preoccupied with their own misfortunes to object on moral grounds to
living under the same roof with them. One was a former governor
of New York, William Sulzer, whom Max Eastman described as a
"gaunt Andrew Jackson of a man with a ten-gallon black hat and
a madly glittering eye." The ex-governor was brooding over having
been impeached and "flung out of the governorship for kicking
down the ladder by which he had climbed into it, a ladder named
Tammany Hall." [1]

On the first floor lived the owner of the brownstone, Major General Daniel E. Sickles, who had lost his leg to a Confederate cannonball while saving (by his own account) the Union army at Gettysburg. During the Civil War, on and off the battlefields, he was one of Fighting Joe Hooker's hard-drinking, hard-wenching lieutenants. The stout old fellow was close to ninety and spent his days in a straight-backed rocker, absorbed, perhaps, in recollecting, if not regretting, a highly colorful career. Fifty-odd years before, having ascended the Tammany ladder much as Governor Sulzer had done, he had been a member of the House of Representatives. One day, on the sidewalk across from the White House, he shot and killed Philip Barton Key, the son of the man who wrote "The Star-Spangled Banner." He claimed that his wife and Key were lovers. He was acquitted on a plea then new to jurisprudence but much employed since: not guilty by reason of temporary insanity. Afterward he served a scandalous term as ambassador to Spain. He was too old to care much what Mrs. Dodge and her young man did on the floor above, and was the last man in New York to object to anything on moral grounds.

Mabel resumed playing hostess at her Wednesday-evening gatherings, and Jack settled down to the increasingly incongruous role of her consort. The imperious Mabel simply could not understand that Jack, at twenty-six, had to pursue his own career and interests, even if this displeased her. "Reed himself was ready for anything!" she recalled in her hyperthyroid style. "Ready at any moment to pop off into some new enthusiasm. He always seemed to have his lungs too full, and he would draw in his round chin in an effort to quiet his excited heart. *Always* there seemed some pressure of excitement going on in him. His eyes glowed for nothing, his brown curls rushed back from his high, round forehead in a furious disorder, and the round highlights on his temples gleamed, his eyebrows went further up. . . ." [2]

Even at breakfast he behaved more like a husband than like an ardent live-in suitor. "I took my breakfast in bed, and he ate his at a little table by my bedside because I wanted him to. But he might as well have been gone from there for all he was with *me*.

He drank his coffee with the morning paper propped up before him, his honey-colored round eyes just popping over 'the news!' Any kind of news as long as it had possibilities for thrill, for action, for excitement." Mabel herself had no interest in the papers except when they carried a story "about myself or some friend or enemy of mine." His habit of burying himself behind the morning paper distressed her immeasurably; "I didn't like that. I felt doomed." That he could be more interested in events far from her elegant boudoir irked her to the point that "I was relieved when breakfast was over, the newspaper fallen to the floor, and he was on his feet eager for the street. Though I hated him to go out and leave me, I hated worse to have him there forgetful of our essential life together. . . ." [3]

Hysterics soon became a regular feature of the household. Mabel hoped that by resuming her "Evenings" and inviting her more interesting friends on other occasions he would be impressed by the attention they showered on her and want to stay at her side all the time. He seemed to be oblivious of these maneuverings, she said, and his cocoon of self-concern remained unbreakable. Instead of becoming more attentive, he began spending more time at the *Masses* during the day and roaming the streets of the lower East Side at night. When he finally made it home, he would be effervescing with accounts of what he had seen and heard on his solitary rambles. Like Stephen Crane, like many young American writers before and since, he was fascinated by prostitutes. A romantic empathy with whores was something that Mrs. Dodge could not understand. Yet Jack, callously unaware of her disinterest in the subject, would come bounding in and recite in elaborate detail his latest encounter with a streetwalker, how he had spent hours talking to her, how beautiful she was, how mysterious in her attitudes, and how sympathetic he felt toward her. In desperation Mabel, more Victorian in that moment than she would have liked to concede, once pretended to faint in the middle of one of his discourses, in the vain hope that he would start thinking about her instead of his latest sidewalk madonna.

He kept urging her to accompany him on his prowling of the

mean streets, but that was hardly what Mabel wanted. She wanted him to share her life, not the other way around. Finally she consented to go along on a ramble through the lower East Side, but at the last moment insisted that they travel by limousine. It was ridiculous, Jack fumed, staring out at the poor from the cushioned ease of a motorcar, and they had a night-long row when they returned to 23 Fifth Avenue.

When Jack brought his own friends to the apartment, Mabel's trancelike silences were unending and discomfiting. After they left, deep in the night, Mabel would keep him up arguing that he was wasting his time on such mediocre and superficial people.

One row reached such a hysterical pitch that Jack walked out on her. She took an overdose of morphine, carefully calculated to alarm him but not to be fatal. He came back to find her in a narcotic stupor. After summoning medical assistance, he fled to Boston, leaving Hutchins Hapgood and Lincoln Steffens to deal with the unhappy woman.

On another quarrelsome occasion, he packed up and stalked out of the apartment. Behind him he left a note reading: "Good-bye, my darling. I cannot live with you. You smother me. You crush me. You want to kill my spirit. I love you better than life but I do not want to die in my spirit. I am going away to save myself. Forgive me. I love you—I love you. Reed."

Mabel found the note, then ran over to the Hapgoods' apartment for comfort. She returned to the empty apartment. "Reed had gone away," she later wrote, "taking the universe with him."

But next day the universe returned, suitcases and all, full of contrition. "Pale, with black shadows under his eyes, his curls on end, he fell on his knees by me and buried his head against me. 'Oh, I couldn't bear it,' he cried. 'I can't live without you. I missed your love, your selfish, selfish love.' " [4]

Jack was living up to his Village sobriquet of "Storm Boy," given him by Art Young, even when he was not quarreling and making up with Mabel Dodge. He had quit the staff of the *American* when he went off to sojourn in Italy, and whatever pocket money he had came from the sale of a very occasional magazine article.

Meanwhile, at the *Masses* Max Eastman, whom Jack had come to admire, was struggling with his various burdens as the sole editor, money raiser, chief executive, editorial writer, and at the same time working on a book about Marxism. To help out with the editorial duties, Eastman hired Harry Kemp, the tramp poet, as he called himself, at fifteen dollars a week. After one day's labor over a pile of manuscripts Kemp sent him a note the next morning saying that he "must live and die a poet" and begging to be relieved of the job.

Jack then volunteered to take over the managing editorship, citing his qualification as a former member of the staff of the *American* and his experience with the various Harvard magazines. He added that he "would gladly give half his time to keep *The Masses* from going under." Eastman accepted, and almost immediately regretted. "Jack had too many wayward ideas, too rich a flow of impulses; he lacked judgment, and he had too much else to do. We agreed almost before he started that his help would be temporary, that what I needed was a paid associate who would sit up to a desk in the office—once in a while at least—and actually be there." [5]

Being desk-bound for even a few hours brought out Jack's prankishness in full spate. One Friday afternoon before leaving for a long weekend in Connecticut, he hoisted the office safe to his shoulder and carried it out to the curbstone on Greenwich Avenue. Then he went capering off to Grand Central. Eastman returned to the office to find his safe in the gutter, tried to manhandle it back into the building, asked the help of passers-by, and still could not manage it. Finally he had to call the Fire Department to get the safe back in the office.[6]

One thing Jack was rather good at was helping Eastman wangle money out of the *Masses'* financial sponsors. Unlike most Village radicals, he was at his ease with rich people and able to treat them as equals even while proposing that they assist in their own downfall by pledging money to keep a revolutionary periodical in business. Mrs. O. H. P. Belmont, E. W. Scripps, the eccentric and wealthy newspaper publisher, and John Fox were among early subsidizers. One day Amos Pinchot called up, just when their money had run out, and volunteered his help. Reed and Eastman dashed over to his offices on Wall Street, and within a few hours were back on Greenwich Avenue with a pledge of two thousand dollars.[7]

Otherwise Jack was Eastman's problem child. Reed's "too spirited help, somewhat like that of a wild colt eager to enjoy the harness, came near to driving me out of the office for good," Eastman wrote. About the time Eastman was ready to give it all up, Floyd Dell, a young literary critic, arrived from Chicago, and Jack was eased out of the managing editorship in favor of Dell.

By now, according to Walter Lippmann, who often met him at Mabel Dodge's soirees, Reed had moved to the left of the various accepted Socialist groupings and was standing with those who believed (like the I.W.W.) in victory for the working class through the violent overturn of established society. "He assumed that all capitalists were fat, bald, and unctuous, that reformers were cowardly or scheming, that all newspapers are corrupt, that Victor Berger and the Socialist Party and Samuel Gompers and the trade unions are a fraud on labor. He made an effort to believe that the working class is not composed of miners, plumbers and working men generally, but is a fine statuesque giant who stands on a high hill facing the sun. He wrote stories about the night court and plays about ladies in kimonos. He talked with intelligent tolerance about dynamite, and thought he saw an intimate connection between the cubists and the I.W.W. He even read a few pages of Bergson. . . ."[8]

He was intoxicated by the prospect of revolution—anywhere, any time, against any form of oppression. The Village was full of wild talk, but none exceeded Reed's in clamoring for action against the oppressors of mankind. He was the terror of Mabel's salon and other places where polite people, vaguely guilty about their own fortunate position, gathered to learn about the storm about to break. It was a masochistic thrill to hear Reed giving his ideological weather forecasts; Art Young's caricature of him in the *Masses* as the "Storm Boy" caught this aspect of him perfectly. Julian Street was probably right about his delight in deliberately shocking conventional people. But, Street noted, even while "loudly proclaiming his disapproval of wealth, he was not above riding in the motors of the rich and dining at their tables, and nothing delighted him more than to set off bombs where members of the capitalist class were gathered. If the lady beside whom he sat at dinner was a pillar of the church, he would find a way to mention casually that he believed in free love, and if her husband had amassed a fortune, he would tell her blandly of the class war that was coming, in which wealth would disappear and the streets would run with fashionable blood.

"If these good ladies tried to reason with him he pelted them with arguments which left them gasping, and if their husbands took up the cudgels they generally regretted it, for Jack was a born debater. Argument was a game at which he loved to exercise his skill, and if facts and statistics were wanted he would invent them to fit the moment's need.

"Sweet sheltered women used to worry about Jack and wonder what was going to become of him. But their husbands didn't worry about him. More than once I have seen a sober man of affairs eye him with an expression suggesting a private hope that the next time this impudent young man rode the brake beams or made uncomplimentary remarks to a policeman, he would get what was coming to him." [9]

By then he was becoming restless in Mabel's gilded cage, and perhaps growingly conscious that some people were finding his position as a rich woman's paramour, who bellowed about the sufferings of the proletariat, a little ridiculous. He needed something to justify himself, a fighting cause to which he could attach himself. That cause, late in November, 1913, became the revolution-within-a-revolution being waged in Mexico on the deserts of Chihuahua State by Pancho Villa and his peon army.

Until then there is nothing in Jack's writings, letters, or remembered conversations to indicate that he had looked into Pancho Villa, or even the Mexican revolution, as a matter of personal or intellectual concern. The Mexican troubles, to this country, were more an irritation than a matter for sympathy or outrage. Reed was wandering around Europe in 1911 when Jack London issued his famous statement to the Mexican revolutionaries: "All the names that you are being called, we have been called. And when graft and greed get up and begin to call names, honest men, brave men, patriotic men and martyrs can expect nothing else than to be called chicken thieves and outlaws. I subscribe myself a chicken thief and revolutionist." [10] Socialism was not immediately engaged because the opening phases of the revolution were mainly a struggle for democracy against the ruling oligarchy. Whatever feelings Reed and his comrades had about it, however, were undoubtedly sympathetic to the revolutionary cause even if it was not motivated by Marxism.

Late in 1913 Pancho Villa and his forces, which might loosely, in later years, be called agrarian reformers, began the uprising in Chihuahua that attracted the full attention of the American public, if only because it washed up against the United States boundary. Carl Hovey, the editor of *Metropolitan Magazine*, at this time an organ of Socialist reform, called Jack in and asked him to go to Mexico as the magazine's correspondent. A few days later the New York *World* also agreed to print his dispatches.

Mabel Dodge tried, of course, to talk him out of the assignment, but Jack was in an elated state which she could not penetrate, "puffed up and excited, his curls tossed back, standing up and declaiming wildly."

Almost absent-mindedly he kissed Mabel good-by and set out for the Mexican border. Mabel was so upset by his eagerness to be off on man's business that she took a train to Chicago and intercepted him there. "When we met I was disappointed that he looked merely rather glad instead of overjoyed," she would remember. "The man in him was already on the job. The woman's place was in the home!"

Mabel clung to him, however, until they reached El Paso, where they took rooms in a "large ugly hotel" and she "began to wonder why I had come." Jack kept rushing away to see various people who claimed they could smooth his way with the contending factions below the border. All he talked about was getting away on his assignment, and Mabel felt that she was only in the way. "I looked at the pale blue mountains on the horizon and somehow I couldn't see what I was going to do in El Paso while he was over there, for I saw soon enough, I couldn't go with him." [11]

They parted in El Paso. Mabel returned to New York, and Greenwich Village's great love affair of 1913 was almost at an end. The passive role of a woman waiting for her adventuring mate to return home was not for Mabel Dodge.

The upheaval in Mexico had begun in 1910, the hundredth anniversary of Father Miguel Hidalgo's "Cry of Dolores," which launched the war for independence from Spain. It was also the year that Halley's comet returned to the earth's view after a seventy-six-year absence—a matter of superstitious note to the Mexican peasantry.

The thirty-four-year rule of President-Dictator Porfirio Díaz had been marked by a widening chasm between Mexico's two classes: the very rich and the very poor. Less than five per cent of the people owned virtually all of the arable land; only twenty per cent of the population could claim something approaching literacy. Periodic uprisings in the remoter sections of the country were quelled by the *rurales*, the gray-uniformed federal police. In the cities, even in the magnificent capital where Díaz and the old men of his government lived in splendor, the wages were minuscule and strikes were smashed with military precision and cruelty.

Elections were rigged in favor of Díaz's continual return to power, and he also kept a firm grip on the puppet strings of all state and municipal officials. His hold on the "republic" which he had helped Juárez to establish after throwing out Maximilian and his foreign mercenaries seemed absolute and unbreakable. In 1910, however, he was opposed in the Presidential election by Francisco I. Madero, the son of a wealthy Coahuila family, a visionary and idealist who had written a book detailing a program by which the

President would be elected to a single six-year term and widespread social reforms would be instituted. During the campaign Madero was thrown in jail for a while, but escaped to temporary exile in San Antonio, Texas. The "Díaz and Death" ticket, as its opponents called the regime, inevitably was continued in office.

A short time later Madero, from his Texas sanctuary, issued a call for a revolution to drive Díaz and the *científicos* from their positions of unchallenged authority. The whole country exploded. In the north, Villa, a former bandit chieftain with a certain political talent and an indubitable native genius for partisan warfare, and Pascual Orozco answered Madero's call, as did a leader of peasant guerrillas, Emiliano Zapata, in the southern state of Morelos. Those three led their ragtag bands in attacks against all the federal army posts, railroad stations, haciendas, and towns within their reach. Each captured garrison provided the rebels with more arms and attracted more recruits. Díaz's authority was crumbling rapidly. The aged dictator was finally compelled to agree to leave the country and allow a provisional government, headed by Madero, to take over.[12]

It seemed as though the revolution had triumphed and Mexico could begin the work of constructing a more democratic society, but actually it was only the beginning of years of turmoil and counterrevolution. Madero's reforms were too mild for the revolutionary leaders north and south who wanted the great haciendas broken up immediately and the land distributed to the peasants. When Madero balked, the peon armies stayed under arms. Somehow Madero had to find a way to disarm them, especially when the partisans began raiding and marching again. Finally Madero turned to General Victoriano Huerta, a ruthless and ambitious schemer, giving him command of the federal forces on his promise to smash the columns now heading toward the capital. Huerta defeated Orozco in the field, then was summoned back to Mexico City to deal with a reported insurrection inside the capital.

General Huerta, a drunkard and cocaine addict who always kept a clear-enough head to advance his own interests, put down the attempted coup, then arrested Madero, supposedly for safekeeping, and transferred him from the palace to the penitentiary. Señora Madero appealed vainly to American authorities to rescue her husband. A day later it was announced that Madero and his vice-president had been shot and killed while under military guard. When Huerta took over as Madero's successor, the murdered Madero was immediately raised to martyrdom by the various rebel leaders who had opposed him for going too slow in social and economic reform, and he "gained a popularity in death which he had never achieved in life . . . became the symbol for the continued struggle against military dictatorship, was canonized and enrolled in the hagiology of the revolution as its first 'apostle.' " [13]

"Bloody usurper" though he was to the masses, Huerta's legitimacy was proclaimed by U.S. Ambassador Henry Lane Wilson, who had earlier maneuvered against Madero in concert with the British. As of March, 1912, Ambassador Wilson insisted in his dispatches to Washington, the Mexican revolution was really over. President Wilson, who had just taken office, refused to act on his ambassador's recommendations that the Huerta government be recognized, and it soon appeared that his temporizing was justified. Orozco and Zapata were still rebelling (though the former soon went over to Huerta), Villa was raising a new army in Chihuahua, and the governor of Coahuila, Venustiano Carranza, had issued a proclamation calling for Huerta's overthrow and announcing himself as the "First Chief of the Constitutionalist Army in charge of the Executive Power."

President Wilson recalled Ambassador Wilson and declared that his administration favored free elections in which Huerta would not be a candidate. Only the government thus elected would be recognized by the United States. Meanwhile, shipment of arms to Huerta and the federal army was forbidden, but U.S. customs inspectors looked the other way when supplies for Huerta's opponents began flowing through the ports of entry on the Texas border.

During the last months of 1913, Huerta, running his government from behind a barricade of cognac bottles at the Café Colón in the capital, struggled to outmaneuver the revolutionaries, who were wresting state after state from his control.

Now began the rise of Pancho Villa, who had acquired the title "Tiger of the North." He was marching all over Chihuahua, its scorching deserts and snow-peaked mountains, seizing everything but the capital city, the vital arterial railway between Juárez and Torreón, and the garrison at Ojinaga, across the Rio Grande from the Texas town of Presidio. In November, 1913, he made a surprise advance northward and captured Ciudad Juárez, across the line from El Paso; then he moved back southward to take Chihuahua City. Shortly before his steeple-hatted legions appeared on the desert horizon, the garrison, under Orozco, a Huerta man now, evacuated the capital and moved north to join General Mercado's federal army at Ojinaga.

Villa by then had captured the American imagination, too, and some American sympathy, by his flamboyant success and his self-portrayal as a Robin Hood acting on behalf of the Mexican masses. This robust appeal did not diminish even when, immediately after taking Juárez, he began acting like a Chinese war lord, living luxuriously on an armored train, and turning over to his brother Hipólito such profitable enterprises as the Juárez bull ring and the red-light district.

To make himself master of Chihuahua State, Villa, at the end of 1913, needed only to crush the Orozco-Mercado force at Ojinaga and wipe out the federal garrison at Torreón, far to the south of Chihuahua City. But that was only the base of his ambitions, which encompassed the whole of Mexico. To achieve them he would have to come to grips with Huerta's main forces, destroy Carranza's pretensions to leading the Constitutionalist cause, come to terms with the rival aspirations of Zapata in the south and of Alvaro Obregón, a new leader who had surfaced in Sonora. Long campaigning and constant intriguing with and against his rivals for power stretched ahead of him, but Villa was supremely confident.

That was the situation in December, 1913, when Jack Reed crossed over the border as war correspondent of the New York

World and the *Metropolitan Magazine*. Now in his twenty-seventh year, with the vigor of youth and a prose style easily adapted to the demands of a war in which he could identify himself with the cause of the oppressed, he was to make himself famous in a few months. Rudyard Kipling would be quoted as saying, "His articles in *Metropolitan* made me *see* Mexico." The *World's* circulation trucks would be emblazoned with the boast, "America's Kipling . . . It's Literature." It was, after all, still the era of Richard Harding Davis. Nothing was more romantic than the war correspondent, brave and dashing in khaki, boots, and sun helmet, careening about in some safely distant conflict. Reed, unabashed at dramatizing himself, played the part with bravura. Gregory Mason, another Greenwich Villager who covered the Mexican revolution, would comment with just a touch of jaundice, "In the Village I heard many exaggerated reports on Reed's belligerent exploits in Chihuahua, and in Chihuahua I heard many exaggerated versions of Reed's amatory exploits in the Village." But, he added in a magazine article, Reed's writing from Mexico was "essentially true in spirit. . . . He caught the spirit of that beloved country, where the fantastic is the commonplace and the impossible is the everyday occurrence." [14]

If Reed created myths about himself, he was also widely credited with being the fabricator of a full-blown Villa legend in the United States. Actually, Francisco Villa was the respected bellwether of the Mexican Conventional Party and therefore a redoubtable political force in his own right, but it was Reed's newspaper dispatches and magazine articles that made him famous. According to Mason, though, the responsibility for starting the legend, if indeed it can be called one, belonged to a nimble operator named Johnny Roberts. "Reed got a great deal of dope on Villa directly or indirectly" from Roberts, Mason related, before he went over the border. Roberts, "one of the most picturesque amalgams of the delightful and the unscrupulous ever produced by the Border," was a correspondent for Hearst when Villa was rolling up his first victories. "Johnny persuaded Hearst that he had pull with Villa, and he persuaded Villa that he had pull with

Hearst." William Randolph Hearst, it might be noted, had a consuming interest in Mexican affairs: he was the largest American
holder of land and mining properties in northern Mexico, and
rightly feared expropriation. His chain of newspapers therefore
vigorously promoted the idea of American intervention. "It worked
beautifully for Johnny, and for all the correspondents who knew
him, for, while Johnny couldn't write much, he could talk amazingly. . . . As Roberts talked the Villa legend, Reed listened,
added an improvement here and there, and made it literature." [15]

Through Roberts, presumably, Reed would be welcome in the
Villista camp, but on his first sortie after news of the federal forces
at Ojinaga, the only organized Huerta resistance left in northern
Chihuahua, he was rudely rebuffed. He went to Presidio, Texas,
and stared across the shallows of the Rio Grande at the garrison
of Ojinaga, which consisted of about thirty-five hundred men. To
command this force, the size of a small regiment, Reed noted that
the federals boasted eleven generals, twenty-one colonels, and
forty-five majors, enough senior officers for a full-sized army corps.

He sent a note across the boundary requesting an interview
with General Mercado. It was intercepted by General Orozco,
who replied, "Esteemed and Honored Sir: If you set foot inside
Ojinaga, I will stand you sideways against a wall, and with my own
hand take great pleasure in shooting furrows in your back." Un-
dismayed, Reed waded across the Rio Grande, avoided meeting
Orozco, and talked briefly with General Mercado, "a fat, pathetic,
worried, undecided little man, who blubbered and blustered. . . ."
He noted that the town was thronged with "sick, exhausted, starving people driven from the interior by fear of the approaching
rebels, a journey of eight days over the most terrible desert in the
world."

On both sides of the border rumors were circulating that Villa's
army was approaching to wipe out the Ojinaga garrison; refugees
scuttled across the Rio Grande laden with gold, to be picked up
in Presidio and whisked away by limousine, and the only comedy
relief for Reed was "the High Sheriff of Presidio County," who
had "read all of Owen Wister's novels, and knew what a Western

sheriff ought to look like: two revolvers on the hip, one slung under his arm, a large knife in his left boot, and an enormous shotgun over his saddle. His conversation was larded with the most fearful oaths, and he never caught any criminal." [16]

Reed wearied of listening to rumors, waiting for the Villistas' approach, and watching the gunrunners, secret agents, and munitions salesmen moving around making their deals. He returned to El Paso shortly before Christmas, 1913. Ojinaga was captured by Villa's army on January 14, 1914, most of the federal troops having fled across the river after putting up a token resistance and gladly surrendering to U.S. internment behind a barbed-wire stockade at Fort Bliss.

At Juárez Reed caught his first glimpse of Villa's forces, two thousand horsemen and five hundred infantry maneuvering out on the desert, and was impressed by them. "These were wild men, well fed, clothed, armed, and mounted, volunteers instead of conscripts like the Federals. A great bunch, believe me." He caught a train for Chihuahua City to find out just why and how their commander aroused such fiery admiration that "Viva Villa" issued from everyone's lips.

His first glimpse of Villa occurred at a ceremony in the governor's palace in which Villa was to be presented a medal for heroism by the officers of his artillery corps. A colonel stepped forward with the medal, and "Villa put out both hands eagerly, like a child for a new toy. He could hardly wait to open the box and see what was inside. . . . Villa looked at the medal, scratching his head, and, in a reverent silence, said clearly: 'This is a hell of a little thing to give a man for all that heroism you are talking about!' " [17]

The following day Reed had his first interview with Villa, the first of a score of such meetings, which he described in a series of seven articles for the *Metropolitan* (and which formed Part II of his book *Insurgent Mexico*, a compilation of his stories from that magazine and the New York *World*). They constituted the definitive profile of the revolutionary as a courageous, lusty, generoushearted primitive whose motive force was a desire to rescue his people from peonage.

He described Villa's animal-like movements, the stiff-legged way he walked, owing to years spent on horseback, the gracefulness of his gestures, the terrible power of expression in his deep-brown eyes. Villa gave him his life story, a vivid account of how he became an outlaw after killing a government official when he was sixteen, how he stole cattle from the haciendas, how he "learned the art of war" as the leader of a small guerrilla band in the mountains of Chihuahua. "Everywhere he was known as The Friend of the Poor. He was the Mexican Robin Hood." Only eight months before Reed met him, Villa had set out from El Paso on his conquest of his native province with "four companions, three led horses, two pounds of sugar and coffee, and a pound of salt."

During the several weeks between the capture of Ojinaga and the campaign against Torreón, Villa busied himself with administrative affairs and made an attempt to restore government services in the vast province now his domain. First there was the problem of money. Farmers were refusing to bring their produce to the market towns because those who had banknotes or silver had buried them. Villa believed in simple solutions: "Why, if all they need is money, let's print some." The printing press in the basement of the governor's palace spewed out two million pesos in currency. How was it to be circulated? Villa called all the poor people of the capital together and gave them fifteen dollars in pesos apiece. To back up his currency and obtain the credit necessary to buy arms and ammunition, he ordered the arrest of Don Luis Terrazas, Jr., a director of the Banco Minero. "When he refused to divulge the hiding-place" of the bank's five-hundred-thousand-dollar gold reserve, Reed reported, "Villa and a squad of soldiers took him out of his house one night, rode him on a mule out into the desert, and strung him up to a tree by the neck. He was cut down just in time to save his life, and led Villa to an old forge in the Terrazas iron works, under which was discovered the reserve of the Banco Minero. Terrazas went back to prison badly shaken, and Villa sent word to his father in El Paso that he would release the son upon payment of $500,000 ransom." [18]

Education for the masses and land for the peasantry were the foundation stones of Villa's program for the country, as Reed reported it. Others in the American press corps, it must be noted, could not believe that Villa had any other program than enriching himself and seizing power. But to Reed, the jovial and plain-spoken Villa was a fellow idealist, with an equal passion for social reform. With his guns taken away from him, his hair combed, and his stocky figure draped in a less military costume, Reed's Villa might have fitted in nicely with Lincoln Steffens, Hutchins Hapgood, and the other "sentimental rebels" who frequented Mabel Dodge's salon. "He believed that land for the people and schools would settle every question of civilization. Schools were an obsession with him. Often I have heard him say: 'When I passed such and such a street this morning I saw a lot of kids. Let's put a school there.'" Villa also established price controls for bread, beef and milk; planned to settle his soldiers on vast co-operatives with a three-day work week, and meanwhile prohibited them from getting drunk or mistreating the civilian population.

Furthermore, Villa took steps toward social justice that could only endear him to his own people and to American liberals and humanists. "The rich Mexicans who had oppressed the people and opposed the Revolution, he expelled promptly from the State and confiscated their vast holdings. By a simple stroke of the pen the 17,000,000 acres and innumerable business enterprises of the Terrazas family became the property of the Constitutional government, as well as the great lands of the Creel family and the magnificent palaces which were their town houses." He told of Villa's "black book," in which were listed the names of oppressors presently beyond his reach, including Americans, Germans, and Englishmen. "Their pages in the black book will be opened when the Constitutionalist government is established in Mexico City; and there, too, he will settle the account of the Mexican people with the Catholic Church."

Reed also conveyed Villa's views on socialism ("I see it only in books and I do not read much"), woman suffrage (he was not opposed to it, but pointed out that "women can be crueller and harder than men." To prove his point Villa called to the current

"Mrs. Villa" and asked her what he should do about three sabo-
teurs who had been caught trying to wreck the railroad. "Oh, well,
shoot them," his current traveling companion replied), and political ambitions (none). With a barefaced impudence which Reed
could not have been expected to detect, Villa affirmed that he was
loyal to Carranza and would support him for the Presidency. "I
am a fighter, not a statesman. I am not educated enough to be
President. . . . I have told you many times there is no possibility
of my becoming President of Mexico."

As a simple guerrilla leader, the guise Villa then preferred, he
was credited by Reed with almost Napoleonic accomplishments.
He invented "an entirely original method of warfare" true enough.
His forked-lightning movements against Huerta's demoralized
troops still stand up as a model of partisan campaigning in open
country. Reed, however, went so far as to claim that Villa invented
the night attack and other innovations that had been practiced for
centuries. "His method of fighting is astonishingly like Napoleon's.
Secrecy, quickness of movement, the adaptation of his plans to the
character of the country and of his soldiers—the value of intimate
relations with the rank and file, and of building up a tradition
among the enemy that his army is invincible, and that he himself
bears a charmed life—these are his characteristics." The Villistas
with their crossed bandoleers reminded Reed of "the ragged Republican army that Napoleon led into Italy." [19]

One of the more illuminating incidents concerning Villa's character occurred while Villa was exiled in El Paso. General Hugh L.
Scott, then commanding at Fort Bliss, sent him a copy of *The
Rules of War* as adopted by the Hague Convention. Villa, Reed
later learned, was "hugely" amused by the pamphlet and commented, "It seems to me a funny thing to make rules about war.
It's not a game. What is the difference between civilized war and
any other kind of war? If you and I are having a fight in a cantina
we are not going to pull a little book out of our pockets and read
over the rules. It says here that you must not use lead bullets [actu-
ally, the pamphlet referred to dumdum bullets]; but I don't see why
not. They do the work." Villa, as Reed confessed, did not abide by

any ground rules in his campaigning. He shot peons captured from the Huerta forces because "no peon would volunteer against the cause of liberty unless he were bad." (Actually, many of the federal troops were pressed into service as unwilling conscripts.) The enemy officers were executed because "they were educated men and ought to know better." Most of the killing of prisoners was performed by Rodolfo Fierro, known as "The Butcher," Reed explained. "In his furious lust for blood Fierro used to shoot down a hundred prisoners with his own revolver, only stopping long enough to reload. He killed for the pure joy of it. During the two weeks that I was in Chihuahua, Fierro killed fifteen inoffensive citizens in cold blood. But there was always a curious relationship between him and Villa. He was Villa's best friend; and Villa loved him like a son and always pardoned him." [20] This should have told Reed more about Villa than he cared to admit to himself or his readers.

Reed could see him only as the folk hero of Mexico, possessing a "passionate dream of peace, justice and plenty" and ambitions limited to building a factory in one of his colonies to manufacture saddles and bridles and living "among my *compañeros* whom I love." Perhaps at that moment Villa really did want nothing for himself, everything for the peon masses; but he would succumb to the universal Faustian impulse and forget that earlier he wanted only to "help make Mexico a happy place." He began as a bandit and ended as a bandit, but by that time Reed was involved in a far greater uprising of the downtrodden, with a sequel immeasurably more tragic.

For two weeks in Chihuahua City Reed spent most of his days hanging around Villa's headquarters. Nights he spent drinking Tom and Jerries at El Cosmopolita to ward off the night chill from the desert. Until Villa took the city, El Cosmopolita was operated by Jacob La Touche, a Turk who had appeared in Chihuahua City twenty-five years earlier with a dancing bear as his only asset. La Touche had owned a mansion on the Paseo Bolívar known as "The Palace of Tears" because it had been built out of the proceeds gained from ruining many men who had a childlike faith in his roulette wheels. Reed and Johnny Roberts spent much time at the gambling tables, especially the stud-poker game, for which they had devised a system that would have gotten them shot in any respectable game north of the border. "Johnny and I would lift a corner of our cards as soon as they were dealt, to show each other. And when I seemed to be drawing ahead Johnny would impulsively push his whole stack over to me; with the next card Johnny's hand would seem to have more promise than mine, and I would push both stacks back to him." Whenever Reed and Roberts prospered too outrageously, the dealer would "whistle shrilly to the two house players and slyly deal them each a hand off the bottom of the pack." [21]

Fascinated though he was by Villa's personality, Jack decided to go south and see what was happening down where the partisans were clashing with the outposts and patrols of the federal army garrisoning Torreón. An American named "Mac" in Reed's accounts of the journey was heading back to his mechanic's job at a mine in the state of Durango and invited Jack to go along. They took the train as far as Jimenez, where they went to Doña Luisa's Station Hotel to spend the night before continuing their journey the next day in a buggy. Doña Luisa, who provided Reed with a chapter for *Insurgent Mexico,* was a salty New England woman of eighty-odd years who inspected them through the Judas window before letting them into the hotel. "There's so many damned drunken generals around today that I've got to keep the door locked," she explained.

Reed traveled as far as Magistral with Mac, then continued in the mule-drawn buggy toward the headquarters of General Tomás Urbina, the leader of a band of Villista partisans. He met five young Americans, who identified themselves as "soldiers of fortune," left to shift for themselves after Villa ordered all Americans discharged from his army. One of them, called "The Major," with his "hard little face and cruel eyes," told Reed, "I always wanted to kill someone with a gun, and I done it at Ojinaga and I ain't got a bellyful yet. They told us we could stay if we signed Mex citizenship papers. . . . I'm going to stay down here till I got enough of a stake to go back to Georgia and start a child-labor factory." Jack decided that Richard Harding Davis' romantic portrayals of the American soldier of fortune were somewhat overdrawn. "I saw few soldiers of fortune—except one—and he was a dry-as-dust scientist studying the action of high explosives in field-guns—who would not have been tramps in their own country." [22]

He finally reached the village of Las Nievas, a collection of adobe huts which looked like "some strange growth of the desert," in northern Durango. Here General Urbina, "the Lion of Durango," rested between campaigns against the *colorados*, the federal army's irregulars, in a house swarming with children and animals. The General's baby daughter was sitting in a corner of the patio using a cartridge as a teething ring. The General, a black-bearded man with small watchful eyes, warmed up to Reed after noticing that the American correspondent carried a camera. "For the next hour I took photographs of General Urbina: General Urbina on foot, with and without sword; General Urbina on three different horses; General Urbina with and without his family; General Urbina's three children on and off horseback; General Urbina's mother, and his mistress; the entire family, armed with swords and revolvers . . . one of the children holding a placard upon which was inked: 'General Tomás Urbina R.' "

A few hours later the General started roaring orders for his irregulars to gather and mount up for an operation. The main force was *La Tropa*, about a hundred hard-riding Indian troopers. Accompanying them was the General's baggage coach, "an exact copy of the Deadwood Stage," in which Urbina carried his campaign necessities: four swords, one of them with the emblem of the Knights of Pythias, a typewriter, three uniforms, the General's personal branding iron, and a twelve-gallon demijohn of *sotol*, that most potent of Mexican firewaters.

Reed himself rode in the coach, rather nervously, since he shared it not only with the General's campaign gear but also with three boxes of dynamite and a case of bombs.

For three weeks he rode with Urbina's band, covering hundreds of miles across the desert and foothills, "sleeping on the ground with the *hombres*, dancing and carousing in looted *haciendas* all night after an all-day ride, being with them intimately in play, in battle." It was, he said later, "perhaps the most satisfactory period of my life." At times the merriment was too hectic even for Reed. One night at La Zarca, when a barrel of *sotol* had been tapped, he was dancing with the camp follower who belonged to one of *La Tropa*; the trooper hit her over the head with his gun butt; another trooper accused the harpist of hitting a wrong note and shot at him, and "there was a snapping of rifle levers all over the place." [23]

At the outpost of La Cadena, while Urbina and *La Tropa* pressed on in their search for the enemy, Reed stayed behind with the hundred-and-fifty-man garrison commanded by a "dreadfully incompetent old party named Major Salazar."

One morning he was awakened by sounds of alarm, troopers saddling their horses, a bugle clamoring, cartridges being slammed into rifles. At last he was going to see a fight. A thousand *colorados*, the Huertista irregulars, had approached during the night and come through the pass that the post at La Cadena was supposed to be guarding. The night guard had been caught sleeping. Reed loaded his camera and ran out to cover his first—and almost his last—battle. The enemy was advancing from the base of the nearby mountain in extended order to surround La Cadena and its garrison. "We could see them now, hundreds of little black figures riding everywhere through the chaparral; the desert swarmed with them. Savage Indian yells reached us. A spent bullet droned overhead, then another; then one unspent, and then a whole flock singing fiercely. Thud! went the adobe walls as bits of clay flew. Peons and their women rushed from house to house, distracted with fear. A trooper, his face black with powder and hateful with killing and terror, galloped by, shouting that all was lost. . . ."

Heavily outnumbered, the outpost was routed, "a wild huddle of troopers" rode past Reed, fleeing for their lives. There was nothing for Reed to do but join the panicky flight across the desert. He stripped off his camera, overcoat, and anything else that might impede his escape from the *colorados*, who knew even less of the rules of war than did Pancho Villa. "I ran on" across the desert floor, Reed recounted, "until I could run no more. Then I walked a few steps and ran again. I was sobbing instead of breathing. Awful cramps gripped my legs." He finally reached a patch of chaparral, which afforded some cover from the pursuers, and was struck by the feeling that "Everything was so unreal, like a page out of Richard Harding Davis. It just seemed to me that if I didn't get away I wouldn't be doing my job well. I kept thinking to myself: 'Well, this is certainly an experience. I'm going to have something to write about.'" He almost didn't. A couple of *colorados* rode within a hundred yards of him and shot down another fugitive from La Cadena. Reed made it to a dense patch of mesquite and hid there until it was safe to start walking toward a ranch where the parents of one of his friends in *La Tropa* lived. The survivors of the battle also gathered there.[24]

Reed took his way back to Chihuahua City, where Villa was making careful preparations for the advance on Torreón. That key railroad junction was strongly held by Huerta's forces; it barred the way to any Constitutionalist offensive toward Mexico City and the south. Huerta's strategy from the beginning of the counterrevolution had been to hold a number of fortified cities on the trunk rail lines—Torreón, Monterrey, Zacatecas, Chihuahua, Saltillo, Tampico, San Luis Potosí, and Guadalajara—leading toward the capital from north and south. Torreón was the passageway through central Mexico, and if it fell Huerta would be dealt a near-mortal blow. His commander in Torreón, General Velasco, had fortified it with a belt of trenches, barbed wire, batteries of field-gun and machine-gun emplacements, and boasted that the city was impregnable.

In February, shortly after returning to Chihuahua from his trip to Durango State, Reed hastened back to El Paso to cover for the New York *World* an incident that had aroused a lot of excitement north of the border. Villa had gone up to Juárez, to superintend the forwarding of arms shipments coming from the United States. There he was confronted by a hot-tempered Briton named William Benton, who owned ranch and mining properties in Durango. Benton accused Villa of rustling cattle from his ranch. The argument ended with Benton shot dead. Who shot him? No one would say, but there were rumors that "Butcher" Fierro had done the deed under Villa's approving eye. In any case, it made for a bad press in the United States and Great Britain. Reed himself merely reported the facts. Then, on orders from the *World*, he went over to Nogales, on the Arizona border, to interview the First Chief of the revolution, Venustiano Carranza, whom he found in his darkened hotel room beside an unmade bed and an ice bucket containing three or four bottles of wine. Reed was not taken by Carranza: "You got the impression of a vast, inert body—a statue." He seemed seven feet tall and wore dark glasses even in the shaded room. The First Chief thrust aside Reed's questions to launch a tirade against American intervention, then being advocated because of the Benton incident, and shouted that such a measure would provoke war and "deepen a profound hatred between the United States and the whole of Latin America, a hatred which will endanger the entire political future of the United States!" [25]

In the first week of March, 1914, Jack and most of the other foreign correspondents gathered again in Chihuahua City. Hundreds of Villa's *soldados*, their wives, children, and camp followers were concentrated in the capital for the boxcar descent on Torreón. A whole train of tank cars was required just to haul the water for the advance. A dust cloud seven miles long arose from the marshaling yards in which Villa's troops and their horses were boarding the cars.

Finally, on March 16, Villa's troop trains and supply wagons began moving out for Torreón. Always obsessed by the need for secrecy Villa "closed the telegraph wires to the north, stopped train service to Juarez, and forbade on pain of death that anyone should carry or send news of his departure to the United States. . . . No one, not even Villa's staff, knew when he would leave Chihuahua; the army had delayed there so long that we all believed it would delay another two weeks. And then Saturday morning we woke to find the telegraph and railway out, and three huge trains, carrying the Brigade Gonzalez-Ortega, already gone. . . ." [26]

The next day, Reed and the other correspondents, traveled in a boxcar with an icebox, two barrels of beer, and a stove, to arrive at

Yermo, the concentration point seventy miles north of Torreón. An artillery park was established, with mules and caissons corralled in the center. The little town swarmed with thousands of Villa's followers, and Carranza's Secretary of War came riding up on a burro with a war map of Mexico strapped to his shoulder.

The Villistas began probing the outer defenses of Torreón. At Bermejillo they rushed into town as Pascual Orozco's irregulars rushed out. That left the telephone system in Villa's hands, and he began conducting psychological war by telephone. His Chapul-tepec-trained artillery commander, Felipe Angeles, got General Velasco, the commandant of Torreón, on the line and suggested that he surrender the city. Villa himself called a federal official in Gómez Palacio, the next objective in his advance, and told him with exaggerated courtesy, "I've covered a lot of territory just to see you fellows."

"Are there many of you up there?" the official nervously inquired.

"No, not many," Villa replied. "Just two regiments of artillery and ten thousand *muchachitos* to entertain you." [27]

The Villistas went to war joyfully, Reed wrote in describing a morning scene in camp. "A hundred breakfast fires smoked from the car-tops, and the women stood turning their dresses slowly in the sun, chattering and joking. Hundreds of little naked babies danced around, while their mothers lifted up their little clothes to the heat. A thousand joyous troopers shouted to each other that the advance was beginning. . . ."

The army continued its advance toward Torreón, frequently held up by the necessity to repair the railroad tracks torn up by General Velasco's retreating forces. Reed accompanied the artillery as it moved up to duel with Velasco's batteries inside Gómez Palacio. He had the true reporter's eye, and the vignettes with which he sprinkled his account of the fighting conveyed to his readers thousands of miles away a vivid sense of reality. "A little farther along I came upon an officer—a German—wandering along, lead-ing his horse by the bridle. 'I cannot ride him any more,' he said to me earnestly. 'He is quite too tired. I am afraid he will die if he does not sleep.' The horse, a big chestnut stallion, stumbled and swayed as he walked. Enormous tears trickled from his half-shut eyes and rolled down his nose. . . ." [28]

Reed followed Villa as that jovially reckless chieftain, clad in a slouch hat and grimy clothes, led his regiments in the assault on Gómez Palacio. It was a surprise attack at night, and Villa himself was in the forefront hurling bombs. He took the fortified town that night, March 26, and Reed wired the *World*, "Seven windrows of men I counted, where seven successive charges failed. The trenches were choked with the bodies of the defenders." Shortly after getting that dispatch off on Villa's military telegraph, he fell ill from drinking unboiled water.

He was still weak and wobbly as he followed the Villa army toward its grapple with the defenders of Torreón. Fortunately the correspondents' private boxcar rolled up and "at last we had our bunks, our blankets and Wong, our beloved Chinese cook." Reed and his colleagues were just beginning to relax over their whisky when the federal artillery began raining shrapnel all around them. The correspondents quieted their fears by keeping the whisky jug in constant circulation. "Every time a shell would explode nearby we would all wince and jump, but after a while we did not mind it. Then we began to congratulate ourselves and each other for being so brave as to stay by the car under artillery fire. Our courage increased as the firing grew far between and finally quit altogether, and as the whiskey grew low." Drunken arguments broke out over who had been the bravest and "one man almost choked a drivelling old fool who was with a moving-picture outfit. Late that night we were still trying earnestly to persuade two of the boys not to sally forth without the password and reconnoiter the Federal lines at Torreon." [29]

For five days Villa drove his assault lines against the main defenses of Torreón. On April 1, fighting block by block, each costing the lives of many men on both sides, Villa's army fought its way into the heart of the city. A last-gasp federal counterattack pushed Villa back to the outskirts, but General Velasco was already fleeing the city under cover of a sudden dust storm. The next day Villa recaptured the city and was able to wire Carranza that the federal troops were in flight and Torreón had been taken at a cost of five hundred Villistas dead and fifteen hundred wounded.

Reed was sickened by the cost of the victory, and had no more stomach for fighting, no matter how just the cause. By the time Villa took his prize, Reed was heading back to El Paso. Accompanied by a photographer, he bribed a railroad hand and acquired the use of a motorized rail car which took them north to Bermejillo, where he caught a hospital train bound for Chihuahua. In El Paso, away from Villa's censorship, he wrote his brilliant account of the battles on the approach to Torreón.

And he found himself famous, nationally famous, for his three months' immersion in the Mexican revolution. This was because, as Walter Lippmann wrote in his essay "Legendary John Reed," "the public discovered that whatever John Reed could touch or see or feel he could convey. The variety of his impressions, the resources and color of his language seemed inexhaustible. The articles which he sent back from the Mexican border were as hot as the Mexican desert, and Villa's revolution, till then reported only as a nuisance, began to unfold itself into throngs of moving people in a gorgeous panorama of earth and sky. Reed loved the Mexicans he met, loved them as they were, danced with them, drank with them, raided with them, risked his life with them. . . . He was not too dainty, or too wise, or too lazy. Mexicans were real people to him. . . . He did not judge, he identified himself with the struggle, and gradually what he saw mingled with what he hoped. Wherever his sympathies marched with the facts, Reed was superb." [30] From a historic rather than a literary perspective, it might be added that Reed perceived the weakness and vanity of the First Chief and glimpsed a foreshadowing of the break between Carranza and Villa that changed the course of the revolution.

On March 23, while Reed was dodging the federal shrapnel on the approaches to Gómez Palacio, the *Metropolitan Magazine* had run a large display advertisement in the New York *Times* to herald his series of articles on the journey to Durango. There was a drawing of Reed wearing a flat-brimmed sombrero, revolver and gun belt strapped around his waist, camera slung over his shoulder. "What Stephen Crane and Richard Harding Davis did for the Spanish-American War in 1898, John Reed, 26 years old, has done for Mexico. You see that beautiful, blood-drenched country. . . . You see glorious, drunken nights of revelry where mirth is turned to tragedy by jealousy fired with too generous gulps of *sotol*. . . . Yes, Reed's story is literature."

It may not have been literature, but it was journalism of the highest order. He had Kipling's word for it that his talent was undeniable, and in July, 1914, the D. Appleton Company published a collection of his Mexican stories and articles under the title *Insurgent Mexico*. Perhaps he was even more flattered by words of praise from Professor Copeland, to whom he dedicated the volume. "It is all good, and more than good," Copeland wrote him, but added in a cautionary postscript, "You are a born writer—I discovered long ago. But I think you don't work hard enough at writing." [31]

Jack worked hard enough, when he worked, but the Professor, in his secluded chambers at Hollis Hall, simply did not understand the demands that fame—and love, and being admired, and having so many causes clamoring for attention—made on the "Golden Boy of the Village."

7

WAR ON
SEVERAL FRONTS

Mabel Dodge was waiting at the border when he crossed to El Paso full of his experiences with Villa and a genuine revolutionary army. It irked her immeasurably that he hardly seemed to notice that she had not played the faithful Penelope during his absence. Fidelity was one quality he did not demand in a woman—did not even seem to notice, either its presence or its absence—and it was also a quality he did not intend to develop in himself. It was too bourgeois a trait to merit serious consideration. Doubtless he had been no more faithful to her than she had been to him, but at least he had the decency not to flourish any other affairs he might have had in whatever hurried circumstances while following the Villistas. But not Mabel. She loved to provoke jealousy, and Gertrude Stein had noted in her "a very old-fashioned coquetry." [1] While still married to Edwin Dodge, she had tormented him by engaging in flirtations quite openly. "Her pleasure lay in Edwin

Dodge's having to be present at the scene of her conquests; the conquests themselves were nothing more than the amusement of the moment. When she tired of Dodge, she tired of the game as well." [2]

But Jack Reed was too infuriatingly self-absorbed to make a satisfactory player in that coquettish "game" of Mabel's. He would only smile vaguely, even encouragingly, when she made a play for some other man in his presence.

When she had returned to New York from El Paso while Reed was chasing after the revolution, she had plunged immediately into an affair with Andrew Dasburg, a painter who had been one of the group invited to the Villa Curonia while Reed was a guest there. During that interim relationship with Dasburg, she later wrote, "I lived in the electric atmosphere that surrounded him. Sometimes he seemed to flame like a star and sparks ran off the breezy hair that aureoled his round head and made him look like a Blake drawing. His body, so slim and broad, was strong, as an organic thing full of terrible forces can be. I felt the wonder of life in him, tempestuous, rising like sap. . . ."

For all the ecstatic adjectives she lavished on Dasburg, he served chiefly as a hoped-for means of arousing Reed's jealousy. "I wrote Reed all about Andrew, and how very attractive he was to me. I sent Andrew to him like a blue ribbon, down there in Mexico where he rode with Villa and his army."

Reed, however, was so full of himself and his own pursuits that he ignored her gloating over Dasburg's charms. "He sent back a letter full of the intoxication of supremacy: 'I will write all our names across the sky in flames,' he wrote. I wish I had his letters— so vivid and alive. . . ." She had to burn her letters from Reed, she added, to "please Maurice, who in his turn loved human sacrifices." [3] Maurice Sterne, painter and sculptor, became Reed's legitimate successor and her third husband.

Mabel and John returned to New York and the apartment at 23 Fifth Avenue, but Mrs. Dodge simply couldn't curb her possessiveness, and the stormy scenes of recrimination and mutual renunciation began all over again. By her own account she made a determined effort to pretend to be the submissive mate and understanding mistress. Yet she could not submerge her own ego eternally, because Reed was so waywardly childish, so exhausting in his boyish enthusiasms. Even the publication of his book was a source of exasperation to her. "He dedicated the book to his mother and this made me silently angry," she wrote. "I myself, obscurely, wanted to be his mother." [4] (Actually, Reed dedicated *Insurgent Mexico* to Professor Copeland.)

If there was an obscure maternal streak in Mrs. Dodge it rapidly wore thin under the pressure of living with Reed. "Desperate, I tried to hold him closer by laments—I grew pale and wept and I held him tighter and tighter." But there was little return for her emotional investment, she later maintained. Her only sexual satisfaction with Reed came that first night they spent together, in the Paris hotel room. The worst of it was that Reed, overweening in his masculinity, seemed to care so little whether *she* was satisfied or not.

When she summoned the members of her group together for a "Reed in Mexico Evening," she observed him from a distance as he spoke before her guests and answered their questions, and was inwardly scornful of his evident sense of self-importance. "He stood up in the crowded rooms, eyes shining and curls bobbing back, temples agleam, and told everybody all about it. I stood off in a corner and looked at him and wondered why he looked so puffed up, as though he had been inflated by a pump. His chest swelled up under his chin and he had to compress it to get the air into his lungs to speak with." She bitterly resented anything that came to Reed without her having arranged it, bought it, or at least planned it for him. It was not so much jealousy of his success as the fact that he had gained it without her help. She was not so overcome by malice, however, that she was prepared to allow another female to move in on her trophy. Her sharp eyes observed a girl named Babs, (who later proclaimed that she was fighting the evils of prostitution by giving herself to any man who wanted her), eying Jack hungrily. Mabel sent her a note admonishing her against making a play for Jack, and eventually extorted Babs' promise to keep her hands off Mabel's property.[5]

Probably it was this exuberance, which he exhibited even in the footling byplay of her salon, that dismayed Mrs. Dodge more than anything else. The kinetic energy of his youth and enthusiasm must have made her feel much more than eight years older than Reed, must have deepened the fears that she could not hold him forever. In the weeks following his return from Mexico, Jack blazed up over the city like a pinwheel. He poured his energy into journalism, poetry, the cause of Pancho Villa, and a dozen other things that caught his attention. Each time he returned to New York from adventures elsewhere the city's fascination for him, which was never quite quenched even by later pilgrimages to the holy city of revolution, was revived and strengthened. The ambivalence of his feelings, torn between admiration for its imperial sky line and knowledge of its cruelty to those who lived beneath, only made its fascination more vivid and compelling. He lyrically expressed them in "Proud New York," which was published by Harriet Monroe in *Poetry*:

> Be proud New York and its man-piled Matterhorns,
> The hard blue sky overhead and the west wind blowing,
> Steam plumes waving from the sun-glittering pinnacles,
> And deep streets shaking to the million river—
>
> Manhattan, zoned with ships, the cruel
>   Youngest of all the world's great towns,
> Thy bodice bright with many a jewel,
>   Imperially crowned with crowns. . . .
>
> Who that had known thee but shall burn
>   In exile till he come again
> To do thy bitter will, O stern
>   Moon of the tides of men!

His restless mind was engaged, seemingly intoxicated by, a constant ferment of schemes, causes, and ideas. In his novel *Venture*, based partly on the character of Jack Reed, Max Eastman described "how full he was of gigantic schemes for diverting rivers out of their courses, upsetting the rhythms of the solar system, making barrels of money."

Julian Street recalled two incidents that displayed Reed in action with his quixotic enthusiasm at furnace heat. One night, Street related, Reed came to his house fuming with indignation. He said he had just met a young girl, an orphan whose guardian had just swindled her out of her inheritance. She was penniless, and Jack swore that he would track the guardian down and wring the stolen money out of him. The next time Street saw Reed he asked how he was making out in the girl's case, but Jack changed the subject. The next time they met the same thing happened. Finally Street asked a mutual friend what had happened. "Oh," the friend told Street, "didn't he tell you? The girl turned out to be cracked— never had any money at all."

A short time later, undaunted, Reed came bounding over to Street's house with another tale of outrage and injustice. "With a group of friends he had gone the night before to an Italian restaurant below Washington Square, and had sat late over coffee and liqueurs. Toward midnight a young woman at another table began to sing. Jack and his friends applauded, and presently, after the fashion of Bohemia, the two groups merged." Jack walked the singer home and almost wept when, under the lamplight on the deserted street, she gave him a haunting rendition of "Home, Sweet Home."

" 'It was an unforgettable experience,' he told me. 'There isn't a voice to compare with hers at the Metropolitan Opera, and when I told her so she wept and gave me her story. There's a clique up at the Metropolitan. They know about her voice, and they realize that if the public once hears hers their regular sopranos are done for; so they've entered into a conspiracy to suppress her.' "

Jack's remedy for this injustice was characteristically charged with direct action; it was the Paterson Pageant, on a less spectacular scale, all over again. "He was raising money to hire a hall and give a recital for her," Street related. "The critics would be there and, having heard her, would force the Metropolitan to take her

in. . . . For the next two weeks we heard of nothing but the recital. Most of Jack's friends bought tickets. A large and warm-
hearted audience assembled. The critics duly arrived. Everything
required to make a memorable musical occasion was there—except
a voice." [6]

The two anecdotes reveal the feckless strain in Jack Reed, his
tendency to go spinning off on tangents like a dismounted fly-
wheel, and they built up the case for Street and his more conservative friends that Jack was something of an irresponsible larrikin.
The playboy image of Reed, particularly in the years before World
War I, was certainly justified in part; he hated to take himself too
seriously, and his sense of humor would always break the most
solemn of surfaces. "He was," wrote Max Eastman, who loved
him as a man even though he came to detest the cause to which
Reed gave his life, "with whatever gifts he had—and their extent
will never be quite known—in the heart of one utterly American
literary tradition, the tradition of imaginative laughter. We are not
so far, I hope, from the great days of Davy Crockett and Artemus
Ward and Mark Twain and Abraham Lincoln that we have to
patronize and excuse and tolerate, and worst of all condescendingly
understand as a 'playboy' a man gifted with an irrepressible and
absolutely divine gift of joking. All the oh-oh-ing about Jack Reed's
joyful, and on the whole superlatively sane exploits in imaginative
laughter, as though they were something that had to be outgrown
before he could become a man . . . has always struck me as suffocating and sanctimonious. There isn't one of John Reed's detrac-
tors as a 'playboy' who wouldn't give his right hand for an occasional glimmer of the wit and gay magnetic humorous fancies that
bubbled out of him in speech and action more than half the
time." [7]

Certainly there was nothing coltish about his professional activities in the several months following his return from Mexico. He
could not forget the sufferings of the people of Mexico, nor would
he allow the American people to forget whatever part of those sufferings were caused by venture capitalism south of the border, nor
was he unmindful of the fact that his experiences in Mexico acted

as a catalytic agent on his talents as a writer. "That four months of riding hundreds of miles across the blazing plains," he wrote several years later in his autobiographical essay, "sleeping on the ground with the *hombres,* dancing and carousing in looted haciendas all night after an all-day ride, being with them intimately in play, in battle, was perhaps the most satisfactory period of my life. I made good with these wild fighting men, and with myself. I found myself again. I wrote better than I have ever written." [8]

Shortly after his return to New York the United States found an excellent excuse for intervention in Mexico. A paymaster from the American naval squadron cruising off Veracruz was arrested by Huerta's officers while buying supplies in the port city. The United States demanded that the officer be released and that the garrison of Veracruz tender a thirteen-gun salute to the American flag in token of its regret for the incident. Huerta refused, perhaps in the belief that the Mexican people would unite behind him if their sovereignty was threatened from the outside. On April 21, President Wilson ordered a naval landing party to occupy Veracruz. There was fighting, in which four Americans were killed. In what Walter Millis has called "a moment either of policy or pique" President Wilson then ordered four army regiments sent to Veracruz and other forces to be mobilized on the border. It looked as though Mexico was about to be invaded again.

Reed was anti-Huerta, of course, but he believed that even a limited intervention would get out of hand and that the United States would proceed from pacification to conquest. In succeeding days, and with an effectiveness that was amazing in a twenty-seven-year-old journalist, Reed did all he could do to counteract the agitation for all-out intervention. He obtained an interview with the aging Joseph Pulitzer, publisher of the New York *World,* and persuaded him to take a more forthright stand against it. And on the following day a *World* editorial reflected his argument that the towering issue was Mexican land for the peons, not Mexican oil for the British and American exploiters. "There will be no permanent peace in Mexico until the peon is on the land that belongs to the peon," it declared. He wrote an article for the *Metro-*

politan Magazine of June, 1914, pointing out that eighty per cent of the Mexican population, possibly an underestimate, was fighting for its rights to a decent life. In reality, he wrote, there was not a series of revolutions, as it appeared in the United States from the tall headlines about Villa, Madero, Orozco, and Zapata, but a centrally motivated uprising. "As a matter of fact, there is and has been only one revolution in Mexico. It is a fight primarily for land." He warned that "the first American soldier across the Rio Grande means the end of the Mexican revolution," and that American concepts of democracy could not be tailored to fit those of Latin America—a pronouncement that continues to echo, almost as futilely, in today's controversies over the affairs of the Southern Hemisphere. "We do not realize that the Latin temperament is different from our own—and that their ideal of liberty is broader than ours. We want to debauch the Mexican people and turn them into little brown copies of American business men and laborers, as we are doing to the Cubans and the Filipinos." An invading army would find it easy enough to roll over the military opposition, but "It is the peons and their women, fighting in the streets and at the doors of their houses, that they will have to murder." In the *Masses* he expressed himself even more strongly, stating that nothing worse could happen than the imposition on Mexico of "our grand democratic institutions—trust government, unemployment and wage slavery."

Some weeks later, when the passion for intervention had cooled slightly, he carried his campaign on behalf of the Mexican revolution to Washington, sought and obtained interviews with Secretary of State William Jennings Bryan and President Wilson. He called on the "Great Commoner" in his home, of which, he later wrote in a magazine article, "I retain an impression of lace window-curtains. Bead curtains separated the parlor from the dining-room, and through these the maid presently passed, still singing." Fittingly enough, in that pious household, the maid was singing hymns. Presently Bryan appeared, with "that familiar and appalling smile." That broad-beamed statesman struck Reed as a monument of American naïveté; he embodied the contemporary view of what a statesman should be—ponderous as an old bull elephant, speaking "in the way a statesman should—slowly, impressively, and with massive seriousness."

Mr. Bryan complained that there was one thing about the Mexicans that troubled him deeply. "Do you know," he inquired in his sonorous voice, "when one faction captures a soldier of another faction, they stand him up against the wall and shoot him down?"

The Secretary of State affirmed, however, that he favored only a program that would insure peace between the United States and Mexico, and he arranged the appointment for Reed to talk with the President.[9]

Both men, as Reed saw them, were well-intentioned liberal-humanists and inclined toward pacifism (Bryan more so than Wilson, as it turned out, for he resigned from the Cabinet in protest against American intervention in World War I). The President, on receiving Reed at the White House, reminded him that he was not to be quoted directly, but he made it plain that he did not intend to intervene more forcefully in Mexican affairs. Veracruz had been occupied, he emphasized to Reed, only to check Huerta. If Carranza's Constitutionalist movement, the umbrella under which all the various anti-Huerta revolutionaries currently were sheltering, succeeded in taking power, the United States would not object to confiscation of the haciendas and the distribution of their land to the peons, though he would prefer that the landowners be compensated for the property expropriated from them. Wilson also emphasized that he was opposed to "the small predatory minorities which balk the people's struggle for intelligence and life." Later Wilson wrote to Reed that he appreciated his "whole spirit" in upholding the cause of the Mexican people.[10]

Even as Jack Reed was making himself the hero of the American left, that loose confederation of anti-imperialists, anarchists, union activists, Socialists, and pre-Soviet Marxists, the ikon of a former hero was being hauled down in sorrow, anger, and disappointment. It was that of Jack London, for so many years the glamour boy of American Socialism. He was a boy no longer—thirty-eight in 1914 and only two years away from suicide on his baronial estate in

California—and success as a popular novelist had corrupted and disillusioned him. London had gone to Veracruz as a correspondent for *Collier's*, as a man who still signed his letters "Yours for the Revolution" but who was shockingly disenchanted by his first glimpse of a real revolution. He enraged his former comrades by writing in *Collier's* that U.S. troops should have occupied Tampico as well as Veracruz, that Mexican oil should be exploited by outside interests, that the only trouble with American intervention, in fact, was that it was not forceful enough. The Mexican revolutionaries, he declared, were simply bandits who were fighting for loot and the pleasures of pillage and rapine. Mexico would continue to be "mismanaged and ill-treated" until the United States "took over the whole country" as the "big brother of the countries of the new world." [11]

Floyd Dell expressed the feelings of most of his fellows when he wrote that Jack Reed was taking Jack London's place as laureate of the left. "My boyhood Socialist hero, Jack London, had died . . . he came back singing the tunes that had been taught him by the American oil-men who were engaged in looting Mexico; he preached Nordic supremacy, and the manifest destiny of the American exploiters. He had, apparently, lost faith in the revolution in which he had once believed. . . . But he died too early. If he had lived a little longer, he would have seen the Russian Revolution. Life would have had some meaning for him again. . . . As it was, the ending which seemed to belong rightfully to his life came to another life, that of a young man who was in many ways like Jack London—Jack Reed." There was something of London's willful immaturity in Reed, as Dell coolly noted; he was "infantile," tended to scatter his energies and "wanted to be everything, artist, revolutionist, adventurer." [12] The curious thing is that Reed—much as he resembled London—seemed to be less aware of him than any of others; there is no record he sought him out on London's occasional visits to New York, or that he was in any way impressed by him.

On the morning of April 22, 1914, while Jack Reed was engaged as usual in excited perusal of the newspapers at the breakfast table in Mabel Dodge's boudoir, a headline in the New York *Times* caught his attention, by both its size and its content:

45 DEAD, 20 HURT

SCORE MISSING

IN STRIKE WAR

The date line was Ludlow, Colorado, which for many years had been serving as a microcosm of the sort of struggle between the oligarchy and the oppressed that Jack London had depicted in *The Iron Heel*. In the coal-mining regions around Trinidad and Ludlow the lives of thirty thousand miners, mostly of Greek, Italian, Slavic, and Mexican descent, were controlled by the Colorado Fuel and Iron Company and several smaller companies. The miners' several attempts to break out of the feudal regime imposed on them by the mining companies, which were supported by a small army of armed deputy sheriffs and private detectives, had always been put down with swift brutality. In 1913, however, the United Mine Workers had moved in scores of organizers, and the miners armed themselves with shotguns and rifles to fight back if another attempt was made to suppress them. It was almost the perfect situation for stirring the juices of a young revolutionary like Jack Reed: even after half a century it is apparent that the workers were entirely in the right, the employers totally in the wrong.[13]

The New York *Times* story told of how a large force of the Colorado National Guard—two companies equipped with machine guns at a time when such weapons were scarce in the regular army —surrounded the tent colony at Ludlow with orders to smash the strike that had begun the previous autumn. "The Ludlow camp," the *Times* reported, "is a mass of charred debris, and buried beneath it is a story of horror unparalleled in the history of industrial warfare. In the holes which had been dug for their protection against the rifles' fire the women and children died like trapped rats when the flames swept over them. One pit, uncovered this afternoon, disclosed the bodies of ten children and two women. . . . A seven-year-old girl dashed from under a blazing tent and heard the screams of bullets about her ears . . . ran into the tent again and fell into the hole with the remainder of her family to die with them. . . . James Fyler, financial secretary of the Trinidad local, died with a bullet in his forehead as he was attempting to rescue his wife from the flames. . . ." The following day the *Times* declared on its editorial page that the Ludlow massacre was "worse than the order that sent the Light Brigade into the jaws of death, worse in its effect than the Black Hole of Calcutta. . . . When a sovereign state employs such horrible means, what may not be expected from the anarchy that ensues?"

Reed immediately made arrangements with the *Metropolitan Magazine* to investigate the strike and the massacre and write a soberly factual and documented account. He was accompanied to Colorado by Max Eastman, who had assigned himself to do a similar job for the *Masses*. They arrived ten days after the rifles and machine guns had done their job, and, as Max Eastman wrote, "Jack Reed and I traveled the whole region in search, you might almost say, of a battle." [14]

What he saw and heard in those embattled mountains, in the company towns and shacks of the miners, Reed reported as "The Colorado War" in the *Metropolitan's* July issue. In Trinidad he found the state militiamen patrolling the streets under arms and observed, "The strikers spoke no words. . . . They just looked, stiffening like hunting dogs." He talked to black-shawled widows who had seen their husbands shot down and who now crouched against a wall like the victims of an Eastern European pogrom.

In Ludlow itself he investigated the "death hole," in which the charred bodies of the ten children and two women had been found. Only debris remained of the tent colony in which twelve hundred persons, the strikers and their families, had lived until the morning the Colorado National Guard surrounded them and opened fire. "Stoves, pots and pans still half full of food that had been cooking that terrible morning, baby-carriages, piles of half-burned clothes, children's toys all riddled with bullets, the scorched mouths of the tent cellars—this was all that remained of the entire worldly possessions of 1,200 people," he wrote.[15]

For several weeks Reed roamed the mining towns of Huerfano and Las Animas Counties and talked to the survivors of the massacre and other strikers, to officials of the mining companies, and in Denver to members of the state government who had ordered the National Guard to descend upon Ludlow. The facts he gathered, and later presented in a straight reportorial style unlike the personal emotions that drenched his reportage from Mexico, amounted to a harsh indictment of the coal companies.

As far as the companies were concerned, it was largely a case of indifferent, absentee ownership allowing its mine superintendents and other executives to wring the most profits at the lowest cost in whatever fashion they thought most efficient. The largest of the companies, the Colorado Fuel and Iron, was controlled by John D. Rockefeller, Jr., who owned forty per cent of its stocks and bonds. Rockefeller had not inspected the property for ten years, had not even attended a directors' meeting in that period, and he told a U.S. Commissioner that he had "not the slightest idea" of the conditions under which the miners worked and lived.

The conditions, as Reed learned from the documents of various investigating agencies, were appalling. The death rate among coal miners in that state was twice as high as the national average. In one hundred and nine deaths investigated by coroner's juries in Huerfano County, the mine managements were found guilty of negligence in only one case. The miners were forced to live in slab shanties rented to them by their employers; the Colorado Fuel and Iron Company owned a dozen towns of that type, complete with stores in which their employees were "expected" to buy all their supplies. Garbage littered the streets, and water was pumped from the mines without being filtered. Anyone who protested was driven out of town. Three strikes previous to the one that started in 1913 were smashed by mine guards and other hirelings of the companies, who patrolled the towns and spied on people suspected of complaining against their employers. The grievances of the miners were endless, but they all added up to the fact that the mining companies had established a medieval fiefdom in the Colorado mountains, stocked it with immigrant laborers ignorant of their rights, and suppressed any attempt to enlighten them or better their conditions.

The flash point in relations between the miners and the coal companies came when the former were organized by the United Mine Workers and drew up a list of demands: wages equal to those paid in the Wyoming mines, an eight-hour day, the right to trade at other than company stores, enforcement of the state's mining laws, and abolition of the mine guards. Though modest enough, they were totally rejected by the coal companies. On September 23, 1913, nine thousand miners went out on strike and marched down the canyons, out of the company towns, to establish themselves in tent colonies. One reaction of the employers was to build the "Death Special," an armored car with a machine gun mounted on it, which menacingly patrolled the tent cities and on one occasion opened fire, killed one striker, and seriously wounded a young boy. Mother Jones, an eighty-year-old Irish-born agitator, appeared in the strike zone, was arrested three hours after she arrived in Trinidad, and was held incommunicado for nine weeks, part of the time in a cellar under the Walsenburg courthouse, in which nightly, she said, "I fought great sewer rats with a beer bottle." [16]

Finally, in desperation, the governor of Colorado called out the National Guard, for which professional gunmen and various other adventurers were, as a U.S. Commission later reported, recruited because they were "economically dependent on and subservient to the will of the coal operators." It was this force of thugs which occupied the high ground surrounding the Ludlow camp on the morning of April 20, opened fire, then poured kerosene on the tents and set them afire. Many of those who escaped the bullets and flames were arrested, and Louis Tikas, a camp leader, was taken before a National Guard lieutenant, who broke a rifle stock over his head and then ordered him shot and killed by one of his troopers. Fighting spread throughout the mountains, thirty people were killed, and Governor Ammons finally appealed to President

Wilson, who sent in six troops of U.S. Cavalry to bring the "Colorado war" to an end.

In Denver, Reed listened to Governor Ammons blandly claim that his National Guard was "composed almost exclusively of young professional and business men, some of them sons of the best families of this state." But Reed also talked to the captain of a militia company, who admitted that ninety per cent of his troopers were former mine guards who had merely changed uniforms. He also listened to the Rockefeller satrap on the scene, J. C. Osgood, president of Colorado Fuel and Iron, who charged that all the violence was caused by "ignorant foreigners" whipped up to an insensate fury by outside agitators.[17]

While compiling his material for the magazine article, Reed joined the agitation himself, and spoke along with George Creel and Judge Ben Lindsey, at meetings for the collection of funds for the strikers' relief. He stopped in Chicago on his way back to New York to speak before newspapermen at Hull House on what he had observed. These and other activities on behalf of the strikers, as well as the compressed fury of the facts he presented in his article, "The Colorado War," helped to counteract the flood of propaganda against "anarchists" and "foreigners" loosed by the Rockefeller interests, their corps of publicists, and other supporters. In part, also, they finally helped to bring about improved conditions in the Colorado coal fields, so that, though the strike was defeated after a fifteen-month struggle, federal investigators were able to report five years later that the miners had better housing and schools, had been accorded their civil rights, had won better working conditions, and were no longer forced to patronize only company stores.

Reed rejoined Mabel Dodge in New York, then later in the spring accompanied her and her household, including her son and her servants, to a summer house she rented at Provincetown. Now, as she later observed in a spattering of capital letters, he was more than ever the Hero, the public figure, and more sought after by claim-jumping Women. He engaged in at least one affair, to her knowledge. But by now she was able to analyze quite coolly her difficulty in choosing a suitable male consort; obviously Jack would never grow into that role. "But why I chose men too immature to satisfy me, or too lacking in essential qualities—ah! that question must be answered later on. Perhaps my unsatisfied maternity helped me choose these younger ones: since I had no maternal feeling for my own son, I must take it out on other women's sons. Certainly Reed was a child compared to myself. . . ." [18]

Off Reed went, home to Portland and his own mother, that summer of 1914, while Mabel journeyed to the Villa Curonia. He was in Portland when the armies of Europe mobilized and then, like mechanical monsters beyond the control of their fabricators, crunched toward each other on the borders of France, Germany, Austria, and Russia. In America, at first, that collision was viewed with detachment. There were vociferous elements who favored the Allies, there were the "hyphenated" Americans who hoped for a victory of the Central Powers because they either sympathized with Germany or (in the case of Irish-Americans) wanted to see Great Britain defeated, but the majority was cozily and insistently neutral. This feeling of aloofness from Europe's problems was expressed on August 19, 1914, two weeks after the war broke out, by President Wilson. "The United States must be neutral in fact as well as in name during these days which are to try men's souls. We must be impartial in thought as well as in action and put a curb upon our sentiments as well as upon every transaction that might be construed as a preference of one party to the struggle before another."

Wilsonian high-mindedness would turn more bellicose in the crucible of events, even pacifists and Socialists and those who sympathized with Germany would be swayed by the sinking of the *Lusitania*, the stories of German "atrocities" in Belgium, the deftness of Allied propaganda as compared with the ham-handedness of the German, the revelation of the Zimmermann telegram, and other mileposts on the road to intervention, but Jack Reed never swerved from the dead-center neutrality prescribed for Americans by their President in 1914. He continued to advocate it even after

Wilson changed his mind and ordered the American Expeditionary Force into the trenches of northern France.

Reed was the subject of one of the free-verse profiles interwoven into the narrative of John Dos Passos' *Nineteen Nineteen,* in which his wartime activities were described with a certain amount of hyperbole but with essential truth:

The war was a blast that blew out all the Diogenes lanterns;
the good men began to gang up to call for machineguns. Jack Reed was the last of the great race of warcorrespondents who ducked under censorships and risked their skins for a story.
Jack Reed was the best American writer of his time, if anybody had wanted to know about the war they could have read about it in the articles he wrote
about the German front,
the Serbian retreat,
Saloniki; . . .
The brasshats wouldn't let him go to France because they said one night in the German trenches kidding with the Boche guncrew he'd pulled the string on a Hun gun pointed at the heart of France . . . playboy stuff but after all what did it matter who fired the guns or which way they were pointed? Reed was with the boys who were being blown to hell,
with the Germans the French the Russians the Bulgarians the seven little tailors in the Ghetto in Salonique. . . .

Reed knew at once where he stood on the question of world war, or any war that was not essentially part of the class struggle. In Europe the Socialists suffered agonies of indecision over whether they should condemn the war and refuse to support their countries' participation or fall in line with all the other political parties in the name of national unity. Only Bolsheviks like Lenin, sitting out his exile in Swiss cafés, and Trotsky, then living in New York City, argued that a true proletarian would refuse to have anything to do with a war fought for the capitalists' purposes. Reed, like the Russians, opted out, discerned the party line before there was a party or a line.

Shortly before the official declarations of war came from European capitals, the editors of *Metropolitan Magazine* asked Reed whether he would be willing to go overseas as its war correspondent. Most pacifists would have avoided further scenes of mass slaughter, and he had departed from the outskirts of Torreón rather than witness any more bloodshed, but he eagerly accepted. The excitement, perhaps, was more than he could withstand. Richard Harding Davis and other rivals in his picturesque craft had already been announced as the representatives of other magazines and newspapers, and Reed, like them, was unaware that World War I would end most of the glamour of war correspondence, as it ended the myth of chivalry and adventure that had encrusted the profession of arms itself.

With the declaration of war Reed was off like a shot, catching the fastest transcontinental train available for New York. The war fever that was spreading across the world did not, however, infect him. On the luxurious train he took eastward, a young Englishman who had been traveling in the Far West and was returning home to join his regiment cut a heroic figure among the other passengers. Well-born and well-tailored, the Englishman said that he was going back home to join the army because it was expected of him, that he came of a family which had borne arms for a thousand years. His simple-minded patriotism aroused little but contempt in Reed, who limned him in an article for the *Metropolitan*. "He was a splendid sight as he stepped along the platform, the pink of young English manhood, the quintessence of that famous English ruling class that has made itself the greatest empire the world has ever seen—without the least idea of what it was doing. He went to glory or the grave, fearless, handsome, unemotional, one hundred sixty pounds of bone and muscle and gentle blood, with the inside of his head exactly like an Early Victorian drawing-room, all knick-knacks, hair-cloth furniture, and drawn blinds." [19]

Before Reed sailed for Europe he made his opinion of the war clear even without absorbing his own impressions of it on the scene. The *Metropolitan*, which had veered leftward sufficiently in the past several years to make Reed its star writer and to take on a near-Socialist tone, was beginning to have second thoughts about its policy as the transatlantic war changed the climate of public opinion; it would not be long before Reed would be considered too "controversial" for its pages. There were misgivings in its offices even as Reed was dispatched overseas, especially after he expressed himself so bluntly in an article titled "The Traders' War" in the *Masses* just before he left.

"The real war," he wrote, "of which this sudden outburst of death and destruction is only an incident, began long ago. It has been raging for tens of years, but its battles have been so little advertised that they have been hardly noted. It is a clash of traders."

In an exposition of radicalism's view of the war that was often to be quoted as the United States indulged in Hamlet-like indecision over whether to sympathize with the Allies or remain strictly neutral, Reed declared that the conflict had come about chiefly through the determination of Great Britain and France to maintain their own colonial systems in Asia and Africa while blocking the expansion of Imperial Germany. He was particularly harsh on the "raw hypocrisy" of the French and English ruling classes when they "shout for a peace which their greed has rendered impossible." The pro-Allies element in the American press was equally hypocritical, he maintained, in advocating that the United States join in a holy war against German imperialism. "What has democracy to do in alliance with Nicholas the Tsar?" he demanded. "Is it Liberalism which is marching from the St. Petersburg of Father Gapon, from the Odessa of the pogroms? We must not be duped by this editorial buncombe about Liberalism going forth to Holy War against Tyranny. This is not Our War." [20]

Considering that the armies of France, Germany, Austria, and Russia were already locked in battle, Reed took a rather circuitous and leisurely route toward the war front. He boarded a ship for Naples and stopped off at the Villa Curonia to pick up Mabel Dodge and her entourage while other American correspondents were hastening to cover the battles in Belgium and on the approaches to northern France. They proceeded to Paris, which was then in danger of capture by the Germans. The French capital was in a state of panic, with a whole German army group swinging down on the Marne after trampling over the Belgian forts. From other correspondents, Reed learned that covering the war was no longer a matter of personal enterprise. Things were going so badly for the Allies that newspapermen were forbidden to venture into the war zone; all they could do was hang around the rearmost headquarters and copy the communiqués, which blandly asserted that the German offensive would soon be halted in its tracks.

It must be said that Reed, in the old traditions of free-enterprise journalism, did his best to circumvent the censorship and the Allied quarantine on correspondents in the battle areas. He teamed up with Robert Dunn, a Harvard man several years older than he, and also a former protégé of Lincoln Steffens, who was trying to cover the war for the New York *Post,* and was also blazing with impatience to see the fighting and find out what was happening on the Marne. Dunn was a venturesome fellow after Reed's own heart who several weeks earlier had tried to infiltrate the Allied battle line on a bicycle but had been captured by the British and sent back to Paris.

Dunn, who described Reed's mistress as "a sloppy lady in lavender" and thought Reed wanted to get away from her as much as he hoped to get a glimpse of the action, agreed to Reed's suggestion that they obtain a pass to see them through the defenses of Paris on the excuse that they wanted to travel to the Riviera, then head northward for the Marne instead. The scheme almost worked. They drove out of Paris, northeastward, and the pass took them past the military-police posts on its outskirts. The first night they came to a British headquarters at Crécy, where they struck up a conversation with several Americans who had enlisted in the British army, two of them motorcyclists from Reed's home town.[21] Later they drank rum with several English soldiers assigned to guard duty at an ammunition dump, and Reed was pleased to report their unenthusiastic attitude toward the war and their amiable feelings toward the enemy. "Lord help us, the Germans as a rule are good enough chaps. It's a silly business, this killing of men. . . . I'm not for war on any account. But us Socialists, we're taking the field to destroy militarism—that's what we're doing. And when we come back again after the war, and Kitchener says to the House of Commons, 'What will we do for these brave soldiers to show our gratitude for saving the Empire?' we're going to say, 'You can jest give us the Empire.' "

The next morning Reed and Dunn were taken into custody by the British provost marshal, along with two English correspondents who had also tried to penetrate the zone of operations, and turned over to the French gendarmery. Treated not much better than spies—and regarded as almost as loathsome by military authorities determined not to let the news of their disastrous setbacks leak out—they were taken to Tours on a train loaded with German prisoners. There, according to Dunn, "we were asked to swear not to re-enter the army zone without leave. 'What if I refuse to swear?' asked Jack, the one time I saw him show some revolutionary gumption." The French officer snapped, "You go to prison," and looked as though he meant it. "So he swore, as I had, and we boarded the next Paris train." [22]

On his return to Paris, immeasurably irked at the new ground rules for war correspondents and observing with disgust how the wealthy and privileged citizens of Paris were heading for safer retreats to the south while Von Kluck's guns echoed from across the Marne, Reed decided to take a look at wartime England. This was not because he was afraid he might wake up one morning and see Uhlans trotting under his window; American citizens, as neutrals, had nothing to fear from the German army, but he found Paris, even under the threat of siege, a boring and apathetic place.

A London inflamed by patriotism, as Paris was not, also disgusted him. Everywhere he looked there were those recruiting posters with Field Marshal Lord Kitchener pointing an index finger and barking for more cannon fodder (Reed considered him "the very Prussian ideal of a military man," who perfectly expressed the imperial policy of "blowing men from the mouths of cannon in order to civilize them"), society women swarming over male civilians on the streets and pinning white feathers on them, territorials drilling in the parks. Kitchener's appeal for six hundred thousand volunteers for the New Army, to replace the regular army, shattered in its retreat from Belgium, had been answered by an overwhelming rush to the recruiting stations. "It is magnificent," Reed observed in an unpublished account of his visit to London, "and infinitely depressing. This patriotism—what a humanly fine, stupid instinct gives birth to it, the sacrifice for an ideal, the self-immolation for something greater than self. Generation after generation surging up to the guns to be shot to death for an ideal so extremely vague that they never know what they are fighting for . . . the English know even less what they are fighting for than the Mexicans." [23] Patriotism as an emotion that would cause a man to sacrifice his life fighting for a country instead of an economic and social class was something he could not understand. He had already announced that he would join Pancho Villa's guerrillas and fight against his own countrymen if the U.S. army invaded Mexico, and he was determined that if his country joined the fighting in Europe he would face a firing squad rather than put on a uniform.

It made him furious that while hundreds of thousands of Englishmen were preparing to throw themselves into the trenches, which would soon extend from the North Sea to the Swiss border, the gilded upper layers of English society continued to enjoy their luxuries and privileges. "The great gray town still pours its roaring streams along the Strand and Oxford Street and Piccadilly; endless streams of omnibuses and taxicabs and carriages pass; in the morning the clerks go down to the City in their carefully-brushed silk hats and thread-bare frock coats. . . . At night the theaters and restaurants are going full blast, thronged with an apparently endless supply of nice young men in faultless evening dress, and beautiful women; along Leicester Square and Piccadilly press the same thousands and thousands of girls, and the hundreds of slim young men with painted lips, which yearly grow more characteristic of London streets." The British aristocracy, he believed, "like a waking lion," was revitalizing itself and "crushes our teeming anthill with a blow of its paw, and shows us again, contemptuously, a servile England split into classes, where every man knows his place. . . ."

England, he declared, bore the major share of "war guilt." In one paragraph he settled to his own satisfaction a question that would engage historians for half a century. "On my map there is a small collection of islands off the northern coast of France, isolated from the continent by a channel, and together a trifle larger than the State of Ohio. From there stretch the wires that control a tenth of the earth's surface. England's guns squat in the mouth of the Mediterranean; Egypt and Malta are hers; she grips the Red Sea, sucks the blood from all India, menaces half a billion human beings from Hong Kong, owns all Australia, half North America, and half of Africa. The fleets of the world salute her ensign on every commanding headland, and her long gray battle-ships steam unopposed from sea to sea. England's word is said in every council, conference, treaty. She is the great intriguer, sitting like a spider in the web of nations and disposing of them to her benefit. And it was England's will that Germany should be destroyed." [24]

And he ended that article, which the *Metropolitan* editors refused and which was consigned to his collection of unpublished manuscripts, with the slogan *"It is not Our War,"* which he sounded in almost everything he wrote about the war.

When he returned to Paris, the battle of the Marne was over, and the field-gray tidal wave of the German armies had washed back to the zigzagging line across northern France they were to occupy, with only occasional variations, until the end of the war. He and Andrew Dasburg—the painter who had temporarily replaced him in Mabel's affections during his months in Mexico, but whom, in the best of Bohemian spirits, he still regarded as a friend—toured the battlefields along the Marne. He was still looking for the sort of usable material that could make his articles for the *Metropolitan* take off on the same high trajectory as his coverage of the Mexican revolution; but the sense of personal involvement, of identification with the mechanized masses of the modern state such as he had felt for Villa's wild horsemen, was entirely missing. It was missing, in fact, from all the reportage of World War I. The miniatures of battle, skirmishes involving a few hundred men, were Reed's style, not the panoramas of endless trench systems, the human-wave assaults over no man's land, the hurricane bombardments of a thousand guns, the drowning of all human individuality. These were best conveyed, eventually, by only a handful of writers—Remarque, Barbusse, Hemingway, Aldington, Ford Madox Ford—who were participants and recast their experiences in fictional form.

Meanwhile, worried as he was about the quality of his work, he was having difficulties with Mabel, and with another woman and her husband. The emotional quadrangle was almost resolved by bullets from the offended husband's revolver. According to the story Reed told his friend and colleague Robert Dunn, he had become involved with a couple he had known in the Village. The girl was a German-American, her husband a dentist who mistreated her. Once, when he went to call on them, he found the young wife alone and ill; her husband had gone off on a trip even though he knew she was not well. Reed nursed her back to health; they fell in love during that process and decided they would marry after the girl got a divorce.

Jack was never any good at keeping things quiet, and shortly both the husband and Mabel Dodge found out about the affair. The husband armed himself and announced that he would shoot Jack on sight. Mabel promptly took an overdose of morphine, "the old trick she keeps for the end of any tether," as Jack told Robert Dunn. "Hours, all night, I fed her black coffee, tramped her up and down the corridor." [25]

By the time Reed got around to telling Dunn about his misadventures, several weeks later in Berlin, it all seemed hilarious. He related with gusto how he was simultaneously engaged in eluding the outraged husband, trying to keep Mabel from killing herself, and sneaking off to rendezvous with his ex-patient. The tale of his essay into French bedroom farce got back to New York, and Walter Lippmann later wrote in his essay on Reed, "He is the only fellow I know who gets himself pursued by men with revolvers, who is always once more just about to ruin himself."

With a fine sense of self-preservation, Reed decided to get away from both importuning women—and the ferocious dentist—by leaving France and investigating the other side of the battle line. Mrs. Dodge went back to New York, convinced that the two-year affair was over, though there would be several anticlimactic encounters with Jack. He journeyed to Berlin, rejoicing, as he told Dunn, at having escaped marriage to either of the women. Getting tied down, he said, was the thing he feared most.

Perhaps getting himself extricated from those emotional entanglements had a therapeutic effect. For the first time since he came to Europe he began getting the feel of the war, and the two articles he wrote for the *Metropolitan* from Germany were far superior to anything he wrote from the Allied side of the line. Possibly because he considered Germany the underdog, arrayed as she was against the overwhelming alliance of France, Russia, and Great Britain, with only Austria on her side, and certainly not because he had any affection for Prussian militarism, he wrote more sympathetically of the Germans than of the French or English. Perhaps, also, he was trying to counteract British propaganda, which was being concocted by the ablest literary men in the empire and was already making a noticeable impact on public opinion in the United States. It helped, too, that the German military authorities did not hamper the activities of neutral correspondents; "you had only to disown any German blame in the event you were hit" by a stray bullet, as Robert Dunn noted, "and take the night train to Metz."

Again with Dunn, Reed journeyed from Berlin to Metz to Lille. In occupied France they found French peasants back at work in their fields while German troops marched along the roads bordering them. "Don't imagine that German soldiers are a cruel, arrogant race," he wrote in his article "German France," which greatly affronted Allied propagandists. "They have done admirable things. I am sure that some of these little northern French towns were never so clean, so intelligently organized. Everywhere they have reopened schools and churches; they have re-established local institutions and local charities; they have scoured whole towns, lighted every house with electricity, placed up-to-date hospitals, served by the finest doctors in the world, at the free disposal of the humblest citizen." [26]

Dunn, less carried away by admiration for German efficiency, painted a somewhat grimmer picture of the occupation. True enough, brick railroad bridges had been replaced by steel-and-concrete structures, but the work was performed by Frenchmen "at forced labor" under overseers with bayonets, and "the streets were empty of citizens; they are ordered home at dark." A conducting officer warned them not to speak in English to strangers, because the French populace was "now very friendly to us," but, even as he said that, a Frenchwoman, overhearing them, muttered "Boches! Sacré boches!" [27] Such observations did not intrude upon Reed's narrative.

As they were being escorted toward the front lines, in the sector of the Bavarian II Corps, Reed and Dunn discussed their views of what the postwar world would be like.

"Times of self-denial, poverty and work—a sort of neo-Puritanism," was Dunn's opinion.

"Rot!" Reed retorted. "Socialism will be in. Pie in the sky, champagne in thundermugs for everyone!"

They went up to the front early in the evening, with German artillery flashing against the sky over Ypres. The German officer with them suggested that they venture no farther than the support trenches, because the French had been throwing in night raids recently and there was always a chance of a mortar shell or a burst of shrapnel catching them in the dugouts of the forward position.

"You want to go?" Dunn asked Reed. "What do you say?"

"What does he think we are," snorted Reed, "Boy Scouts?"

They stopped in a ruined village behind the lines to buy a couple of bottles of champagne, and then pressed forward. French machine-gun fire whipped overhead as they crawled along a communications trench toward the front line. Finally they reached a dugout in the main trench with the French only a few hundred yards away, and a young Bavarian lieutenant told them, as Dunn recalled, that "three weeks ago the Spahis opposite had tried to rush this position, and fifteen men had been killed here, in today's firing." German howitzers were replying to a barrage from French artillery; flares shot into the night sky, and occasionally an outbreak of rifle and machine-gun fire added contrapuntal effects to the roar and blast of the big guns. Obviously it was a nervous night on both sides of the line. To ease the tension, Reed and Dunn broke out their champagne and settled down to a poker game with the German officers in the dugout.[28]

Later in the evening one of the German officers genially suggested that their guests might like to take a shot at the French just for the hell of it. The champagne had done its work, and both Americans agreed, though they knew that under the rules of war they were noncombatants and forbidden to bear or fire any weapon. They stepped into the trench, peered across no man's land through a slit in the armor-plating, and each fired a shot with a Mauser rifle in the general direction of the French army. Both, Dunn said, fired "high into the air."

No one would have heard about this minor indiscretion, but for the fact that Dunn committed a major indiscretion. In his next dispatch to the New York *Post*, he told of the incident.

When he mentioned to Reed that he had done so, Jack shook his head and said, "It could get us in a jam." [29]

That was one of the few understatements of Jack Reed's career.

8

"THE MAD DEMOCRACY
OF BATTLE"

Of all the shot and shell that exploded on the Western Front, the stray Mauser shots fired by Reed and Dunn caused an inordinate amount of controversy and recrimination. Behind the uproar was undoubtedly the unsympathetic tone of Reed's writing from the Allied side of the line. Had the two correspondents idly aimed at the Germans instead of the French there would certainly have been less protest in the United States and elsewhere.

Dunn described their action in the New York *Post* on February 27, 1915, in a blithely unrepentant fashion: "Be it on our heads, we did it, both fired twice, turn and turn about, wicked, full-fledged franc-tireurs. . . . That Reed should have done so, with his scorn of force and soldiering, is sufficient, if sophistical, excuse for me."

The French government immediately announced that neither correspondent would be permitted to return and would be arrested if they appeared on French soil. "By his own confession," *Le Temps* of Paris declared, "Dunn is an assassin and should be treated as such." [1] Naturally the same went for Reed. President John Grier Hibben, of Princeton, was quoted as protesting "this cold-blooded and inhuman proceeding." [2] Richard Harding Davis, in his rather stuffy fashion, denounced Reed and refused to speak to Dunn when they happened to meet. Being "cut" by Davis in those days was the journalistic equivalent of being drummed out of the regiment. Editorials in the pro-Allied newspapers condemned Reed and Dunn for committing an act that not only was nonneutral but was also pro-German. Theodore Roosevelt told Dunn that he would have had him and Reed "shot on sight" for larking about in German trenches.[3]

One of the few voices raised in their defense was that of Lincoln Steffens, who wrote to the editors of the New York *Post*, "It would have been 'discreet' to suppress any mention" of the shots they fired in a moment of exhilaration. "But Dunn mentioned it; of course he did; he couldn't help it. And neither should you have cut it out, as you wished you had. It is one of the most significant facts reported from the front. It shows that you and I, and Dunn's critics, would fall in the trenches into the spirit of actual war; the careless spirit of passionless shooting into the dark." [4]

The *Metropolitan* meanwhile wanted Reed to return to France as its correspondent. Toward this end it enlisted Theodore Roosevelt—who had joined its staff as a regular contributor in February, 1915—in the effort to whitewash Reed and make him acceptable to the French. The former President applied himself to this task with understandably divided feelings. He had always respected and admired Reed's late father, who was one of his most vocal supporters in the Pacific Northwest, but found it rather difficult to stomach C. J.'s son and his outspoken opinions. Further, there was the fact that the younger man showed no deference to Roosevelt's years and position in the world. For his part, Reed resented Roosevelt's presence in the *Metropolitan's* offices and his name on its masthead as a contributing editor: it was a symptom of the magazine's change in attitude since the beginning of the war. The

Metropolitan was swerving away from its Socialist position and taking a more pro-Allied stance. It provided space for Roosevelt to denounce Pancho Villa and those Americans who supported him, which was "literally like defending an oldtime Apache chief"; to clamor for universal military training, and to rage at "the peace-at-any-price people, the professionalist pacifists."

Whenever Roosevelt and his young antagonist met in the magazine's offices, they went for each other like a couple of pit bulldogs. One of the politer exchanges recorded ran like this:

ROOSEVELT: "Villa is a murderer and a bigamist."
REED: "Well, I believe in bigamy."
ROOSEVELT (extending his hand to shake Reed's): "I am glad, John Reed, to find that you believe in something. It is very necessary for a young man to believe in something." [5]

Nevertheless, Roosevelt agreed to write a letter of introduction to Jean Jules Jusserand, the French ambassador in Washington, which Reed could present in making a personal appeal for renewing his credentials as a correspondent with the French armies. "The letter of introduction," wrote Julian Street, "dictated by Roosevelt in Reed's presence, was a curious document. It stated that Jack was sorry he had fired toward the French, that he wished to go to France, and that if permitted to do so, his writings would doubtless benefit the French cause. But that was not all. At the end came a sentence somewhat as follows: 'Nevertheless, I am bound to say that if I were Marshal Joffre and Reed fell into my hands I should have him court-martialled and shot.' . . . Jack took the letter to Washington and saw the ambassador, who told him nothing could be done for him and strongly advised him not to set foot on French soil." [6]

While waiting for a new assignment on the war fronts, Jack worked on articles, short stories, and a three-act play, *Enter Dibble*, which he had started two years earlier. One of his stories, "The Barber of Lille," about a German officer murdered in occupied France, was published by the *Metropolitan*; another, "Daughter of the Revolution," about a prostitute descended from people who had fought for the Commune and led strikes and was herself living testimony to the "intolerable degradation of the human spirit by the masters of the earth," was published by the *Masses*. They were more successful, certainly, than the play, which was a sort of proletarian comedy about a man who intended to be "the greatest ditch-digger the world has ever seen." Shavian in tone but not in theatrical effectiveness, *Enter Dibble* was never produced, though his one-act play *Moondown* was presented by the Washington Square Players and was well received.

When the *Metropolitan* sent him to cover one of Billy Sunday's soul-saving crusades in Philadelphia, the result was an article, "Back of Billy Sunday," that explored the motives of the Philadelphia bigwigs who formed the evangelist's local committee. Significantly, they included an even dozen industrialists, a dozen bankers, and four corporation lawyers. One member was Alba B. Johnson, the president of the Baldwin Locomotive Company, which was notorious for its methods of breaking strikes and for keeping wages low. "People's minds are obsessed by material things," Johnson told Reed. "Billy Sunday makes people look to the salvation of their own souls" and forget the "selfish desire to become rich." The naïve instrument of Johnson's designs against materialism, Billy Sunday himself, was gently treated in Reed's article. Billy put on a good show, Reed conceded. "We went away unconverted," he concluded, "but Philadelphia was saved." [7]

Despite their falling-out in Paris, he and Mabel Dodge made another attempt to obtain extramarital happiness. Something, perhaps no more and no less than sexual attraction, drew them together in spite of Mabel's hysterics and Jack's infidelity. Jack simply could not help behaving like a yo-yo. After moving back in with Mabel, he went off on an amorous tangent with a woman Mabel identified in her memoirs only as "N." Then, contritely, by her account, he returned to Mabel's bed and board.

"Well! Well! Well! Yes, there was no one like me," she recounted. "Once a man loved me, he said, he could never get over it. . . . He could not live without me. So he had come back to me. . . . He was like a little boy come home to his mother after an escapade, disarmingly anxious to tell her all about it. Here he was home again, the hunter home from the hills." [8]

He kept talking about marrying her after he returned to America from his next assignment to the war fronts. The *Metropolitan* had already decided to send him to the Balkans, since the French and British would not have him. The prospect of returning to the battle fronts unnerved and depressed him, she said, picturing him on the verge of a nervous breakdown. This does not quite jibe with other accounts of his happy-go-lucky attitude on leaving for Europe. But according to Mabel he bought her a wedding ring and insisted that she wear it, and he instructed Carl Hovey, his editor, to refer to her any decisions to be made on his behalf.

The dramatic leave-taking, Mabel insisted, left her cold and emptyhearted. She went to bed with him as a farewell gesture but "without emotion." And when he left for the docks, "after a long, passionate, more loving farewell than he had ever expressed when I had really cared for him, I forgot him before the day was over: nothing had happened so far as I was concerned." [9]

Before he left for Southeastern Europe, Jack was somewhat annoyed by Walter Lippmann's celebrated dissection of the Reed career and what motivated it, which was published in an early issue of the newly established *New Republic*. It treated him, in effect, as something of a trifler, a seeker after thrills and adventures rather than a man dedicated to social and political reform, a creature largely devoted to self-indulgence. "By temperament he is not a professional writer or reporter. He is a person who enjoys himself. Revolution, literature, poetry, they are only things which hold him at times, incidents merely of his living. Now and then he finds adventure by imagining it, oftener he transforms his own experience. He is one of those people who treat as serious possibilities such stock fantasies as shipping before the mast, rescuing women, hunting lions, or trying to fly around the world in an aeroplane. . . . Reed is one of the intractables, to whom the organized monotone and virtue of our civilization is unbearable. You would have to destroy him to make him fit. At times when he seemed to be rushing himself and others into trouble, when his ideas were especially befuddled, I have tried to argue with him. But all laborious elucidation he greets with pained boredom. . . . I don't know what to do about him. In common with a whole regiment of his friends, I have been brooding over his soul for years, and often I feel like saying to him what one of them said when Reed was explaining Utopia. 'If I were establishing it, I'd hang you first, my dear Jack.' But it would be a lonely Utopia." [10]

Reed did not publicly reply to the Lippmann essay, and certainly he was not visibly shaken or dismayed by the judgment pronounced by his rather solemn and longheaded former classmate. Perhaps, in moments of introspection, he was convinced that his own method of seeking after the truth, even if it sometimes resembled the gamboling of a spring lamb, was the right one for him. It was an instinctive rather than an intellectual process. With considerable perception Max Lerner has written of that wayward journey of Reed's: ". . . through all his wanderings and explorations Reed was led, by some hard and uncanny inner sense, to discover truths and solutions that remained hidden from wiser minds than his, like Lincoln Steffens's, and from subtler minds, like Walter Lippmann's. He often got the right answers on the basis of the wrong reasons. Part of his genius lay in being so terribly unfooled." Lerner was referring at that point to Reed's refusal to be misled by war propaganda. " 'This is not our war,' he kept saying, when everyone else was getting lost in a maze of sophistry and propaganda. He was no thinker but a man of action. But it was his good fortune to be led to the most desirable of all fates for a man of action who is also a writer and a poet—the chance at once to write history and to make it." *

* The temptation to quote more of Mr. Lerner is irresistible. Writing in *The Nation* on April 29, 1936—his subject being the recently published biography of Reed by Granville Hicks—Lerner declared that it was unjust and misleading to emphasize Reed's legendary characteristics. "One of the best ways to damn a man . . . is to build a legend around him. That makes him a hazy and unreal figure and takes the edge off whatever sharp meaning his life might otherwise have. John Reed was a dangerous man. His life traced a pattern which, if it were followed by other middle-class lives, would burst the bounds of our present social system. And so those who have feared him, unable to fight his influence in any other way, have welcomed the chance to make him incredible . . . condescended to his Faustian thirst for life. . . .

Certainly the Lippmann essay did not send Reed off to Europe for his second, and more oblique, view of the war with any resolves to be more circumspect, less of an "intractable" character. Once again he vibrated with a schoolboyish enthusiasm; he had persuaded himself, as he wrote to his mother on disembarking in Italy, that covering the war in Eastern Europe would be more rewarding than witnessing the organized slaughter on the western front. It was a nostalgia for the war of movement, of men fighting in the open as individuals rather than parts of a gigantic military machine, that even then was afflicting certain romantics in the British and French war ministries who were launching amphibious forces against the Turkish peninsula of Gallipoli. With only the vaguest notions of where his travels would take him, or perhaps a faulty sense of geography, he told Mrs. Reed, "The Caucasus is something like Mexico, they say, and I'm sure I'll like the people. It will be great to get on a horse and ride over the mountain passes where Genghis Khan invaded Europe." [11]

Reed was accompanied on his assignment to the Balkans by Boardman Robinson, who had been an artist on the New York *Tribune* staff for many years. The red-bearded Robinson, English born but a naturalized American citizen, was an admirable choice for a traveling companion. With a matching lust for adventure and a similarly uproarious sense of humor, they complemented each other like those contemporary comic-strip heroes the Katzenjammer Kids. If Jack needed anyone to help him get into trouble, he had an excellent collaborator in Boardman Robinson. Thus in the view of Reed's staider friends, such as Julian Street, the whole idea of venturing into the typhus-ridden backwaters of the European war was a "stupendous piece of foolhardiness." [12] There would be no press officers to provide comforts, no billets arranged for them, no conducting officers to make sure they did not stray into danger. In the maelstrom of the Balkan war, which was

Walter Lippmann set the pattern . . . and Reed's enemies have followed the pattern, as his friends have often stumbled into it." Lerner, incidentally, believed that Hicks's biography should receive the Pulitzer Prize for biography in 1936, "but it will not. That, too, is part of John Reed's story."

merely a local extension of blood feuds dating back to tribal days, there was no proper front, only a rapid ebb and flow of battle. It was the sort of mountain-feuding country where a strange face was enough to earn a bullet between the eyes from some invisible sniper far away.

And that was just what he and Robinson were looking for, a war whose magnitude was not so vast that it could not be encompassed by the solitary imagination, as Reed explained in the introduction to *The War in Eastern Europe*, a collection of his writings and Robinson's sketches. The fighting in the Balkans was just sporadic enough so that "we were able to observe the more normal life of the Eastern nations, under the steady drain of long-drawn-out warfare. In the excitement of sudden invasion, desperate resistance, capture and destruction of cities, men seem to lose their distinctive personal or racial flavor, and become alike in the mad democracy of battle. As we saw them, they had settled down to war as a business, had begun to adjust themselves to this new way of life and to talk and think of other things." As in Mexico and behind the Allied lines in France, Reed was interested in the ordinary life of the people, what they thought and felt, as much as the life of the soldiers. As a magazine correspondent he did not have to concern himself with the minutiae of war, the communiqués, the minor advances and retreats; he was able to concentrate on the human side. Thus his articles in the *Metropolitan* and his book—with Robinson's admirable sketches—form an invaluable picture of Southeastern Europe early in the war.

It was the forgotten front from then until the end, although it was the arena in which the continental war started. Hardly a valley was not soaked in blood and the race memory of conquest, oppression, and liberation. The First and Second Balkan Wars, involving Ottoman Turkey and its provinces, then the provinces against each other, had served as a curtain raiser. Then had come the assassination of Austrian Archduke Franz Ferdinand at Sarajevo, and the invasion of Serbia by the Austrian armies.

Now, in the spring of 1915, much of Serbia was occupied by Austrian troops. Worse yet, perhaps, a massive epidemic of typhus had swept the region. Bulgaria was trembling on the brink of joining the Central Powers, though this would mean alignment with the ancient enemy Turkey. Rumania soon would jump in on the opposite side. Greece was divided to the point of civil war between factions favoring the Germans and Austrians and those with French and British sympathies. An Allied expeditionary force was in the last stages of preparation for landing on Gallipoli, taking Constantinople, opening up supply routes to Russia through the Black Sea, and, incidentally perhaps, sweeping up the Balkans and threatening the Central Powers from the rear.

Without any clear idea of how they would approach their assignment, since so much had to be left to chance, Reed and Boardman wandered from Italy to Salonika, which was thronged with refugees from the fighting in the mountains to the north. Finally they headed north, toward the remnants of unoccupied Serbia, despite reports that a thousand persons a day were dying of abdominal typhus, spotted fever, and recurrent fever.

A Standard Oil executive in Salonika, on being told their destination, remarked to them, "Too bad. So young, too. Do you want the remains shipped home, or shall we have you buried up there?"

Proceeding north toward the mountains of Macedonia, they heard tales of the typhus epidemic, which had reached its peak in February, when there were "hundreds dying and delirious in the mud of the streets for want of hospitals." A lieutenant attached to the British medical mission told them, "The truth about the typhus is that no one knows anything about it, except that about one-sixth of the Serbian nation is dead of it." And a deadly companion, cholera, was also coming down the roads from the combat zone to the north.

Train service had been suspended to prevent the spread of cholera, so they traveled on whatever military conveyance was available across the gorge of the Vardar. The violence of the scenery and the Macedonian people was matched only by the beauty of the mountains. "From every canyon burst rapid mountain streams. In this valley the air was hot and moist; irrigation ditches, lined with great willows, struck off from the river, across fields of young tobacco plants, acres upon acres of mulberry-trees, and ploughed land of heavy, rich clay that looked like cotton country. . . . Here every field, every shelf of earth, was cultivated." Nearby were neat villages of white houses with red-tiled roofs.

But the stigmata of war were all around. The Serbian soldiers were dressed in rags, with kepis the only part of a military uniform they wore. A Serbian trooper told Reed, "We Serbians have no longer any uniforms. We have fought four wars in three years— the First and Second Balkan Wars, the Albanian revolt, and now this one. For three years our soldiers have not changed their clothes." [13]

Boardman and Reed caught a military train bound for Nish, the capital of unoccupied Serbia, and passed railway flatcars loaded with troops, each regiment accompanied by a small gypsy band playing fiddles and bagpipes. And they saw a hospital outside which hundreds of Austrian wounded lay on piles of drying mud.

Nish was a city of mud, disease, and intrigue, people starving in the streets, and "sudden windows ablaze with expensive jewelry and extravagant women's hats." The streets were thronged with "gypsies, poverty-stricken peasants, gendarmes with great swords, in red and blue uniforms, tax-collectors dressed like generals, also with swords, smart army officers hung with medals, soldiers in filthy tatters, their feet bound with rags—soldiers limping, staggering on crutches, without arms, without legs, discharged from the overcrowded hospitals, still blue and shaking from the typhus— and everywhere the Austrian prisoners. Government officials hurried by with portfolios under their arms . . . army contractors hobnobbed with political hangers-on over maculate café tables."

With the help of the local U.S. consul, the two men stayed at the Diplomatic Club, and found it an oasis of cleanliness and comfort, with an Austrian prisoner, a headwaiter at the Carlton in London before the war, presiding over its dining room. The entrance to the club was through a pigpen, Reed wrote, and "To see the British Minister sail majestically past the pigsty and mount the club stairs as if it were Piccadilly was a thing worth coming miles for." [14]

They journeyed to the Serbian army headquarters at Kragujevac and rode on horseback over the mountain battlefields nearby, where the Austrian army had recently been hurled back across the River Sava and out of the old capital, Belgrade. The Serbs greatly impressed Reed, who considered them "the strong, virile stock of a young race not far removed from the half-savagery of a mountain peasantry, intensely patriotic and intensely independent." (It was an odd facet of his character that he could admire the patriotism of small nations, but not that of the more powerful ones, though the difference, certainly, was merely one of degree.) A military train took them to within half a dozen miles of Belgrade, the stations in and around the city having been wrecked by Austrian bombardment. The city had only recently been recaptured, and the Austrians were just across the river. An artillery duel was being fought even as they entered Belgrade.

Much of Belgrade had been shattered in the fighting of the past eight months. As they passed the Royal Gardens "a draggled peacock . . . stood screaming in a ruined window, while a laughing group of soldiers clustered on the sidewalk underneath were imitating it." An English gunboat had just sunk an Austrian monitor in the Sava, and the city was expecting an Austrian bombardment at any moment. "The Austrians usually take it out on Belgrade," they were told. They came across batteries manned by Serbia's allies—French marines, Russian sailors, English naval gunners—which replied to the Austrian guns on the other side of the river. At night an Austrian searchlight swept the city, "then the invisible guns of the highland across the Save spat red; for an hour heavy missiles hurled through the sky, exploding miles back about the smoking English guns—the ground shook where we stood."

In the next several days they toured the Serbian trenches up the river and wandered through woods full of wild pigs and dotted with the cenotaphs of Turkish beys, pashas, and hadjis. They drank *raki* and Turkish coffee with the villagers, sang American songs for them, listened to tales of atrocities committed by the Hungarian contingents in the Austrian army. In Shabats they were shown a photograph of a hundred women and children who had been chained together and then decapitated by the enemy. Town after town had been gutted and lay in ruins. At a typhus hospital in Loznica the stricken, mostly soldiers, "lay packed closely shoulder to shoulder upon foul straw spread upon the floor." It was a question whether the massive, scientific bloodletting of the western front was worse than the human suffering on this forgotten front where disease was as deadly as modern military technology and Balkan hatred more virulent than that between Teuton and Gaul. Here, too, there was none of the heroic idealism Reed had found among Villa and his *compañeros*. Even a solitary Socialist, the captain of a Serb battery, whom he came across at Obrenovac, disappointed him when he confessed that he had lost his "faith" after four years of war. "I spend all day thinking of those guns; I lie awake at night worrying about the battery." [15]

After he and Robinson returned to Belgrade, Reed was stricken with crippling pains in his lower back. A Serbian doctor diagnosed his trouble as venereal disease, but an English army surgeon suggested that he was suffering from an infected left kidney—a return of the illness that had blighted so much of his boyhood. He was advised to return to America and have an operation performed. The pain lessened, however, and he decided to remain on the assignment. This showed not only his courage but also his fatalism, of which one of his editors remarked, "He had the nerve to face a firing squad believing he could kid his way out."

Instead of nursing the infection, or at least staying close to places where it might be treated if it worsened, he and Robinson decided to cross the devastated Balkans and investigate the Russian front. At the end of May, 1915, the czarist armies had just ended a two-hundred-mile retreat from the Carpathians after a series of disasters inflicted by the Austro-German armies. Although Reed and Boardman had no permission from Russia to enter that country, they decided to journey by train to the frontier where the Rumanian province of Moldavia, Austrian Bucovina, and

Russian Bessarabia came together in the bend of the River Pruth. They traveled over the Rumanian railway to Dorohoi, its northern terminus, where the chief of police offered to drive them to the Russian side of the Pruth in his automobile. The Moldavian hills were brown and gold, and over in Bucovina were "white winding roads, dazzling villas set in green, an occasional shining town— order and prosperity," while across the Pruth was visible nothing but Russian shabbiness, "the wet tin roofs of a clump of wooden shacks, thatched huts the color of dirt, a wandering muddy track that served as a road."

Their way was smoothed by the Rumanian police chief, who had friends at the headquarters of the Third Russian Army. Suddenly, passing a meadow in which a unit of the Russian army was bivouacked, they had ventured into Asia. Around the campfires were "men with Chinese eyes and cheek-bones polished like teak, robed in long caftans and crowned with towering shaggy hats of fur"—Turkomans from the Asian steppe, descendants of the warriors who had followed Genghis Khan, Tamerlane, and Attila.

The commandant of Novoselitsa poured glass after glass of tea for them, and other officers gathered around to converse in snatches of French and German. A lieutenant gave them an inkling of how corroded the czarist army was with nepotism and favoritism, how hopeless were its chances against the cold efficiency of the Teutonic armies, which humiliated it in every encounter. The young officer told them of a well-connected colonel who had performed ignobly in the war against Japan, yet was made chief of staff to General N. Y. Ivanov, of the Third Army. "It was he who forced the beginning of the retreat from the Carpathians; when Ivanov was absent he ordered the retreat of an entire army corps— exposing the flank of the next army. There wasn't any reason for it. People say he is insane. . . . However, the thing was hushed up, and he became chief of staff to General Dimitriev and did the same thing over again! You'd think that would finish him? Ah, no! He had powerful friends in Petrograd—and now he is chief of staff to another general!" Another officer said, with Russian fatalism, "It is like that. Advance, retreat. Advance, retreat." Reed asked a captain how long he thought the war would last. "What do we care," replied the captain with a grin, "so long as England gives money and the earth gives men?" [16]

A lieutenant in a Crimean Tartar regiment told of how his men, during the retreat from East Prussia in the first months of the war, had wanted to pull down a statue of Bismarck standing in a Prussian town, but the colonel forbade it because "it might cause an international incident." The Tartars disobeyed orders and stole the bronze statue. At Tilsit a general found it in a baggage wagon and threatened to court-martial those who stole it, so that night the Tartars removed it from the wagon and set it up in a field, where they toasted it in looted champagne. Next morning they found it had been stolen from them by a Siberian regiment. "Who knows where it is now?" the lieutenant said. "Perhaps retreating across Galicia with the Siberians."

The two men traveled by carriage along roads clogged with the horse-drawn wagons and ox carts that supplied the Russian army, day after day jolting over rutted roads toward Tarnopol, where it would be decided whether they had any right to be where they were. Tarnopol was the army-group headquarters. Polish began to replace Rumanian as the native tongue, and Slavonic crosses gave way to Catholic crucifixes. At Zaleshchki they were permitted to board a troop train for Tarnopol, and a colonel obligingly showed them the current positions of the Russian army and its opponents. So ill-prepared was the Russian army that the colonel was using captured German maps, explaining, "At the beginning of the war we had no maps at all of Bucovina or Galicia. We didn't even know the lay of the land until we had captured some."

At Tarnopol, on the "boundless Galician steppe, heavy with golden wheat and with ploughed land deeper than velvet," they were greeted with consternation. A staff major refused to believe they could have journeyed from Serbia, through Rumania, then across Bessarabia and Galicia without being stopped and thrown into jail. A General Lichinsky decided that they would have to proceed to Lemberg and state their case before the governor general of Galicia. Again they boarded a train that carried them across the wheat fields of Poland. The rail lines were clogged, and often they had to wait for hours on sidings. "One had the impression of vast forces hurled carelessly here and there, of indifference on a grand scale, of gigantic waste." Reed could not help contrasting the Russian forces with the "faultless German machine" operating in northern France, where "the Germans had built new four-track lines plunging across country and cutting through cities, over bridges made of steel and concrete, erected in eighteen days. In German France trains were never late. . . ."

In royal and ancient Lemberg "immense modern German buildings bulked across the noble skyline," and Reed discovered that the Poles were "the ugliest race in the world." The two men presented themselves at the chancellery and were told to wait in an anteroom, along with "one dashing boy in a hussar uniform telling in French a story about himself and a Polish countess whom he had met in Nice," a "gentle-faced pope of the Russian church," and a "bull-necked colonel covered with decorations." They were interviewed by the governor general's aide-de-camp, Prince Troubetskoi, "a great handsome youth with shining teeth." The urbane princeling sighed. "Americans! What's the use of regulations when Americans are about?" [17]

Prince Troubetskoi gave them a choice: they could go either to Petrograd to receive permission to visit the front from the supreme command or to General Ivanov, at Chelm, the headquarters of the Russian armies on the southwestern front. Chelm was closer to Lemberg and to the battle front. It was only a hundred miles from Lemberg by any direct route, but three hundred miles by railroad. They chose this, though they would have to make a detour into Russia and then back into Poland.

It was a hectic journey. They had to share a compartment with a crotchety old general who was being invalided home. The general had what Reed called "a morbid fear of fresh air." This led to a violent disagreement between them. As Robinson later told the story to Julian Street, he was awakened during the night by the sounds of a violent scuffle in the compartment. It was Jack and the general, who had closed the window Jack had just opened.

"Jack leaped up, seized the general by the back and jerked him away from the window. 'You damned old fool,' he cried, 'don't you know you'll suffocate?' At intervals during the night the struggle was resumed, and it is difficult to say why the railroad police, who were finally called aboard the train to interfere, did not put Jack in jail, for a general in the Czar's army was not a person to be trifled with, especially in time of war." [18]

At Rovno they had to change trains, and during the nine-hour wait they explored the local ghetto. Reed marveled at the endurance of the Jews in this hostile land. "Here in Rovno," he wrote later, "were thousands of Jews shut in an impregnable world of their own, scrupulously observing a religion incessantly purified, practising their own customs, speaking their own language, with two codes of morals—one for each other and the other for the Gentiles. Persecution has only engendered a poison and a running sore in the body of the Russian people. It was true what Miroshnikov [the Russian officer who acted as their guide in the Pale of Settlement] said, as we drank *kvass* in a little Jewish bar—that all Jews were traitors to Russia. Of course they are." [19] The pogroms had left them with little reason to love Mother Russia.

They were arrested by military police at the Rovno station, but were released in time to catch the train for Chelm. As they resumed the journey, Reed brooded over the "mysterious and somber" Russian forest, "leagues and leagues of it. . . . Hours apart are little thatched towns, mere slashings in the primeval woods," in which the most pretentious building was always the government vodka shop. Already he had noted the mystic feeling of the Russians for their land. "They do not seem to realize that there is any world outside of Russia; that is why they fight so badly on an invasion of the enemy's country . . . that is why they fight so well on defense."

He had come to the conclusion that, despite the heavy hand of czarist repression everywhere, "Russian ideas are the most exhilarating, Russian thought the freest, Russian art the most exuberant. . . . Russians themselves are, perhaps, the most interesting human beings that exist." Already he was a Russophile; already he was well along the road that would link his destiny inextricably with the Russians. "In America," he wrote, "we are the possessors of a great empire—but we live as if this were a crowded island like England. . . . Our streets are narrow and our cities congested. . . . Russia is also a great empire; but there the people live as though they knew it were one." [20]

Presumably this feeling was undimmed by their inhospitable reception at Chelm. Immediately after checking into the English hotel there, they were ordered to be put under house arrest and placed in a stuffy windowless room in the attic, where Reed rapidly developed symptoms of claustrophobia. Cossacks mounted guard outside their door. They could not go to the front; they could not see General Ivanov; they were suspected of being German spies. They would have to wait while Chelm conferred by telegraph with Petrograd on what to do with them. Reed was not at his best under confinement, as Robinson later confided to Julian Street. He was especially enraged by "an obnoxious Cossack guard who spat upon the floor of their room. Warned not to repeat the offense, he did repeat it. Instantly Jack sprang upon him, and pinioning his elbows, threw him out, bolting the door just as a saber point came through." [21]

After fourteen maddening days, they were informed that they could proceed to Petrograd, where the commander in chief himself would decide whether they could go to the front. It did not seem auspicious that they were accompanied to the capital by armed guards.

Nor was it. On arrival in Petrograd they checked into the Astoria Hotel, where, as they immediately realized, they were under constant surveillance by the secret police. Grand Duke Nicholas, as supreme commander of the Russian armies, was agitated by the manner in which they had managed to penetrate the Russian front and see for themselves the disorganization and inefficiency in the rear of the armies. He had already started an investigation and ordered that punishment be meted out to the officers who had failed to take them in custody and had, instead, extended hospitality. The reason was simple enough. Reed and Robinson were more dangerous than German spies. In their accounts of their journey, they could destroy the myth of the "Russian steamroller," the immense and inexorable military machine, a myth still being carefully (and understandably) preserved in the Allied countries. The truth they could tell was dangerous; it would encourage Russia's enemies, and discourage the Allies from increasing their vast shipments of gold, munitions, and supplies to their fumbling eastern ally.

Reed immediately took his case to the American Embassy, a two-story building on the Fourstatskyia Oulitsa, in which a former Baltimore banker, George T. Marye, presided in a dim and distracted fashion. To Ambassador Marye, as that fussy, white-mustached little man made apparent immediately, Reed and his companion were simply an embarrassment. His advice to Reed was to leave Russia "by the shortest route." [22]

Later, Reed told Negley Farson, then an American businessman in Petrograd, later a celebrated correspondent and author of the best-selling *The Way of a Transgressor*, how Ambassador Marye dithered whenever he and Robinson approached him for help as American citizens entitled to whatever protection he could afford them. He quoted Marye:

"Gentlemen, I regret exceedingly—the, ahem—shall we say, unfortunate predicament you find yourselves in, but—ahem—I would like to point out to your attention that you have willfully, needlessly and may I say—ahem—quite unwarrantably created this—ahem—situation yourselves. Therefore,—ahem—I regret to inform you that the Embassy of the United States cannot take up your case. You have placed yourselves beyond the—ahem—outside my province—ahem, ahem—sorry."

Reed demanded to know whether that meant Marye was refusing to help them in any way.

The Ambassador replied that there was nothing he could do.

"Oh, yes, you can, Your Excellency," Jack retorted. "You can go to hell!" [23]

Negley Farson, as a sympathetic member of the American colony in the capital, often ate and drank with Reed and Robinson at the

Astoria, and found them a rollicking pair for all their worries. "Reed," as Farson remembered, "was shooting his hands upward through his rumpled waves of chestnut hair. Robinson was tugging at his red beard. Both were making jokes about the Russian officers and American businessmen around them and laughing uproariously. They were dressed in rough corduroy breeches, as if they had just come down from a fishing trip in the Maine woods."

Farson, like Walter Lippmann, observed that fighting with the authorities—any authorities—acted like champagne on Reed's anarchistic spirit. "An arrest of any sort, even an anaemic open-arrest that allowed one to eat sterlet and caviare with the courtesans of the Astoria was balm to John's soul."

" 'The Grand Duke Nicholas is threatening to shoot us!' John exulted.

" 'Silly ass,' laughed the ex-Englishman, Boardman Robinson, who, with masterful strokes was drawing a caricature of a firing-squad on the tablecloth. 'It's perfectly gorgeous publicity!' "

For "about a week," Farson recalled, "we did nothing but pick each other's brains all night over the open-air dining table in the courtyard of the Hotel Angleterre," to which they had moved. Reed listened with great interest as Farson told him of Russia's crippling problem of munitions, of watching Russian regiments entrain for the front without rifles or weapons of any kind.[24]

Finally Reed and Robinson were advised that the Foreign Office was charging them for having entered Russia on false passports, breaking the military regulations on civilian movement behind the front lines, and carrying messages to revolutionaries. Furthermore, word had reached Petrograd that Reed had been prohibited from entering France for having fired a shot from the German lines. "The French," Farson noted, "had too much power in Russia for either John Reed or Boardman Robinson to let themselves feel comfortable over that blot on John's escutcheon."

Grand Duke Nicholas, related Farson, finally "gave them an ultimatum that they could leave Russia, *via Siberia*, within a stipulated time, or—face the consequences. The consequences were alternatively imprisonment or a firing-squad. And this last was not far-fetched by any means. Men were shot for less than John Reed had done." Compared to allowing the Americans to spread the news of Russian military weaknesses—from the Grand Duke's viewpoint—"an 'accident' to two American newspaper correspondents was a mere nothing, and even an execution would be justified." [25]

In those days, vexatious at best, Reed showed one of the most admirable parts of his character. It was not only courage in the Hemingway definition, but gaiety under pressure. Most men, faced with the possibly fatal displeasure of the Grand Duke Nicholas, then the most powerful man in a country where power could be used with the most brutal indifference to human consequences, would have at least shown signs of wilting. Not Jack; nor, for that matter, Boardman Robinson. They behaved as though the Cheka were a bogeyman to frighten naïve tourists. Only Petrograd itself, with its immense boulevards, its great canals and stone quays along the Neva, its "immense silent squares and wide streets," in which "the people are lost," the "splendid front of palaces yellow and barbarically red" along the broad river, overawed them.

One day Farson went up to their room to take them out to lunch. "I found John and Boardman in an uproarious mood. They were amusing themselves by throwing pop bottles at a Russian secret service 'plainclothes' man who was watching them from the street.

" 'You can always tell a Russian Detective,' said John, 'because he wears a bowler hat like Charlie Chaplin, carries a little Charlie Chaplin cane, and wears patent leather shoes—like that!' As he said this, he stepped back from the window and threw another pop bottle in a neat parabola into the street. Charlie Chaplin had moved to another lamp-post from which he was glaring at us. 'They replace them at regular intervals,' said John. 'We ruin their morale.' 'We've had a gorgeous morning,' said Boardman, with his deep-chested laugh. 'They've been chasing us all day.' "

After listening to Reed's description of the games they had been playing with the secret police, Farson thought it little wonder that the Grand Duke Nicholas, a towering fellow with rages to match, was seriously considering having them shot. Reed described "one of their usual mornings of taking *droshkies* and giving them an address they never intended to go to—for the benefit of the lurking Charlie Chaplin's ears—then leaping out on either side as the *droshky* was galloping down the Nevsky. The frantic effort of Charlie Chaplin's pursuing *droshky* to turn and 'dog' them—how they would make a hurried rendezvous and then dart off in different directions, a frantic Charlie Chaplin not knowing which to follow. Jumping on and off tram-cars and nearly breaking little Charlie Chaplin's neck. Going into the big Army and Navy store, and, for the benefit of an eavesdropping Charlie Chaplin, asking the price of machine-guns, rifles, daggers and dynamite. Then going up and trying to speak to Charlie Chaplin. Little Charlie Chaplin becoming almost terrified at this unorthodox behaviour of the man he had been set to shadow . . . Charlie Chaplin on the run . . . dodging like hell to get away from Boardman and John!"

After he finished this recital, Jack tossed their last pop bottle at the Cheka agent, then turned to Robinson and yelled, "Order some more soda, Boardman, the battery is running low." [26]

When they were not bedeviling the Grand Duke's watchdogs, they made life miserable for Ambassador Marye. Every time Marye appeared in public, Reed would step up to him and loudly inquire, "Well, what are you going to do for an American citizen?," a refrain which considerably lowered His Excellency's prestige in the American colony. Robinson drew a cartoon, later published in the *Metropolitan,* showing the Ambassador in the admiral's uniform one of his aides had busied himself designing for the American diplomatic corps of Petrograd, his plumed hat dwarfing his small head, his huge ornamental sword dangling between his tiny legs, and his hand pointing to a sign above the American Embassy reading NO AMERICANS NEED APPLY.

As the Grand Duke's ultimatum came close to enforcement, Robinson went over to the British Embassy and sought the assistance of its capable counsellor, Benjamin Bruce. Even though Robinson was no longer a British citizen and Reed never had been,

Bruce agreed to help them. "I was sitting in their bedroom in the Angleterre," Farson recounted, "when Bruce brought over . . . the telegram which the British Embassy in Petrograd had sent to the Grand Duke. It was over a page long, and it was to the effect that, in spite of their having violated Russian regulations by appearing behind the Russian front without the proper credentials, and as much as it was to be regretted that such a thing had happened, they were nevertheless two very eminent and respected American newspapermen; that there could be no question of their having anything but the most impeccable attitude towards Russia, and that it would be an act of the greatest magnanimity if His Imperial Highness, the Grand Duke Nicholas Nicholaivitch, could see his way to permit them to leave forthwith. . . ."

Bruce suggested that meanwhile they "leave those poor wretched secret service men in peace." [27]

A few days later word came from the Grand Duke's headquarters that they would be granted exit permits. When these arrived, Reed and Robinson immediately caught a train for Moscow, Kiev, and Bucharest. At their stopover in Moscow the two men wandered around the Kremlin square, rather depressed by its red-stone and monolithic magnificence, then took a steamer up the river to the Sparrow Hills, on which Napoleon had stood to watch Moscow burning. They had hardly resumed their journey southward when police boarded the train and removed them. Orders from the Grand Duke! They were not to leave Russia by the southern exit, but must, on pain of a military court-martial, return to Petrograd and leave the country via Siberia and Vladivostok—a roundabout journey three-quarters of the way around the world that would take weeks to complete. Once again Ambassador Marye refused to consider helping his two fellow citizens; once again the British Embassy interceded for them, and they were allowed to catch the next train for Bucharest.

Their Russian odyssey had been profitless so far as reaching the battle lines was concerned, but Reed was not disillusioned with the country itself. Perhaps intuition told him this fateful attraction would bring him back, and back again, because he was attuned to the national rhythm "that has in it all the deep solemnity and mad gayety of Russia." [28]

Bucharest, with certifiable claims to being the Paris of the Balkans, was still the capital of a neutral nation in midsummer of 1915. Reed and Robinson took adjoining rooms at the Athénée Palace Hotel, indubitably the Ritz of the Balkans, and settled down to writing and sketching the *Metropolitan* series. Occasionally, they would quibble noisily over the impressionism in Reed's writing and in Robinson's sketching. Robinson would read a passage in one of Reed's articles and complain that it had not happened that way at all. "What the hell difference does it make?" demanded Jack, whose passion for exactitude was intermittent and entirely governable. Then he would snatch up one of Robinson's drawings and point out that his collaborator had exaggerated a detail here and there. Haughtily, Robinson would reply that he wasn't a mere photographer. "Exactly," Jack would retort, "that is just what I am trying to do."

Reed left his companion still sketching away at the Athénée Palace while he continued on alone to Constantinople. The French and British had clawed out a toehold on the Gallipoli Peninsula, and Reed hoped that he would be allowed to visit the front from the Turkish side.

He boarded the Orient Express, and was not impressed by whatever vestiges of its prewar glamour remained. What did impress him was the "international company" aboard, which, encapsulated from the sound of guns and the barrage of propaganda, got along amiably enough and proved, to Reed, his point that the war spirit was a poison manufactured by the capitalistic system which lost its potency when isolated. In the various compartments were three English officers in mufti, a French engineer, a Bulgarian military mission, a Russian school teacher, an American tobacco-buyer, a pretty Viennese dancer, two Hungarians, and at least a hundred Germans, civil and military, all trained for their role in the "Teutonic Empire of the East." It was a unique company that thundered through the night toward Constantinople. And how bitterly

ironical that, on neutral ground, these men of all the warring nations could revert to the civilized habits of peacetime the moment
circumstances permitted.

"It was curious," Reed wrote, "to watch the ancient habit of
cosmopolitan existence take possession of that train-load. Some
ticket agent with a sense of humor had paired two Englishmen
with a couple of German embassy attachés in the same compartment—they were scrupulously polite to each other. The French-
man and the other Britisher gravitated naturally to the side of the
fair Austrian, where they all laughed and chattered about youthful
student days in Vienna. Late at night I caught one of the German
diplomats out in the corridor gossiping about Moscow with the
Russian teacher." [29]

He was entranced by Constantinople, with the purple-and-gold
splendor of antiquity still lingering on its seven hills and with its
ability, as the focal point of so many wars and invasions through
the centuries, to wait out still another with a weary and blasé patience. The Germans were running the country, and warships with
German sailors in fezzes were lying in the Golden Horn and the
Bosporus. The pro-German semidictator Enver Pasha had his secret police nosing about everywhere, including Reed's hotel, in
the Pera quarter, where the Italian porter told him, "Excellency,
the secret police have been here to inquire about your Excellency.
Would your Excellency like me to tell them any particular thing?"

The cosmopolitan throng of Constantinople repelled him. He
characterized it as "a crowd of no nations and of all bloods, clever,
facile, unscrupulous, shallow—Levantine." Off the streets frequented by tourists, back among the incredibly old and ramshackle
wooden tenements and narrow twisting streets lived "the fakirs
and the thieves and the vicious and unfit of the Christian Orient"
with "whole quarters given over to a kind of weak debauch."

His guide was a wealthy young Turk named Daoud Bey, to
whom he had been given letters of introduction and who epitomized for Reed much that was graceful and much that was corrupt
in the closing scenes of the Ottoman Empire. At the age of nineteen, simply as a mark of his family's influence, the epicene youth

had been commissioned an admiral in the Turkish navy. Several years later, when a British mission had attempted to reorganize the Turkish fleet, Daoud was asked whether he cared to take up active duty to justify his rank. "I should like to very much," the young bey replied, "provided I never have to set foot on a ship. I can't bear the sea." When Reed asked him why he had not volunteered to serve with his countrymen in their desperate defense of Gallipoli, Daoud languidly replied, "No Turk of any prominence could afford to be seen in the army"—that was a privilege reserved for the Anatolian peasantry. "Why, my dear fellow, if I were to serve in this war the disgrace would kill my father." [30]

Antimilitaristic and proudly unpatriotic though he was, Reed could not help but approve his compatriots' success in street brawls between sailors from the U.S. station ship in the Bosporus and German soldiers and sailors. He dwelled lovingly, as befitted a pacifist with an odd taste for armed combat, on "the night that Seaman Williams broke the German lieutenant's head with a stone beer-mug, and was transferred back to the United States as being 'unfit for diplomatic service.' And then there is the wonderful history of the two sailors who laid out seventeen attacking Germans in a café, and were led back to the American Sailors' Club by congratulatory police. . . ." [31]

After two weeks of waiting around his hotel and strolling the streets with Daoud Bey, Reed was informed by Enver Pasha's headquarters that he would not be permitted to go to Gallipoli. It was unofficially suggested that he leave the country; his neutrality was unquestioned, but the Turkish police had become suspicious because they had seen him talking with too many Armenians.

He left Constantinople for Sofia, where he and Boardman Robinson met again. Of all the Balkans, Jack liked the Bulgarians best, for their honesty and simplicity of manner. He also preferred Sofia to the ancient corruption of Constantinople and the fake-French pretentiousness of Bucharest, where a "dinky little German King lives in a dinky little palace that looks like a French prefecture, surrounded by a pompous little court." He also disliked the Rumanians for violently insisting that they were not a Balkan nation, and he quoted the typical Rumanian as saying, "Rumania is not a Balkan state. How dare you confuse us with half-savage Greeks or Slavs! We are *Latins*." Perhaps what he really admired about Bulgaria was its Russian flavor.

"It is wonderful," he wrote of Sofia, "to see again the simple, flat, frank faces of mountaineers and free men, and to fill your ears with the crackling virility of Slavic speech. Bulgaria is the only country I know where you can speak to anyone on the street and get a cordial answer—where if a shopkeeper gives you the wrong change he will follow you to your hotel to return a two-cent piece."

Most of the country's political leaders, he noted, had been educated at Roberts College, founded by American missionaries, in Constantinople. That was why "so many American methods are used in Bulgarian politics—even our kind of graft!" But the Bulgarian court and many of the military were pro-German, and Reed predicted well in advance of the event that Bulgaria would join the Central Powers in a war—again a correct prognosis—"from which they cannot emerge except as losers." [32]

He and Robinson continued their wandering: to the temporary Serbian capital of Nish, where their warnings that Bulgaria would soon join the drive to expunge Free Serbia were ignored, and then back to Salonika.

They had missed all the spectacular, headline-making aspects of the war, arriving just after the Austrians had been driven from Belgrade, after the Russians had retreated on the Balkan front, just before the Allied landings on Gallipoli, before Bulgaria fell upon Serbia and then Rumania.

Reed was satisfied, however, with having been under fire only during the Austrian bombardment of Belgrade. He had seen enough of the massive bloodletting of modern war; even the comparatively minor operations on the outskirts of Torreón had sickened him. He was satisfied, he wrote in the preface to *The War in Eastern Europe*, with "finding out how the different peoples live" and trying to "give our impressions of human beings as we found them in the countries of Eastern Europe, from April to October, 1915." That he did, and brilliantly.

9

"THE FIRST PERSON
I EVER LOVED"

John Reed at twenty-eight had traveled the world from the deserts of Chihuahua to the sweet waters of Asia, and had made himself available in such romantic places as Florence, Paris, Constantinople, the Riviera, and the decks of various transatlantic liners, without finding any lasting romantic love. It was the supreme irony of his personal life that he tumbled so precipitously in the last place he would have expected—in his prosaic and unloved home town.

Doubtless it was not for lack of trying in other places. A poet, even one who had to turn his hand to journalism most of the time, had to be endangered by consuming passions or the whole history of literature was a lie. Much of the storminess of his relationship with Mabel Dodge probably was caused by his effort to persuade himself, through melodramatic scenes, that he really was involved in a great love affair. The fact that Mabel was able to lend herself so wholeheartedly to those scenes, and even to improvise on her own (though mock suicide attempts were going too far), prolonged the affair and provided it with an artificial tropical heat.

When Reed returned to New York late in the fall of 1915, he found that Mabel had discarded the wedding ring he had placed on her finger and had taken up with Maurice Sterne, whom she married the following year. There was a brief reconciliation, and Reed went to stay with her at a small white house she had rented on Mt. Airy, near Croton-on-Hudson. Max Eastman and his first wife, the former Ida Rauh, were also house guests of Mabel's. Jack's final leave-taking, as Eastman recalled, took place on a fittingly stormy night. "I remember his stamping out of her bedroom in the small hours of the night, slamming the door and plunging away in a heavy rainstorm, none of us knew where. I felt that Mabel was on the hunt again, and that I was in a conveniently dangerous position. She seemed to be sending out waves of more than the usual potency in my direction, but I may be wrong about that. All she ever said was: 'Why don't you arrange your life?' " [1] *

Dampened both literally and emotionally, Reed stormed back to the city and continued working on his articles about Eastern Europe for the *Metropolitan*. He lectured on his experiences to two widely different audiences, the Harvard Club and the inmates of Sing Sing, and perhaps was not greatly surprised by the contrasting reception. At the Harvard Club he was accorded a hostile disbelief because of his conviction that the whole European war was madness, while at Sing Sing he was given an enthusiastic reception, perhaps because he brought up his own police record, a series

---

* After her short-lived marriage to Maurice Sterne, Mrs. Dodge was married, for the fourth and last time, at the age of forty-four, to Tony Luhan, a Pueblo Indian, whose silence was perhaps comforting in contrast to the articulateness of her former husbands and lovers. Her home in Taos, New Mexico, for years was an intellectual mecca. Among those lured to it was D. H. Lawrence, certainly the prize literary trophy of her lion-hunting career. In Taos she fought for domination of Lawrence's creative personality with an equally formidable opponent, Lawrence's wife, the former Baroness Frieda von Richthofen. "I wanted to seduce his spirit," Mrs. Dodge later explained, "so that I could make him carry out certain things. . . . I did not want, particularly, to touch him." In this effort at spiritual seduction she was not particularly successful. She died in Taos, in 1962, at the age of eighty-three.

of arrests over half the world which no one in his audience could match.

Late in November he left New York for a visit with his mother and brother in Portland. After a few days of being enclosed, if not quite smothered, by his mother's love and need for him, which had always been intensified by the fact that he was her first-born son, by his ailing childhood, and perhaps by his later waywardness, Jack was bored and restless. He wrote to a friend in New York that being home, in the Oregon city whose atmosphere had always stifled him, was "suspended animation." He could not wait to return to New York.

All that changed a few days later.

The reason was a sprightly young woman named Mrs. Louise Bryant Trullinger, who could have served admirably as a transplanted model for Carol Kennicott in Sinclair Lewis' *Main Street*. She was the New Woman heralded by the novelists of the time, the restless heroine of Jack London and Frank Norris yearning for wider and more significant experience and daringly anticipating the moral and intellectual freedom of the postwar years. Louise Bryant had been raised by her grandfather, the traditionally migrating younger son of a baronial Anglo-Irish family, and was educated at the universities of Nevada and Oregon. She was red-cheeked and freckle-faced, with beautiful gray eyes and a questingly romantic disposition; a near-miraculous feminine counterpart to Reed himself. She also shared his fickleness, his independence of spirit, his vulnerability and tendency toward self-punishment, and his absolute fecklessness. For a while she taught school on an island in Puget Sound, but soon gave up that respectable post to work in the more gregarious and stimulating atmosphere of a cannery. She next took up newspaper work as a feature writer and illustrator of fashion articles. Then, as though seeking a sure containment of her rebellious spirit, she became the wife of a Portland dentist.

As Mrs. Paul Trullinger, however, she refused to conform to what must have been expected of her. Parlor radicalism was her escape from the stodginess of the middle-class environment. She was an enthusiastic reader of the *Masses*, and according to Max

Eastman, "Louise had been sending us prodigious bundles of sub-
scriptions before he [Reed] ever discovered her." [2] One of her intellectual heroes, naturally, was the home-town boy who had made
such a name for himself as a crusader, poet, and war correspondent.

When she heard that Reed had come home on a visit, she appealed to mutual friends, Mr. and Mrs. Carl Walters, to arrange a
meeting. They invited Reed to dinner with Louise and several
other friends. The day of the dinner party, apparently by coincidence, Louise was introduced to her hero elsewhere, and she took
him to her home to look over various things she had written. By
the time they appeared together at the Walters home, everyone
there knew they were in love. In a few days Jack was writing to a
friend in New York that he had fallen for Louise. "She's wild,
brave, and straight—and graceful and lovely to look at." He could
not understand how "in this spiritual vacuum" of Portland such a
flower of beauty and intellect had blossomed. Furthermore, she
had agreed to leave her dentist husband and join him in New
York. Louise, he thought, was "the first person I ever loved without reservation." [3]

There was no talk of marriage at first; that was a bourgeois convention of no importance to two such unfettered spirits. Eventually
she would be divorced by Dr. Trullinger, but that inconsequential
legal matter did not enter into their calculations. They would live
together in Greenwich Village, work for the revolution, and create
great works of literature.

Shortly before New Year's, 1916, Jack left Portland for New
York, and Louise joined him there a few weeks later. They set up
very light housekeeping in Jack's apartment on Washington
Square. Bursting with pride, Jack showed her off to all his friends.
Among them, apparently, was Mabel Dodge, who sized up Louise
and predictably found her shallower and less charming than did
Jack's less intimate friends. Mabel conceded that "the girl was
clever with a certain Irish quickness, and very eager to get on."
Jack was mainly her passport to the great world, where she intended to shine at least as brightly as he did. "I think Reed was a
stepping stone, and through him she met a lot of people she would

never have known otherwise. It had not seemed to me that she cared very much for him." [4]

But Jack was unaware of any element of opportunism in the eager and vivacious young woman who now shared his life, and was delighted by the way she managed to charm most of his friends. Hard work, hard play and love without claims or responsibilities was their prescription for happiness. His journalistic career was divided between well-paid articles for the *Metropolitan* and an almost equal, but unpaid output for the *Masses*. As war fever took hold in America, he became one of the most eloquent and ubiquitous of those who agitated and propagandized against it. A certain amount of maturity had begun to make itself evident in him early in 1916; it did not quench his lively humor or his love of laughter, but it tempered them. "Jack was a steadying influence on me—though he would be the most surprised to hear me say it," Max Eastman said years later. "Not that he had stability, but he was more easefully daring than I, more instinctively belligerent. He did not have to fall back so often, in the class war we were waging, on naked resolution. He actually liked battle; he liked dust and smoke—he liked the town! One day during that year 1916 he called up and asked permission to dedicate a volume of poems to me. I stammered a yes that must have sounded more abashed than complimented. . . . His understanding was subtle—his dedication, when it appeared, proved to be a celebration of this very difference between us. He had turned that squeamish timorousness which made me admire him extravagantly into a cause of his admiring me." [5] *

There was one pathetic footnote to his affair with Mabel Dodge. One night Mabel could not resist the temptation to drop in on Jack and Louise and find out just how they were getting along.

---

* The poem dedicated to Eastman read in part:
    "There was a man who, loving quiet beauty best,
    Yet could not rest
    For the harsh moaning of unhappy humankind,
    Fettered and blind—
    Too driven to know beauty and too hungry-tired
    To be inspired."

She decided to use as an excuse the need to borrow a typewriter. When she knocked on the door of their apartment, Louise came, holding a lighted candle.

"Is Reed here?" Mabel asked.

Louise nodded. A moment later, Jack, surprise showing on his face, perhaps apprehensive that Mabel had come over to cause a scene, appeared behind Louise.

The dialogue was not quite up to the brittleness required of a scene involving sophisticated people in a situation that Greenwich Village playwrights would handle with considerably more panache in the nineteen-twenties.

"Reed," Mabel explained, "I came to ask you for your old type-writer, if you are not using it."

"Louise is using it," Jack told her.

"Oh, all right, I only thought . . ." Mabel could not find anything else to say. She turned and walked away.[6] They never met again; one of the Village's more spectacular love affairs ended not with the thunder of the gods in anger, but with a spasm of banality.

Reed's antiwar activity increased during the spring of 1916 as American intervention either to the south or across the Atlantic became more likely. With the French army bleeding to death before Verdun, with the Russian armies all but immobilized by their lack of supplies, the pressure for the United States to join the struggle, both from within the country and from the Allied propaganda machines, was reaching the explosive point; America was steadily being convinced that civilization would collapse if she did not help to prevent a German victory. In Mexico, too, the revolution was endangering American interests, and the split between Carranza and Villa, which Reed had foreseen, was giving American interventionists a chance to plead their case more effectively. In January, 1916, nineteen Americans were taken from a train in Chihuahua and shot to death. Villa was blamed, of course, and little credence was given to his protest that the atrocity was committed by a former lieutenant who had turned renegade. Villa had begun skirmishing against the Constitutionalist army, commanded by

Carranza, whose government had been recognized by Washington. Since Carranza was the more manageable, many in Washington were arguing that the United States should intervene on his side and help him eliminate Villa.

It was one of Villa's reckless forays—this time across the American border—that finally brought about intervention. Early in the morning of March 9, 1916, Villa and hundreds of his horsemen, without warning, attacked the town of Columbus, New Mexico, and the headquarters of the Thirteenth Cavalry. They killed eighteen American soldiers and civilians, wounded eight others, and wrecked the town. A punitive expedition, under General John J. Pershing, was immediately organized and launched in pursuit of Villa.

Reed had once threatened to join Villa and take up a rifle among his *compañeros* if the United States invaded Mexico, but he had now come to the conclusion that Villa had strayed from the path of social reform and reverted to banditry. He still admired Villa personally, however, and refused all offers to accompany the Pershing expedition as a correspondent. "I don't care if he is only a bandit," he told a friend, "I like him just the same." [7] If he went to Mexico, he said, he would report the campaign from Villa's side.

Instead of involving himself in the Mexican troubles, he concentrated on the home front by fighting militarism and all its aspects. Speaking before a Columbia University student organization, he warned the young men that going to war would only give them a taste for killing, not a repugnance for it. Before labor groups he denounced the "preparedness" campaign of Theodore Roosevelt and other pro-Allied elements who were urging an industrial and citizen-soldier mobilization for the coming involvement in the European war. Before the Intercollegiate Socialist Society he warned that a "drilled nation in the power of the capitalist class is dangerous, but a drilled nation in the hands of the workers would be interesting. For instance, if the men employed in the munitions factories should take it into their heads to train a little now and then, if they should familiarize themselves with guns, isn't there just a chance that their demands for better conditions would be listened to with somewhat more attention and respect?" [8]

He also found time to come to Emma Goldman's defense when that anarchist leader was arrested for having given public lectures favoring birth control. A protest meeting was held at Carnegie Hall to raise funds for her defense. Reed was one of several speakers, Miss Goldman later wrote, who upheld birth-control measures and praised their "social and human value as a liberating factor, particularly in the lives of proletarians." [9]

The 1916 Presidential campaign was meanwhile taking shape, with Woodrow Wilson's supporters proclaiming his worthiness for re-election on the grounds that he "kept us out of war." Reed evidently did not believe that Wilson would continue his course of neutrality, which in fact was veering steadily toward collaboration with France and Britain. Perhaps to bolster his case against what he considered Wilsonian hypocrisy, he went to Florida on an assignment for *Collier's* early in the spring of 1916 to interview William Jennings Bryan, who had resigned as Wilson's Secretary of State in protest against the administration's unneutral bias. He joined Bryan on his lecture tour of Florida, accompanying him on a trip up the Saint Johns River during which Bryan spoke to the people gathered on the boat landings along the way. In between speeches, Reed questioned Bryan on his attitude toward involvement in the European war. What would Bryan do and say if the United States fought in an unjust cause? Bryan refused to be trapped by what he called hypothetical questions, but said that he was still opposed to war. Reed, as on their first meeting, when Bryan was still Secretary of State, was half irritated, half amused by Bryan's overflowing platitudes, but conceded in his article that Bryan had always "been on the side of democracy," that he had long ago advocated the income tax, low tariffs, regulation of big business, and the popular election of senators when such reforms were "considered the dreams of an idiot . . . and remember that he is not yet done." [10]

A massive "preparedness" parade held in New York, with society women and Wall Street magnificoes, among others, marching behind militant banners, was a symptom of the war fever that aroused Reed's strongest efforts to keep the United States out of the European trenches. In an article for the *Masses* titled "At the Throat of the Republic," he dissected the movement that was attempting to drag the country into war, and declared that the enemy was not Germany and her allies but "that two percent of the people of the United States who own sixty percent of the national wealth," that self-described patriots "who have already robbed him [the workingman] of all that he has . . . are now planning to make a soldier out of him to defend their loot." The chief supporters of the "preparedness" campaign, he showed, were its principal beneficiaries. The National Security League, he claimed, was a creation of Hudson Maxim, the munitions maker. The Navy League was sponsored and directed by the Morgan interests, United States Steel, Bethlehem Steel, the Baldwin Locomotive Works, and W. A. Clark's copper interests, all of which would benefit enormously from war production. Nor did he spare the *Metropolitan Magazine*, his chief source of income, in which the controlling interest was held by Harry Payne Whitney, and Theodore Roosevelt was allowed to set the tempo for the martial drumbeat.[11]

It was a definitive exposé of the elements that were trying to influence Congress and the President toward sending an army overseas. The *Masses'* circulation, however, was too small and its viewpoint too suspect to cause any great alarm among the citizenry, which had committed itself to an emotional anti-German attitude following the sinking of the *Lusitania* by a German U-boat. The chief effect of the article was to widen the split between Reed and the editors of the *Metropolitan*, who were beginning to wonder whether his fame as a writer was as great an asset as his extramural activities in opposition to the magazine's current policies were a liability.

Reed was quite frank with his colleagues on the *Metropolitan* in predicting that the day would come when they would be bitterly and personally opposed. He told H. J. Whigham, who had replaced Carl Hovey as editor, "You and I call ourselves friends, but we are not really friends, because we don't believe in the same things, and the time will come when we won't speak to each other. You are going to see great things happen in this country pretty soon. It may kill me and it may kill you and all your friends, but it's going to be great!" [12]

Despite their differences, the editors of the *Metropolitan* appointed Reed to cover the national political conventions that summer. He was almost unable to accept the assignment, because his malfunctioning left kidney was troubling him again. The doctors told him he would probably have to have it removed, but meanwhile he was well enough to continue working. In Chicago he witnessed the nomination of Charles Evans Hughes as the Republican candidate for the Presidency. Julian Street, who was also covering the convention, said that Jack paraded his convictions with his usual aggressiveness. "He was wearing a conspicuous red badge and was indignant because no one took exception to it. Lunching with Mark Sullivan, Wallace Morgan and me at the Blackstone Hotel, he threw off a veritable spray of provocative remarks, but we declined to take issue with him, and when in response to one of his sallies, Sullivan gave him an indulgent smile, Jack got up and left us for a poor, mean-spirited lot."

Street believed that Jack had become much less the laughing cavalier of the revolution-to-be and was beginning to assume some of the humorless and dogmatic qualities of the doctrinaire Marxist. "If you agreed with him, that was all right; if you disagreed with him, that was better still, because it gave him a chance to argue; the one thing you must not do was to take him lightly, and to laugh at him was the unforgivable sin." [13]

Perhaps some of Reed's uncharacteristic grimness, his unwillingness to josh about issues he considered beyond the realm of humor, was caused not only by his illness but also by the news he had just received of the death of Alan Seeger. He and the young poet had been closer while Seeger shared quarters in Greenwich Village with Reed and his friends than during their years at Harvard. Like many of their contemporaries, Reed believed that Seeger would have had a great career: he was considered the most promising of a class that included T. S. Eliot and Conrad Aiken. All that promise was ended on the night of July 4, 1916, when Private Seeger, of Battalion C, 2nd Marching Regiment of the French Foreign Legion, was wounded in a bayonet attack on the German lines at Belloy-en-Santerre and died begging his comrades for water. To Jack Reed, the death of the moody and taciturn Seeger was not heroic, but shameful.

Reed covered the renomination of Woodrow Wilson at the Democratic convention in St. Louis, and the convention of the Progressive Republicans, which collapsed in disarray when Theodore Roosevelt refused the nomination for another Bull Moose campaign. In their absurd faith in Roosevelt, which had once been shared by his father, the Progressives were, according to Reed, "unenlightened," mere "backwoods idealists." [14] He summed up his impressions of the political conventions in the title of his *Metropolitan* article, "The National Circus."

Before returning to New York, he stopped in Detroit and spent two days talking to Henry Ford. They got along well, and even talked of establishing a newspaper which would convey their views on labor-management policy and world peace. From hindsight, the confrontation may seem to have had its outlandish aspects; the secular saint of American Communism collaborating with an industrialist who in later years became a bitter-end antiunionist. In 1916, however, there were several areas in which their views coincided. Two years earlier, Ford had established a minimum wage of five dollars for an eight-hour day, a voluntary move which shocked his fellow industrialists and made those in the labor movement regard him as an enlightened employer. Judging from what Reed wrote about him in "Industry's Miracle Maker" for the *Metropolitan* and in another article, for the *Masses*, he believed that Ford was willing to go much farther along the road of industrial democracy. Ford also was a somewhat eccentric standard-bearer in the peace movement. He had contributed a million dollars toward establishing a fund to be used to bring about peace in Europe, and with tremendous fanfare had launched the Ford Peace Ship's expedition to The Hague. A whole boatload of idealists, reformers, pacifists, journalists, and crackpots sailed for Europe with Ford, who proclaimed, "We'll get the boys out of the trenches by Christmas." The ship and its illusions soon foundered on the rock-bound realities of a Europe determined to continue fighting. After his long talks with Ford, Reed was willing to believe, momentarily, that social and economic justice might be attained without revolution. The hope did not long survive, nor did Ford give more than momentary consideration to publishing a newspaper with Reed. Yet there was a certain odd sympathy between the two men, both radical offshoots of an innocence and idealism peculiarly American.

The rest of that summer Reed spent with Louise and many of their friends at Provincetown, embraced by the enthusiasm surrounding the Provincetown Players. In the group, which was presenting one-act plays in an improvised theater on a rickety wharf, were Susan Glaspel and her husband, George Cram Cook, Mary Heaton Vorse, Eugene O'Neill, Mr. and Mrs. Hutchins Hapgood, and Mr. and Mrs. Max Eastman. One of the offerings on the first bill was Reed's satirical one-act play *Freedom*, about four prisoners plotting an escape.

It was a glorious summer for most of the Villagers working and playing in the sea-washed outpost of Bohemia on Cape Cod. Jack and Louise took a house across from Max Eastman's, and, as Eastman remembered it, "the home they made never seemed to draw me except as a spectacle." A highly Bohemian household, it also contained Hippolyte Havel, the "conscientiously irresponsible anarchist," who acted as major-domo, and his anarchist-comrade Terry Carlin. The latter met Eugene O'Neill, then half-bum and half-genius, in a Boston saloon and persuaded him to come along to Provincetown. "These men," Eastman recalled, "used their belief in anarchism, as artists often use their talents, to justify a loafer's life." Havel, in particular, "outwitted work instead of attacking it head on." Louise Bryant had the emancipated woman's attitude toward housekeeping, and the place she shared with Reed and their guests was "barn-like in its physical aspect," as Eastman recalled. "A large assortment of interesting males was provided with abundant nutrition, however, and beds to sleep on." They included Robert Rogers and Robert Edmond Jones, Jack's Harvard classmates.[15]

The most striking work to emerge from the Players' workshop that summer was O'Neill's play *Bound East for Cardiff*, with Jack one of the members of the cast. It appeared on the same bill as Louise Bryant's one-act *Thirst*, in which she and O'Neill both played roles. Artistic collaboration evidently developed into something of an emotional triangle between Reed, O'Neill, and Miss Bryant.

The gaunt and tubercular O'Neill, handsome in a smoldering way, had been a seaman, a prospector in South America, an alcoholic waif on the New York water front, and, more recently, a student in Professor George Pierce Baker's playwrighting class at Harvard. His tuberculosis had only recently been arrested, and he was under a doctor's orders not to drink anything alcoholic. Some of his binges around Provincetown, in defiance of those orders, were the talk of the summer colony for years afterward. Once, he smashed all the crockery in the Reed-Bryant household, hurling it at a green mouse he claimed was staring at him from a corner of his room. When all the dishes were broken, he picked up the fragments and threw them, too, at the hallucinatory mouse, then passed out.[16]

The vivid impression made by *Bound East for Cardiff* suddenly raised O'Neill to the position of the Players' prophet and leading talent. Gene O'Neill, it was decided, must be saved from himself and his destructive thirst for alcohol.

The one who took this mission most seriously was Louise Bryant. Some members of the group felt that the darkly beautiful Louise, with her pensive profile, and O'Neill, who one of his friends said was irresistibly "hardboiled and whimsical, brutal and tender" to women, were pairing themselves and freezing out Jack Reed. If so, Jack gave no signs of noticing it. He liked O'Neill and spent hours arguing with him over the future of American radicalism, Jack holding that the workers would finally be led to rebel, O'Neill cynically maintaining they lacked the spirit and would always be placated.

Jack evidently took it very coolly when Louise spent hours sitting on the beach with O'Neill. Some members, citing the fact that women often threw themselves at the playwright, believed that she had fallen in love with him. Others, including Eastman, insisted that she was merely trying to straighten him out, to get him to stop drinking so heavily. Mabel Dodge, who was spending the summer nearby on the Cape with her new husband, was not so preoccupied with her honeymoon that she ignored reports about the romance and passed along the gossip that O'Neill and Louise were having an affair. In her memoirs she wrote that they had "a brief passage of passion" while Jack was down in New York on magazine business.

If there was a romance, it apparently ended with the summer. When they all returned to New York, however, Jack and Louise continued their interest in the Provincetown Players; Jack, in fact, is credited with having pushed the idea that the theater group should take advantage of momentum achieved mainly through the production of O'Neill's *Bound East for Cardiff*. At a meeting on September 5, with Louise taking down the minutes, he proposed that the group continue producing in the winter. During the winter season, it was decided, "active members must either write, produce, act, or donate labor." A somewhat egotistic proposal of O'Neill's that the group call itself the Playwrights' Theater was voted down. The group became O'Neill's vehicle to supremacy among American dramatists, but was little more than an occasional distraction for Reed.

That fall he devoted more time to the national election than to the considerably involved affairs of the Provincetown Players. He had decided that President Wilson was sincere in his protestations that he was doing all he could to keep the United States out of the European war, and he joined a group of liberal and Socialist writers and intellectuals urging Wilson's re-election. In an article written for distribution by this committee, he declared that Wilson had "dared to stand for rights of weak nations" and "opposed the doctrines of militarism"—words he would gladly have retracted less than eight months later. He took the occasion to attack Theodore Roosevelt as a "believer in war for its own sake, the leader of the munitions makers' party, and a traitor to the people."

Shortly before the election, which returned Wilson to the White House, it became apparent to Jack and his doctors that his left kidney would have to be removed. For months he had been suffering sporadically intense pain and was subject to melancholy moods, reflections on mortality unusual in a man who had not yet reached his thirtieth birthday. Undoubtedly it was in one of his elegiac moments that he composed one of the simplest and most moving of his poems—"Fog."

> Death comes like this, I know—
> Snow-soft and gently cold;
> Impalpable battalions of thin mist,
> Light-quenching and sound-smothering and slow.
>
> Slack as a wind-spilled sail
> The spent world flaps in space—
> Day's but a grayer night, and the old sun
> Up the blind sky goes heavily and pale.
>
> Out of all circumstance
> I drift or seem to drift
> In a vague vapor-world that clings and veils
> Great trees a-row like kneeling elephants.[17]

Perhaps something of the same foreboding was clinging to him, foglike, when he decided that he and Louise should be married. It was possible that the nephrectomy, to be performed at Johns Hopkins Hospital, might cost his life. Louise had obtained her divorce from Dr. Trullinger in Portland. Ambitious for a literary career, she evidently was not as much in love with Jack as he was with her, and was not eager to legitimatize their relationship. But Jack at this point was conventional enough to insist on marriage— perhaps as much for the practical aspects of passing along whatever income there might be from his books as on moral grounds. They took a train up to Poughkeepsie one afternoon and were married in the city hall. None of their friends were invited to come along. They were almost shamefaced at such a conventional denouement to almost a year of living proudly in what was called "sin," and Louise insisted on keeping her maiden name.

She was so unimpressed by the sanctity of the occasion that when the city clerk had finished mumbling the marriage lines she started to leave without the certificate attesting to her new respectability. "Here, lady," the clerk called, "hang on to this. You may need it some day." [18]

On November 12, Reed entered the Baltimore hospital, and ten days later his left kidney was removed. His recovery was slow at first, but on December 13 he was well enough to be discharged. He kept his mind off the pain, typically, by writing poetry. One of his poems in blank verse dealt with two patients in adjoining rooms, one the head of the local ice trust, with "orchids to ease his soul," and the other a bricklayer, doped with morphine and in the terminal stages of his illness, dying "without love, or battle, or any glorious suddenness."

Early in 1917 the *Metropolitan* announced that it would send John Reed to China, to "hold up the mirror to this mysterious and romantic country." The expense of sending its star correspondent to the other side of the world, with very little to report there compared with what was happening in Europe and the Middle East, was an indication of how embarrassing his presence had become. The people who financed the *Metropolitan* undoubtedly were inquiring why its editors tolerated a man who spent so much of his energy and used the fame he had acquired as its war correspondent to spread himself over the *Masses* with its attacks on established opinion and institutions. Who was the fellow working for? And why, so long as the *Metropolitan* was employing him, did he have to outrage most of his fellow citizens in his spare time?

Certainly there was no equivocation in such broadsides as Reed's "Whose War?" in the *Masses*: "I hate soldiers. I hate to see a man with a bayonet fixed on his rifle, who can order me off the street. I hate to belong to an organization that is proud of obeying a caste of superior beings, that is proud of killing free ideas, so that it may more efficiently kill human beings in cold blood."

Was that the kind of talk the country wanted to hear at a time when its young men were going off to citizen-soldiers' training camps to prepare themselves for the day when they would have to defend the flag against the Kaiser's war machine? Was it not more important to whip up the national spirit than to proclaim, "I have been with the armies of all the belligerents but one, and I have seen men die, and go mad, and lie in hospitals suffering hell . . ."?

Some of his older and more farsighted friends were advising him to express himself less freely, less openly against the administration's policy, particularly after Germany announced late in January that it was going to resume unrestricted submarine warfare and a few days later Washington replied by breaking off diplomatic relations with Berlin. "You do wrong to buck this thing," Lincoln Steffens wrote to Reed. "In the first place the war was inevitable; in the second place the consequences of the war, its by-products, are normal and typical; in the third place, the public mind is sick. I know it is hard. I think it is undemocratic to try to do so much now. Write, but don't publish." The word was getting around that Reed was actually pro-German, and men he had known for years looked the other way when they passed him on the street. Even his old mentor Professor Copeland, though still friendly, was "in a frame of mind that thinks no one is a he-man who hasn't gone into naval aviation."

After the United States broke off relations with Germany, the *Metropolitan*'s editors decided against sending Reed to China, even though all arrangements had been made for the trip, both for him and for his wife. He was not fired outright; Hovey and Whigham were old-fashioned liberals who could not bring themselves to do anything so forthright and brutal. Instead, he was put on the shelf, given to understand that his work was not acceptable to the magazine until either the times were less disjointed or he went along with the consensus. No more of his stories or articles appeared in *Collier's*, his second-best source of income. Professionally, he had been placed in Coventry. His career as a journalist had suffered a serious setback, but he showed no signs of dismay.

Some of his friends, disaffected by his continuing agitation against American intervention, were convinced that he had acquired a taste for martyrdom. There may have been an element of conscious self-sacrifice in his persistence in an unpopular cause, but his actions were all of a piece, true to form, when considered against the background of the half-dozen years following his graduation from Harvard. What mattered most to him was not professional or literary advancement, but the steady progress of the American radical movement. All his actions were shaped toward that goal. All his fame was at its disposal. His vocation was the revolution, which he firmly believed would come about once the attention of the working classes was focused on their own grievances and not on war or war prosperity.

The evening of April 2, 1917, was one of the most momentous in American history: the night a great invisible bell tolled for the end of American innocence. President Wilson had summoned a joint session of Congress to recommend a declaration of war against Germany, to end American isolation from Europe's recurring fevers of hatred and revenge, and, in effect, to assume the burdens of a world power. "The day has come," the President told Congress, "when America is privileged to spend her blood and her might for the principles that gave her birth and happiness and the peace she has treasured." Then the President went back to the White House, far less exultant than the words he had uttered to Congress, and wept.

Jack Reed did not weep. That evening he was in Washington to attend an antiwar rally sponsored by pacifist groups of all coloration but dominated by the liberal-humanist element rather than the Marxist socialists. The chairman was Dr. David Starr Jordan, the chancellor of Stanford University, who had led American peace movements for many years but never on a political basis. He was determined to keep the tone of the meeting on an elevated, idealistic level, and in consideration of that mandate the speeches were mild, uninflammatory, gently protesting.

The rally was nearing its close, and Reed had not been called to the platform. Dr. Jordan ignored occasional mutterings from the audience of "We want Jack Reed." They came from his supporters, carefully planted at strategic locations in the crowd.

Finally Dr. Jordan himself addressed the meeting, evidently hoping to close it without hearing from the more radical voices. "We were for peace," Dr. Jordan said, "but we will follow our country."

Reed and his partisans had no intention of participating in a requiem for the peace movement. Its fight, in their view, had just begun and would not subside gracefully, patriotically, reproachfully, to merge itself with the supposed majority. "Jack Reed, Jack Reed," his supporters kept chanting with increasing volume.

Dr. Jordan shook his head and said there was no time left for further speechmaking. The clamor from Reed's partisans rose. Unbidden, he strode down the aisle toward the platform. "This is not my war," he shouted after jumping on the platform, "and I will not support it!"

In those words he sounded the keynote of the hard-core American left. It would fight the war, come what may. The Socialist Party, at an emergency convention, would adopt a resolution decrying American participation, and such Socialist leaders as Eugene V. Debs and Congressman Victor Berger, of Wisconsin, would be imprisoned for seditious activities, but many other leading Socialists, including William English Walling, J. G. Phelps Stokes, and John Spargo, like many German Socialists before them, would split away on the issue and support their country's side in the war.

Reed stayed in Washington to testify before the Congressional committees considering various war measures. On April 12, with Harry Weinberger, of the Free Speech League of America, and Jane Addams, president of the Women's Peace Party of America, he appeared at the hearing of the House Judiciary Committee on the Espionage Bill (H.R. 291, an act to "punish acts of interference with the foreign relations, the neutrality and foreign commerce of the United States").

He told the committee that if the bill was passed, the President could marshal all the powers granted him and "could become a virtual dictator of what we could say about anything in connection with the war." He pointed out that in England George Bernard Shaw and Norman Angell had been permitted to criticize their government, that in France Clemenceau assailed his government's conduct of the war in his newspaper, and that even in Germany Karl Liebknecht and Maximilian Harden had spoken out "quite freely." He continued:

Almost every country, it seems to me, has had to adopt Prussianism to defeat Prussianism. I think that war regulations of this kind in this country will destroy democratic institutions. We have had some fore-taste of Prussianism in this country already. On April 4, the police of Philadelphia forbade any public meeting in the City of Philadelphia against a declaration of war or to talk for peace.

In Chicago, on April 5, a man was arrested for defaming the Presi-dent. Defaming the President consisted in saying that the President wanted war, and this man disapproved of the President. If there is any difference between this new, unheard of charge of defaming the Presi-dent and the Prussian lèse-majesté, at which we have all laughed for a great many years as a ridiculous manifestation of aristocracy, I would like to know what it is.

If the people of this country are prevented from speaking their minds out loud, they will speak them secretly, by underground methods. . . . Free speech cannot be stopped by suppressing it.

Two days later he appeared at a hearing on the Conscription Bill, and this time he came under a crossfire of questions from the committee.

Asked whether he would refuse to serve in the nation's armed forces—a purely academic matter for a man who had just had one kidney removed—Reed replied, "I am not a peace-at-any-price man, or a thorough pacifist, but I would not serve in this war. You can shoot me if you want and try to draft me to fight—and I know that there are ten thousand other people—"

One congressman interrupted to say that he did not want to hear any more from Reed, and another commented, "We should be thankful that the country" did not have to "depend on that kind of man." The chairman, however, insisted that Reed had a right to be heard.

Another member wanted to hear his "personal reasons" for not wanting to fight.

"I was trying to state them," Reed replied.

"It is not your *personal* objection to fighting?"

"No," Reed rejoined, "I have no personal objection to fighting. I just think that the war is unjust on both sides, that Europe is mad, and that we should keep out of it." [19]

He was then excused, and went back to New York to continue his agitprop activity in an atmosphere of increasing hostility. It was dangerous work. War hysteria never ran higher in the United States than during those years; German-Americans, even those who did not oppose the majority, were often mobbed, dachshunds were frowned upon, and sauerkraut became Liberty Cabbage. Those who openly opposed American participation were risking their lives as well as their personal liberty. Aside from such physical risks, Reed was assailed by pleas from his family in Portland to stop disgracing himself. His brother, Harry, enlisted in the army and wrote to him that he wished "you could see a little more clearly just what the situation is in this country and how useless it is to try to buck what can't be changed." And his mother expressed her shock at Jack's disavowals of any patriotic sentiment, at his joining with anti-Americans "of foreign birth." Bitterly she added, "I do not want you to fight, heaven knows, for us, but I do not want you to fight against us, by word and pen, and I can't help saying that if you do, now that war is declared, I shall feel deeply ashamed." [20]

Reed was not deterred for a moment by the appeals from home. With his other sources of income cut off, he joined the staff of the New York *Mail* as a reporter and feature writer. A later investigation showed that the *Mail* was secretly financed, in part, by funds from the German government. None of its staff was aware of this, but they could hardly have ignored the pro-German bias of its editorial columns. "By John Reed" appeared over a variety of stories fed into the daily gristmill—the life story of lightweight champion Benny Leonard, a campaign for the application of an excess-profits tax, mood pieces on the lower East Side, Central Park, Hoboken, and the Bowery, "Giddy Saratoga Throngs Forget All About War," and a biting description of a society benefit party held in MacDougal Alley: "It was New York's last real laugh. Within a few months now the casualty lists will be appearing, and in the rotogravure sections of the Sunday papers there will be pages of young, high-bred faces with the caption 'The Roll of Honor.' "

When he was not running down assignments from the *Mail's* city desk, he was appearing at antiwar rallies and working for the *Masses*. One night early in June, at the Hunt's Point Casino, in the Bronx, a phalanx of police descended with warrants against Emma Goldman and Alexander Berkman, who were on the platform denouncing the conscription laws. Before the police could make their move, a group of soldiers in the rear of the hall started throwing light bulbs to break up the meeting, then tangled with police when they charged toward the platform. In the melee Reed jumped up on the stage and helped to cover the escape of Goldman and Berkman. Next morning, however, the two anarchists were arrested down in the Village. Reed appeared at their subsequent trial as a character witness.

One day, in the *Mail's* city room, he came across a brief article in the New York *Tribune* reporting that a surprising number of young men drafted into the army were suffering nervous breakdowns. He clipped out the article and later that afternoon took it down to the *Masses* office. Pasting the clipping on a sheet of paper, he scrawled a caption over it: KNIT A STRAITJACKET FOR YOUR SOLDIER BOY! And the *Masses* published it without further comment. That grim little experiment in slogan-making was to haunt its author in later brushes with authority.

Early in June he and Louise quarreled bitterly and separated. She sailed off for France as a free-lance correspondent. In discussing the matter with Lincoln Steffens, as Reed later wrote to Louise, his father-confessor told him he had been "a cad and a fool." The reason for the breakup apparently was an extramarital affair of Jack's which Louise learned about. Almost every day he wrote her a detailed account of his doings, explaining, "I just tell you all this stupid history, my honey, so you may know all that I've been doing, and that you may believe that nevermore is there going to be any chance of any girl coming between me and my honey." [21]

The summer of 1917 was his season of discontent and despair, as he indicated in the stream of letters to Louise in Paris. A weekend cottage they had bought at Croton-on-Hudson was "terrible without you." And all his friends, he wrote on June 14, looked upon his working for the *Mail* as "a fatal mistake on my part." In letter after letter he appealed for a reconciliation. "O my dear lover I wish we could have gone together. I don't suppose I'll ever be convinced that you had to go so far away! . . . It isn't you who must learn, my honey, but me. In lots of ways we are very different, and we must both try to realize that. . . . You thought you were getting a hero—and you only got a vicious little person who is fast losing any spark he may have had." Wherever he went on assignment for the *Mail*, he took time to dash off a note or send her fifty-dollar checks in care of American Express in Paris. "I'm in Baltimore," he wrote on June 19, "waiting for a damned actress, Lillian Lorraine, whom I've got to interview about her damned marriage to a damned prizefighter."

Apparently warming to his pleas, she began sending him her stories about the first American troops reaching France. He rewrote or polished them, then gave them to John Wheeler's syndicate for sale to the New York *American* and other papers. "All stories of the life of American troops at the front," he wrote to her on July 8, "their actions in Paris, what they think of the war and the French, why they are in the war, etc., is the best stuff for the papers here now."

By then he had begun trying to arrange a trip to Russia, which was in the grip of revolution and counterrevolution, and he asked Louise whether she would consider meeting him in Petrograd. She was to go directly, via Stockholm, while he would travel there via Vladivostok and the Siberian railroad. He assured her that he could "shut down on his temptations," adding, "All this absence, my darling, did not make me love you any better—it could not. . . . It was never necessary for you to go away in order to make me conscious of my love." He worried over her constantly, knowing that her intrepidity matched his own, and he cabled her on July 17: DON'T GO ENGLAND IF DANGER HAVE YOU ENOUGH MONEY LOVE.

In the self-doubt and despondency of that summer he wrote his introspective essay "Almost Thirty." With his thirtieth birthday only a few months away, he sadly reflected on the end of his youth, which seemed to coincide with "the end of the world's youth, too." His career was bogged down; the antiwar movement to which he had committed it seemed to be going no place, with the people it was trying to save unwilling to listen, rushing to join the American Expeditionary Force and plunge into the organized slaughter. In Europe, except for rebelling Russia, there was no indication that either side had sufficiently wearied of the killing. In Russia, at the moment, the revolution was a democratic one pledged to continue fighting Germany. The class struggle was moribund, the "masses" for which it was waged were bedazzled by temporarily higher wages, striped silk shirts, and cheap motorcars.

He felt that at "almost thirty" he had "little that I can hold to." Even the future of his marriage was in doubt. Yet he also believed that there were great days ahead because "the world we live in is so full of swift change and color and meaning that I can hardly keep from imagining the splendid and terrible possibilities of the time to come." [22]

These "possibilities" were to burst upon him, as they did upon the people of Russia, before the year was out.

10

THE NOVEMBER DAYS

To revolutionaries scattered all over Europe and America the news coming out of Russia, though muffled by Allied censorship, was underlined by the tremors that could only signify a great and spreading upheaval. Aleksandr Kerenski's provisional government was tottering under the impact of German offensives from the west which it was unable to fend off; Lenin and his Bolshevik following had been gathering power since the day (April 18, 1917) he had arrived at the Finland Station in St. Petersburg aboard a sealed train from Switzerland supplied by the Germans; Leon Trotsky had arrived there on May 17 from his exile in New York City, and, shortly, the last gasp of the czarist reaction would expire with the failure of General Kornilov's counterrevolution. The first echoes of "All power to the Soviets" were beginning to be heard in Russia and beyond its borders.

Until that summer, Jack Reed had considered the overturn of

czarism a "bourgeois" affair, a mere imitation of western democracy. Stronger medicine was needed, and by the summer of 1917 he was confident that it would be supplied according to Marxist prescription. Not far in the offing, as he wrote in the *Masses*, was "the real thing," the "long-thwarted rise of the Russian masses, as now we see with increasing plainness; and the purpose of it is the establishment of a new human society upon the earth."

And that was something that Reed had to see with his own eyes, the great event for which he had been training himself in the half-dozen years since he had left Harvard. Louise Bryant returned from France early in August, eager to join him in the venture, willing to forgive his lapse in fidelity, swayed perhaps by the heart-felt appeal contained in one of the letters he wrote her while she was in Paris. "No one I love has ever been able to let me express myself fully, freely, and trust that expression." [1]

The means of getting them both to Russia at first presented a serious problem. A press syndicate was willing to accept Louise as its correspondent in Petrograd, but none of the newspapers and magazines that could afford to send a man to Russia would consider Jack, with his well-advertised sympathies, as its representative. That left the project up to the leftist organs, which were then finding their sources of revenue drying up. Max Eastman wanted him to represent the *Masses*, but that particular till was now empty. Finally the backing for the Reeds' trip was obtained through a fund raised by Eugen Boissevain, a loyal supporter of the *Masses*, with a society woman named Mrs. McCullough the principal contributor. If it had not been for Mrs. McCullough's two thousand dollars, as Eastman has pointed out, the classic account of the Bolshevik Revolution might never have been written.[2] By the time Jack and Louise sailed aboard the Danish steamer *United States*, on August 17, the Socialist New York *Call* and the magazine *Seven Arts* had also agreed to publish whatever Reed might send them. Three days before sailing, he had been examined by army doctors and exempted from military service because of the kidney that had been removed; the State Department then granted the passports. At Halifax, the ship was held up for a week while intelligence officers searched it from keel to crow's-nest for contraband and questioned the passengers bound for Christiania (now Oslo), the voyage's terminus. A boarding party of English marines, apparently tipped off from Washington to give Reed and his effects a thorough shakedown, searched the cabin occupied by Jack and Louise just after he had concealed a number of letters of introduction to Swedish Socialists under the carpet.

British arrogance had expanded to the point where it seemed "perfectly natural," Reed wrote in a newsletter to the *Masses*, that his ship should "sail first to Halifax and stay there as long as London wishes, without any explanation." [3] The article appeared in the last issue of the *Masses*, which also carried an advertisement on its back cover proclaiming "John Reed is in Petrograd. . . . His story of the first Proletarian revolution will be an event in the world's literature." *

Aboard the *United States* were a number of American college graduates being sent as clerks to an American bank in Petrograd, Russians going back home to test the new climate, and assorted Scandinavians. The Dutch captain posted a notice warning: "As this ship belongs to a neutral nation, the passengers are requested, on receipt of war news, to avoid all public manifestations of political sympathies or antipathies." It was unnecessary, according to Reed, because most of those aboard were thoroughly sick of the war.

The *United States* arrived safely in Christiania, and Jack and his wife hurried on to Stockholm after learning, on September 3, that the Germans had taken Riga and the route to Petrograd might be closed off if and when the offensive continued. They crossed Sweden by train, caught a small steamer to Finland, entrained again for the journey across the forests and lakes to Petrograd. On arrival they found an apartment and looked up various Americans in the city who could bring them up to date. These included Alex

---

* The *Masses* correctly predicted the classic quality of Reed's account of the Russian Revolution, but had not forecast its own demise in its last issue. Eastman closed up shop after the post office ruled it "unmailable." He and his sister then established another magazine, the *Liberator*.

and Zorin Gomberg, Boris Reinstein, Bill Shatov, Albert Rhys Williams, and others they had known in Socialist and I.W.W. circles in the United States. Most were convinced that the revolutionary tide could not be stemmed.

Reed was exhilarated by what he saw and heard, and on September 17 wrote to Boardman Robinson that the great stone city had changed for the better. "Joy where there was gloom, and gloom where there was joy. We are in the middle of things, and believe me it's thrilling. There is so much dramatic to write that I don't know where to begin. For color and terror and grandeur this makes Mexico look pale." [4]

He could not speak Russian—except to identify himself, "Ya amerikanski sotsialist!," to everyone he met—but there was always someone in the colony of American sympathizers to interpret for him. Everywhere he went he saw signs that the most violent faction of the revolutionary spectrum, the Bolsheviks, was coming out on top in the struggle for power. The Mensheviks, just to the right of the Bolsheviks, the Social Revolutionaries, and all the democratic parties were pinning their hopes on the Constituent Assembly scheduled to convene in December. The slogan "All power to the Soviets" was rising from a murmur to a shout. "Meanwhile," Reed wrote, "the soldiers began to solve the peace question by simply deserting, the peasants burned manor-houses and took over the great estates, the workers sabotaged and struck. . . . The policy of the Provisional Government alternated between ineffective reforms and stern repressive measures." Kerenski's efforts to hold the country together, keep the soldiers and sailors under arms against the Germans, and build the foundation for a democracy were, he observed, "supported by the 'moderate' Socialists and their leaders in the Ministry, who considered it necessary to cooperate with the propertied classes." But that was not good enough for the Russian masses: "The people rapidly deserted them, and went over to the Bolsheviki, who stood for Peace, Land, and Workers' Control of Industry, and a Government of the working-class." [5] This, of course, was overstating the case for the Bolsheviks, numerically a small splinter group, but so tightly organized, so cohesive and single-minded, so brilliantly led by Lenin and Trotsky that their influence on events swelled out of proportion to their influence on the inert mass of the Russian people.

A week after Reed arrived in Petrograd, he summed up the situation in a letter to Boardman Robinson's wife intended for publication as an article. The revolution had coalesced into the class struggle "as predicted by the Marxians." The middle-class liberals, also predictably enough, had "definitely aligned themselves with the capitalist elements." Except for the novelist Maxim Gorky, the "intellectuals and romantic revolutionaries . . . are shocked at what revolution really is" and had either opted out or gone over to the other side. Other veterans of the revolutionary movement were also disaffected; "their real concern was with a political revolution, and the political revolution has happened, and Russia is a republic, I believe, for ever—but what is going on now is an economic revolution, which they don't understand nor care for. Through the tempest of events tumbling over one another which is beating upon Russia, the Bolsheviki star steadily rises."

While the red star was rising, the white one of an old regime unable to comprehend what was happening in Russia was sinking fast. A month after his arrival Reed interviewed Stepan Georgevitch Lianozov, a capitalist known as the "Russian Rockefeller," whose obtuseness seemed incredible.

"Revolution is a sickness," Lianozov told Reed. "Sooner or later the foreign powers must intervene here—as one would intervene to cure a sick child, and teach it how to walk. Of course, it would be more or less improper, but the nations must realize the danger of Bolshevism in their own countries—such contagious ideas as 'proletarian dictatorship' and 'world social revolution.' . . . There is a chance that this intervention may not be necessary. Transportation is demoralized, the factories are closing down, and the Germans are advancing. Starvation and defeat may bring the Russian people to their senses." Bolshevism would be destroyed, Lianozov said, by one of two methods. "The Government can evacuate Petrograd, then a state of siege declared, and the military commander of the district can deal with these gentlemen without legal formalities." Or the Constituent Assembly, if it showed radical tendencies, could be permanently adjourned "by force of arms." [6]

In the house where Jack and Louise rented a small apartment, as among the propertied class as a whole, a German occupation was preferred to a Bolshevik seizure of power. Their landlord and others of the middle class even preferred the Germans to the provisional government. "The subject of conversation at the dinner table was almost invariably the coming of the Germans, bringing 'law and order' . . . One evening I spent at the house of a Moscow merchant; during tea we asked the eleven people at the table whether they preferred 'Wilhelm or the Bolsheviki.' The vote was ten to one for Wilhelm." [7]

Looking back on the October days when the ancient edifice of Muscovy was cracking from foundations to roof, these people seemed "incredibly conservative" to Reed on later reflection—"so quickly did we adapt ourselves to the newer, swifter life; just as Russian politics swung bodily to the Left." As an example he cited the visit of a group of Social Revolutionary leaders to the British ambassador and their plea that he not mention their visit because they were "considered too far Right." The urbane Sir George Buchanan murmured in reply, "And to think that one year ago my Government instructed me not to receive [Prince] Miliukov, [leader of the right-wing Cadets Party], because he was so dangerously Left."

To Reed the political situation was glowing with the red dawn, but Petrograd in that transitory period was overcast with the leaden gloom of approaching winter and suffering from shortages of all kinds.

"Under dull grey skies, in the shortening days, the rain fell drenching, incessantly," he later wrote. "The mud underfoot was deep, slippery, and clinging, tracked everywhere by heavy boots, and worse than usual because of the complete breakdown of the Municipal administration. Bitter damp winds rushed in from the Gulf of Finland, and the chill fog rolled through the streets. At

night, for motives of economy as well as fear of Zeppelins, the
street-lights were few and far between; in private dwellings and
apartment-houses the electricity was turned on from six o'clock
until midnight, with candles forty cents apiece and little kerosene
to be had. It was dark from three in the afternoon to ten in the
morning. . . . Robberies and housebreakings increased. In apartment houses the men took turns at all-night guard duty, armed
with loaded rifles. . . . Week by week food became scarcer. The
daily allowance of bread fell from a pound and a half to a pound,
then three-quarters, half, and a quarter-pound. . . . Sugar one
was entitled to at the rate of two pounds a month—if one could
get it at all, which was seldom. A bar of chocolate or a pound of
tasteless candy cost anywhere from seven to ten rubles—at least a
dollar. There was milk for about half the babies in the city. . . .
For milk and bread and sugar and tobacco one had to stand in
queue long hours in the chill rain." But the theaters were open:
Chaliapin was singing, Karsavina was appearing in a new ballet,
and Tolstoy's *Death of Ivan Ilyitch* had been revived at the
Alexandrinsky Theater.

The "petty conventional life of the city" carried on, "ignoring
the Revolution as much as possible." Privileged young ladies from
the provinces still came to Petrograd to learn French and other
social graces, and "gay young beautiful officers" paraded dashingly
around the hotel lobbies trailing their gold-handled Caucasian
swords. "The ladies of the minor bureaucratic set took tea with
each other in the afternoon, carrying each her little gold or silver
or jewelled sugar-box, and half a loaf of bread in her muff, and
wished that the Tsar were back, or that the Germans would come,
or anything that would solve the servant problem." A well-born
young woman he knew "came home one afternoon in hysterics because the woman street-car conductor had called her 'Comrade!' " [8]

But a new wind was rising and could be felt on such occasions
as the mass meeting at the Cirque Moderne, one of the assem-
blages that were becoming more numerous night after night to
show support for Alexander Berkman, Emma Goldman, and other
American radicals then in jail. "The bare, gloomy amphitheatre, lit

by five tiny lights hanging from a thin wire, was packed from the ring up the steep sweep of grimy benches to the very roof—soldiers, sailors, workers, women, all listening as if their lives depended upon it."

Reed was one of those introduced to the meeting, which cheered him as a spokesman for the American Socialist Party and a man under indictment for having opposed capitalism in America. (He was not in reality a "spokesman" for American Socialists, but by then he had indeed been indicted, as an editor of the *Masses*, along with Eastman and others, for seditious utterances.)

His appearance at the Cirque Moderne naturally attracted the attention of the American Embassy, which had an agent in the audience. The American Ambassador, David R. Francis, had ordered a watch kept on Reed and other Americans who openly sympathized with the revolution. He had been understandably perplexed when Reed presented himself at the Embassy shortly after arrival in Petrograd bearing a letter of introduction from Dudley Field Malone, who was Collector of the Port of New York and an appointee—like Ambassador Francis—of the Wilson administration.

The Ambassador, a wealthy Missouri businessman, had arrived in Russia a year before with his Negro valet, his portable cuspidor with the lid that operated by means of a foot pedal, his chests of cigars and boxes of poker chips, his Ford touring car. He was a homely figure "more attuned to the world of O. Henry than the Czarist Court," as Alan Moorehead described him in *The Russian Revolution*, and he was ill-equipped to understand a firebrand like Jack Reed. What business did a young American have throwing himself into the activities of a revolutionary rabble? What concern was it of an American citizen that Russians were trying to overturn the provisional government (which the United States had been among the first to recognize, largely at Francis' urging)?

Obviously Reed was a dangerous young man and must be watched, especially after Francis' agent reported that Reed was telling the Bolsheviks that Berkman would probably be executed, and that he, Reed, had succeeded in having the Associated Press correspondent turned away from meetings on the grounds that the A.P. was the conduit for the capitalistic press, which would garble the news coming out of Russia anyway.[9]

Meanwhile, an agent of the Russian secret police stole Reed's wallet and passed along its contents, including a letter from Morris Hillquit, the Socialist leader, and another from Camille Huysmans addressed to the Scandinavian Socialist Committee, to the American Embassy.

About this time Reed's friend from the earlier visit to Petrograd, Negley Farson, ran into him and Louise at the Hotel de l'Europe. Jack told him how his pocket had been picked by a Russian agent "in connivance with the American Embassy in Petrograd." Although a businessman at the time, Farson sympathized with Reed, if not with his convictions, and considered the action "peevish" on the part of the U.S. government. Reed's letter of credit had been stolen with the other contents of his wallet, so Farson lent him two thousand rubles.

The next day Reed showed up in Farson's room at the hotel and handed him back his check. "Most amazing thing," Farson quoted Jack as saying. "I went into the Consulate this morning—and the very first thing they did was hand me back my wallet! The letter of credit was there, and all that was missing was a few hundred rubles in cash!" [10]

Farson said that the letters Reed carried were photostated and that the people to whom they were addressed were "watched." He was leaving Russia shortly, and spent the last night with Jack and Louise. He saw them to the pier from which their droshky was placed on a barge and towed back across the Neva. "That night," Farson would recall, "he had tried until the last minute to persuade me to remain with him and see the real revolution in Petrograd. I remembered this and I cupped my hands. 'Goodbye, John,' I called. 'You'll need more luck than I will, I think.' Those were the last words I said to him, and I could not see him even then. They were prophetic words." [11]

Certainly no earthly power could have torn Jack Reed from the scene of what he was convinced would be the turning point in human history. A man on fire, he roamed the imperial boulevards, the mass meetings called by Bolshevik agitators, the factories where the various Socialist factions (Bolshevik, Menshevik, Social Revolutionary) were trying to capture the allegiance of the workers to support them in their separate bids for power at the Second All-Russian Congress of Soviets, which would convene in Petrograd on November 2. Lenin, as the co-ordinator of the Bolshevik plans, was hiding out in Finland until his scheming for power was ready to bear fruit. On October 22, he secretly returned to Petrograd.

The day before that, Reed went out to the Obukhovsky Zavod, a huge government munitions factory on the Schlusselberg Prospekt, where Lunacharski and other Bolshevik leaders addressed a Sunday mass meeting. "The meeting took place between the gaunt brick walls of a huge unfinished building, ten thousand black-clothed men and women packed around a scaffolding draped in red, people heaped on piles of lumber and bricks, perched high up on shadowy girders, intent and thunder-voiced. Through the dull, heavy sky now and again burst the sun, flooding reddish light through the skeleton windows upon the mass of simple faces upturned to us." Lunacharski told the workers it was necessary for the Soviets to take power to "guarantee the Revolution against its enemies," and a haggard veteran of the Rumanian front told the crowd, "We are starving at the front, we are stiff with cold. We are dying for no reason." [12]

The following day, at a session of the Council of the Republic, through which Kerensky was attempting to rule the country, Reed saw how the "gulf between the two sides of the chamber deepened day by day," the Socialist factions on one side, Kerensky and his supporters on the other. "Kerensky himself came twice, to plead passionately for national unity, once bursting into tears at the end. The assembly heard him coldly, interrupting with ironical remarks." It was disunity the Bolsheviks sought. They were only a faction within the left wing, yet they hoped that through constant agitation, by inflaming the mob spirit, and by applying their limited but essentially military force they could seize total power. The Congress of Soviets was delayed five days, to November 7, to make sure enough delegates would be on hand and that all preparations were made for the overthrow of the provisional government.

By October 29, Jack had seen enough of those preparations to cable the New York *Call*: IT IS POSSIBLE THE PROLETARIAT WILL FINALLY LOSE ITS TEMPER AND RISE.

A political hurricane was being whipped up through plans long perfected in exile, and Reed was in its eye. Night after night he went without sleep, racing from one meeting to another, then taking his turn at guard duty with the other men in the house in which he and Louise rented rooms. He was in a fever of exaltation. Not only would he witness and participate in a revolution, but he also would observe it from the inner councils as well as the streets and meeting halls—the perfect journalistic vantage point. At last the revolutionary and the journalist in him would function at the highest pitch. The reportorial eye, the poet's perception, the revolutionary's grasp of the significance of the events he was witnessing, all were combined in those November days to produce one of the world's great feats of recording history as it was made. The only missing element was objectivity. What he produced was passionately one-sided, unabashedly partisan, saved from being mere propaganda only by the artistry of its presentation.

As the opening of the Congress of Soviets approached, the tension in Petrograd was growing unbearably. In the barracks of the restless garrison there were, Reed recorded, "meetings every night, and all day long interminable hot arguments." At night the crowds on the Nevsky were "pouring in slow voluble tides . . . fighting for the newspapers." The privileged classes sensed that their time was drawing to a close. "Gambling clubs functioned hectically from dusk to dawn, with champagne flowing and stakes of twenty thousand rubles. In the centre of the city at night prostitutes in jewels and expensive furs walked up and down, crowded the cafés." At the Smolny Institute, formerly a select school for the daughters of the nobility, under carvings of the imperial coat of arms, the various Bolshevik task forces worked around the clock,

THE NOVEMBER DAYS 207

while upstairs in the great hall the Petrograd Soviet met in constant uproarious session.

In the center of the vortex, the dominating figure, was Lenin—"great Lenin," as Reed called him. "A short, stocky figure, with a big head set down in his shoulders, bald and bulging. Little eyes, a snubbish nose, wide, generous mouth, and heavy chin; clean-shaven now, but already beginning to bristle with the well-known beard of his past and future. Dressed in shabby clothes, his trousers much too long for him. Unimpressive, to be the idol of a mob, loved and revered as perhaps few leaders in history have been. A strange popular leader—a leader purely by virtue of intellect; colorless, humourless, uncompromising and detached, without picturesque idiosyncrasies—but with the power of explaining profound ideas in simple terms, of analysing a concrete situation. And combined with shrewdness, the greatest intellectual audacity." [13]

From Friday, November 2, to Monday, November 5, the left wing of the Bolshevik faction, headed by Lenin, made the tactical moves toward insurrection. Even the Bolshevik minority was rent by factionalism, and on November 2 Zinoviev, soon to be followed by Kamenev, both members of the right wing of the Bolsheviks, publicly recanted his opposition to Lenin and the latter's plans for a forcible seizure of power. Then all regiments of the Petrograd garrison were provided with Bolshevik commissars, who maintained liaison between the barracks and the tactical headquarters at Smolny Institute, ready to give the signal for an uprising. On November 4, the Bolsheviks called out the workers and soldiers to make a nonviolent show of strength on the streets of the districts. On November 5, the various regiments were ordered to be ready to occupy strategic points in the city. That same day Kerensky declared a state of emergency, banned the Bolshevik newspapers, strengthened the guard at the Winter Palace, but, fatally for himself and Russian democracy, he failed to attack the Bolshevik headquarters in the Smolny Institute. In that moment, with insurrection a certainty, the divided and indecisive leaders of middle-class democracy lost all hope of prevailing.

Fascinated by the mechanics of revolution, Reed followed every move the Bolsheviks and their opponents made. He watched Russian democracy crumbling on that day of indecision, as in the great hall of the Smolny Institute Bolshevism's opponents wrangled, taunted each other, and ranted hour after hour. "As I went down the stairs," he wrote, "it seemed to me that in spite of the bitter wrangling, no real voice from the rough world outside could penetrate this high, cold hall—and that the Provisional Government was wrecked. . . ." That night he and Louise went to a motion-picture show near the Kazan Cathedral, "a bloody Italian film of passion and intrigue." Down front there was a crowd of soldiers and sailors "totally unable to comprehend why there should be so much violent running about, and so much homicide." Outside the theater "the tides of people flowed endlessly. . . . It was always like that in Petrograd just before trouble. . . ."

Meanwhile, the delegates to the Congress of Soviets were slowly assembling. On November 2, only fifteen were on hand, but next day there were a hundred, and on November 4 there were a hundred and seventy-five present, of whom, Reed noted, "one hundred and three were Bolsheviki." The day before the Congress was to open, there were five hundred and sixty-four, of whom two hundred and fifty were Bolsheviks. Mostly they were bearded soldiers in their uniforms, workmen in their long black blouses, with a few long-haired peasants among them. "The depths of Russia had been stirred up, and it was the bottom which became uppermost now." [14]

The evening of November 6 the Congress of Soviets held a preliminary meeting in the great hall of the Smolny Institute. "As night fell the great hall filled with soldiers and workmen, a monstrous dun mass, deep-humming in a blue haze of smoke." It was midnight before the excited delegates were called to order, and Dan, the Menshevik leader, rose to speak in a tense and menacing silence. With great courage he spoke out against an armed uprising, arguing, "The masses are sick and exhausted. They have no interest in the Revolution. If the Bolsheviki start anything, that will be the end of the Revolution. . . . All power to the

Soviets—that means death! . . . Those who are urging this are committing a crime!"

Tumult arose from the Bolshevik delegates. Opposition, then and evermore, must be drowned out. The Menshevik's pleas were lost in an uproar of shouts, laughter, whistling, stamping, and howling. "Then for the Bolsheviki, Trotsky mounted the tribune, borne on a wave of roaring applause that burst into cheers and a rising house, thunderous." He would be heard. "His thin, pointed face was positively Mephistophelian in its expression of malicious irony. 'Dan's tactics prove that the masses—the great, dull, indifferent masses—are absolutely with him!' (Titanic mirth) . . . 'No. The history of the last seven months shows that the masses have left the Mensheviks. . . . Dan tells you that you have no right to make an insurrection. Insurrection is the right of all revolutionists! When the downtrodden masses revolt, it is their right. . . .'"

About 4:00 A.M. Reed left the hall and met a Bolshevik leader in the corridor. " 'We're moving,' he said calmly but with satisfaction. 'We pinched the assistant minister of justice and the minister of religion. They're down in the cellar now. One regiment is on the march to capture the telegraph agency, another the state bank. The Red Guard is out. . . .'" Outside the Institute Reed saw the "huddled group of boys in workmen's clothes, carrying guns with bayonets," who composed the armed vanguard of the revolution. "Far over the still roofs westward came the sound of scattered rifle fire where the *yunkers* [military cadets loyal to the provisional government] were trying to open the bridges over the Neva, to prevent the factory workers and soldiers of the Viborg quarter from joining the Soviet forces in the centre of the city. . . . Behind us great Smolny, bright with lights, hummed like a gigantic hive. . . ." [15]

Next day Jack and Louise awakened late, he wrote, and "the noon cannon boomed from Peter-Paul as I went down the Nevsky." In effect, the Bolsheviks, on the eve of the Congress called to deliberate what must be done, had gone ahead and done it. During the night they had seized control of the city, its communications, its bridges and means of transportation. Kerensky had hurried out to the headquarters of the Third Cavalry Corps, hoping to rally it in defense of the government. At 10:00 A.M. Trotsky, as head of the Military Revolutionary Committee, issued a proclamation stating that the government had fallen— which was true, of course, only as far as Petrograd was concerned.

Jack and Louise wandered the streets that day watching the activity outside the Winter Palace and Smolny Institute. He was present, with Louise and several other Americans, when the Congress of Soviets opened late that evening. Protesting that the Bolsheviks had "anticipated the will" of the Congress, a number of Mensheviks and Social Revolutionaries rose and left the great hall. Let them go, Trotsky told the delegates, "letting out his rich voice in cool contempt," as Reed reported. " 'They are just so much refuse which will be swept into the garbage-heap of history!' "

While the delegates to the Congress were gloating over their triumph, one anti-Bolshevik bastion in the capital was still holding out. It was the Winter Palace, the ramparts of which were manned by a pathetic handful of cadets and one hundred and thirty members of the Women's Battalion who had refused to desert. They were under bombardment from the gunners in the Fortress of St. Peter and St. Paul; an ineffective display which merely knocked down a few stones. Jack and Louise, with several other Americans, left the great hall at Smolny to hurry over to the Winter Palace and witness its capture. They were given passes by the Military Revolutionary Committee in the room beneath the meeting hall where, antlike, the committee had succeeded in hollowing out the provisional government's power of resistance in Petrograd.

They entered the Winter Palace on the heels of an assault wave of Red Guards, soldiers, and sailors. "Carried along by the eager wave of men," Reed wrote, "we were swept into the right hand entrance, opening into a great bare vaulted room, the cellar of the East wing, from which issued a maze of corridors and stair-cases. A number of huge packing cases stood about, and upon these the

Red Guards and soldiers fell furiously, battering them open with the butts of their rifles, and pulling out carpets, curtains, linen, porcelain plates, glassware. . . . One man went strutting around with a bronze clock perched on his shoulder; another found a plume of ostrich feathers, which he stuck in his hat."

The sack of the palace was just beginning when Bolshevik monitors appeared, bawling up and down the corridors, "Revolutionary discipline! Property of the people!" and snatching back what the looters had taken. The young cadets and the Women's Battalion surrendered quickly and bloodlessly. Upstairs Reed and his companions found many of the chambers ransacked, every desk and cabinet in the offices, and "in the living rooms beds had been stripped of their coverings and ward-robes wrenched open. The most highly prized loot was clothing, which the working people needed. In a room where furniture was stored we came upon two soldiers ripping the elaborate Spanish leather upholstery from the chairs. They explained it was to make boots with. . . ."

Reed, elated with the spectacle of Romanoff splendor trampled by the mob, did a little souvenir-hunting himself. He found a short jeweled sword and stuck it under his coat. Louise later described it as "a silver Caucasian dagger" which had been presented by the Czar to some vanished loyalist.

In a gold and malachite chamber with a green baize table the Reeds stumbled on the scene of deliberations by Kerensky's ministers just a few hours earlier. The conference had been disbanded by the cannonade from the Fortress of St. Peter and St. Paul. As another keepsake Reed snatched up a paper on which one of Kerensky's ministers—soon to vanish in the dungeons of the fortress—had started to write a proclamation, "The Provisional Government appeals to all classes to support the Provisional Government—"

They were strolling through the immense picture gallery when a crowd of a hundred men erupted suddenly from a corridor and surrounded them.

"One giant of a soldier stood in our path, his face dark with sullen suspicion. 'Who are you?' he growled. 'What are you doing here?' The others massed slowly around, staring and beginning to mutter. 'Provocatori!' I heard somebody say. 'Looters!' I produced our passes from the Military Revolutionary Committee. The soldier took them gingerly, turned them upside down and looked at them without comprehension. Evidently he could not read. He handed them back and spat on the floor. 'Bumagi! Papers!' said he with contempt. The mass slowly began to close in, like wild cattle around a cow-puncher on foot."

In this delicate moment, with the Americans finding their beloved proletariat suddenly assuming the aspect of a lynch mob, they were saved by the appearance of an officer. He spoke French and thus must have belonged to the formerly privileged class. Sweating with fear, he held up their passes and told the crowd: "Comrades! These people are foreign comrades—from America. They have come here to be able to tell their countrymen about the bravery and the revolutionary discipline of the proletarian army!"

The mob continued to press closer, until the officer's appeals finally persuaded the men to allow him to escort them out a side door opening on a quay by the Neva. "You have narrowly escaped," he told them, wiping the sweat from his face. [16]

After that brush with "revolutionary discipline," Reed and his friends pushed on toward the welcome lights of the Nevsky, where "the only signs of war were Red Guards and soldiers squatting around the fires." It was three o'clock in the morning. "The city was quiet—probably never so quiet in its history; on that night not a single hold-up occurred, not a single robbery." *

Before going to bed, too keyed up by all they had witnessed that night, they went over to the City Duma building. There, all uncomprehending, the anti-Bolshevik elements were joining to form a Committee for Salvation of Country and Revolution, still unaware that the Russian passion for committee-forming, proclama-

---

* Three days later Reed again reported, with some exaggeration, that revolutionary peace had descended upon Petrograd. Actually, as Antonov-Ovseenko, the leader of the assault on the Winter Palace, recorded, one regiment "got completely drunk while guarding the wine cellars of the Palace," and there was much drunken disorder throughout the city.

tion-drawing, and agenda-composing was undoubtedly one reason for the collapse of all efforts to put down an insurrection fomented by one numerically insignificant fraction of the left wing. Russian democracy, like the Russian empire it had succeeded, died with a scratching of pens and a murmur of debate over the wording of a proclamation.

Next, at Reed's insistence, and it is easy to imagine him, with flushed face and feverishly glowing eyes, excitedly rallying his exhausted wife and companions, they found a cab that took them back to the Smolny Institute. The driver was an anti-Bolshevik who demanded thirty rubles for his fare, then dropped them two blocks from their destination. The Congress was still in session, delegate after delegate clamoring for the floor and a moment in history. It was 5:17, as Reed meticulously wrote in his notebook, when tremendous news came from the front. There was still a great fear that the army, after all, might turn on them. That fear was quieted when a Bolshevik climbed up on the platform with a telegram in his hand and announced that the Twelfth Army, on the northern front, closest to Petrograd, was joining the revolution. The *coup d'état* engineered by Lenin was being solidified; on the floor men wept and embraced each other.

Now, Reed later wrote, "there was all great Russia to win—and then the world!"

They went home just as the winter night was paling before the dawn. To Jack it was "the shadow of a terrible dawn grey-rising over Russia. . . ." [17]

The next morning the city was amazingly calm on the surface. Most of the citizens of Petrograd got up and went to work as usual; the streetcars were running, and the stores, restaurants, and theaters opened. Except for the Red Guards on patrol, there were few signs that the revolution had taken a new and more violent turning. "Nothing," Reed wrote later, "is so astounding as the vitality of the social organism—how it persists, feeding itself, clothing itself, amusing itself, in the face of the worst calamities. . . ."

Beneath the surface, however, rumors were circulating that Kerensky was rallying the support of the army at the front, that

General Kornilov would return at the head of the Third Cavalry Corps. At Smolny Institute, Lenin and his associates on the presidium were feverishly planning how to consolidate their control of the capital and extend it to all of Russia. They were also hard-pressed to keep the Congress in line and argue down suggestions that the Bolsheviks arrange a compromise with the more moderate Socialists, so that taking over the vast administrative apparatus could be done as smoothly as possible. Some hint of future blocks in the path of the revolution came when the Union of Railway Workers that day demanded that the government be formed of a coalition of all the Socialist parties, and not just the Bolsheviks; it threatened to strike and tie up the whole railroad system if Bolshevik intransigence should result in a civil war. "Smolny was tenser than ever," Reed noted. "The same running men in the dark corridors, squads of workers with rifles, leaders with bulging portfolios arguing, explaining, giving orders as they hurried along, surrounded by friends and lieutenants . . . living prodigies of sleeplessness and work . . . so much they had to do, so much! Take over the Government, organise the city, keep the garrison loyal, fight the Duma and the Committee for Salvation, keep out the Germans, prepare to do battle with Kerensky, inform the provinces what had happened, propagandise from Archangel to Vladivostok . . ." [18]

The second session of the Congress was delayed from 1:00 P.M. to 8:40 P.M. At the press table in the great hall, while they waited for the presidium to appear, Reed listened to the correspondent for a "bourgeois" paper denounce the Bolsheviks as "common, rude, ignorant persons, without aesthetic sensibilities."

Finally Lenin, with his Asiatic calm, appeared on the platform with his collaborators. A number of speakers stood on the podium and presented a confusion of reports, alarms, proclamations.

Then the Congress was electrified as Lenin advanced to the center. The charismatic effect on his followers, as Reed defined it, was an ability to simplify, to lead them out of the bog of dialectic and theory created by the party intellectuals. "Now Lenin, gripping the edge of the reading stand, letting his little winking eyes travel over the crowd as he stood there, apparently oblivious to the long-rolling ovation, which lasted several minutes. When it finished, he said simply, 'We shall now proceed to construct the Socialist order!' Again that overwhelming human roar." He promised peace on the "basis of Socialist terms"—no annexations, no indemnities, the right of self-determination for all peoples, and the repudiation of all secret treaties. "The war is ended!" a delegate shouted. The assemblage then sang the "Funeral March" and the "*Internationale.*" Lenin proceeded to read a decree on the abolition of private ownership of land and the seizure of all Crown and church property. He was followed by Kamenev, who read a list of the Council of People's Commissars, headed by Lenin, as president, and Trotsky, as commissar for foreign affairs. Way down the list was "Stalin, Chairman for Minority Nationalities." The latter was so inconsiderable a figure that he is mentioned only twice in Reed's account of the revolution, then and as cosignatory of a decree guaranteeing the rights of the minority peoples of Russia.[19]

When he returned home early in the morning, Reed was greeted by his landlady, who told him "the House Committee has again asked that you take your turn on guard-duty with the rest of the men." Reed resigned on the spot as a sentry. "I solemnly affirmed that the Consul had forbidden all American citizens to carry arms —especially in the neighbourhood of the Russian intelligentsia."

On Friday, November 9, the atmosphere was more menacing as reaction to the Bolshevik coup began to make itself felt. In a continuing state of feverish excitement Reed raced around the city listening to rumors that Cossack squadrons were preparing to descend and attending a meeting of the armored-car regiment at the Mikhailovsky Riding School whose loyalty was in doubt. "Inside only a single arc-light burned dimly, high up near the roof of the enormous hall. . . . Around dimly squatted the monstrous shapes of the armoured cars. One stood alone in the centre of the place, under the light, and round it were gathered some two thousand dun-colored soldiers, almost lost in the immensity of that imperial building. A dozen men, officers, chairmen of the Soldiers' Committees, were perched on top of the car, and from the central turret

a soldier was speaking." The soldier was arguing against precipi-
tating a civil war. "Never have I seen men trying so hard to understand, to decide. They never moved, stood staring with a sort of
terrible intentness at the speaker."

In the end it was a Bolshevik, N. V. Krylenko, the new commissar for military affairs, who moved them with his appeal: "The
government is in your hands. You are the masters. Great Russia
is in your hands. Will you give it back?" [20]

Otherwise the fate of Russia was still unsettled. It was still touch
and go. The military garrisons and army camps were divided between the haranguing Bolshevik commissars who appeared among
them and the appeals of the Committee of Salvation. So were the
labor unions, the navy, the people themselves. The Allies rejected
the Bolshevik note declaring that Russia was leaving the war and
refused to recognize the new self-proclaimed government. And all
that came out of Smolny were bales of new proclamations to be
plastered over the city's walls.

During the next three days the whole nation seemed to be holding its breath. The suspense would be ended only when the major
army units around Petrograd followed the lead of the Twelfth
Army, or refused to. Over the weekend, November 10-11, it almost
seemed as though a new counterrevolution might sweep away the
Bolshevik claim to power. Reed heard reports that a column of
Cossacks was only eight *versts* from the city. All civil servants went
on strike, as did telephone, telegraph, and post office employees. Petrograd was isolated from Russia and the world. An air-
plane dropped leaflets bearing Kerensky's signature that ordered all
men of the armed forces to assemble in Mars Field and "threatened terrible vengeance on all who did not submit." The news
from the provinces was equally alarming to the Bolsheviks: in
Moscow the provisional government still held the Kremlin, and
in Kiev the Cossacks had overthrown the local Soviet and arrested
its leaders. It was expected that whatever forces Kerensky could
rally would approach over the open plains to the south of Petrograd, and an unorganized volunteer force, using all available means
of transport, rushed out to dig trenches and prepare to defend the

capital. On Sunday a group of cadets loyal to Kerensky rushed the telephone building, seized it, and held it all day, before the Red Guards took it by storm. The only thing that encouraged Reed was the way the people rallied to the Bolshevik banners. "South and southwest they poured through the shabby streets toward the Moskovsky Gate, men, women and children, with rifles, picks, spades, rolls of wire, cartridge belts over their working clothes. . . . Such an immense, spontaneous outpouring of a city never was seen!"

In his memoirs, Trotsky admitted that during that weekend the new revolution was in mortal danger. The Committee of Salvation was gathering adherents by the hour. Kerensky was advancing on Tsarskoe Selo, riding a white horse, with Cossack squadrons strung out behind him. Reed went out to that suburb, from which could be seen "the sprawling grey immensity of the capital spread along the dreary plain, and beyond, the steely Gulf of Finland." And there Kerensky blundered. He gave the defending Second Rifles ten minutes to lay down their arms; they refused, and the Cossack artillery opened fire on their barracks and killed eight men. "From that moment there were no more 'neutral' soldiers in Tsarskoe. . . ." [21]

Reed had become separated from Louise that Sunday, and when they were reunited that evening in their apartment he learned that she had come under fire, while crouching in an archway in St. Isaac's Square, from a machine gun mounted on an armored car. It had killed seven persons nearby, including a British officer.

November 12 was a "day of suspense," as Reed recalled it, with "the eyes of all Russia fixed on the grey plain beyond the gates of Petrograd, where all the available strength of the old order faced the unorganized power of the new, the unknown."

It was not until the next day that Kerensky's threat, borne on Cossack sabers, was blunted for good. His advance came up against a mixed force of detachments of the old czarist regiments, Red Guards, sailors, and a few armored cars. After a brief clash, Kerensky's Cossacks broke and fled, and the Bolshevik forces reoccupied Tsarskoe. Kerensky himself, disguised as a sailor, fled from the scene, and eventually, with the help of a British agent, from Russia. The news reached the Smolny Institute Tuesday morning in the form of a message from Trotsky, who had gone to the front. He reported to the Congress: "The night of November 12/13 will go down in history. Kerensky has been decisively repulsed. Kerensky is retreating. We are advancing."

From Smolny, Reed wrote, the new rulers of Russia were "hurling out to the world paeans of triumph."

He went out to the scene of the battle and came to a crossroads swarming with the triumphant defenders of Petrograd, where the "earth was trampled into mud half a mile around. The fighting had been furious here. . . . In the distance riderless Cossack horses circled hungrily, for the grass of the plain had died long ago. . . ." Tsarskoe was "bustling with the swaggering heroes of the proletarian horde."

When he returned to Petrograd that evening, the driver of the truck in which he rode cried out as the lights of the capital came in view, "Mine! All mine now! My Petrograd!" [22]

During the next two days the Bolsheviks rapidly consolidated their grip on the state. News came from Moscow that the provisional forces defending the Kremlin had surrendered. Reed exulted that Bolshevism had won against the middle and upper classes, the merchants and professional men, the landowners, even "the other Socialist parties," who "hated the Bolsheviki with an implacable hatred." He noted that only "a few—a very few—intellectuals" sided with the Bolsheviks.

Meanwhile, he had not neglected his professional duties. Days before, he had cabled Max Eastman: "This morning I was at the scene of the dispersal of the Junkers defending the Winter Palace by the Soviet troops, in the afternoon I was present at the opening of the All-Russian Assembly of Soviets, in the evening I witnessed the assault of the Winter Palace, entering with the first Bolshevik troops." Eastman was promised exclusive rights to Reed's dispatches, and was properly pleased with the prospects they offered. "His articles were worth thousands of dollars," Eastman recalled in his memoirs, "and I was in fact offered thousands for them. With that asset, and the subscription list—and yet more, the infamy—of the old *Masses*, and its brilliant staff of contributing editors, the opportunity to start a magazine [the *Liberator*] was irresistible." [23]

Reed began mailing a series of articles on all he had witnessed, under the general title "The Rising of the Proletariat," still unaware that the *Masses* had been closed. His articles eventually appeared in the *Liberator*. He also cabled to the New York *Call* a message from Lenin to American Socialists.

Thereafter he divided his time between working at the typewriter in his apartment and going around to the various offices of the new government. On November 18 the first snow fell on Petrograd, and "joy swept the city. . . . Everybody was smiling; people ran into the streets. . . . The life of the city grew gay, and the very Revolution ran swifter. . . ."

The historically famous "ten days"—actually eight, November 9 to 16—were over, and though Jack and Louise lingered in Russia a couple of months longer, what followed was comparatively anticlimactic. On November 21 they made a hazardous trip to Moscow to investigate reports that much of the city had been destroyed in the fighting. They found the reports highly exaggerated; the Kremlin was pocked with a few shell holes, but there was little other physical damage. Many had been killed, however, and the streets were filled with funeral processions.

They returned to Petrograd a day later. All they had witnessed so far convinced them that the revolution had been saved by the Bolsheviks, that the old tyranny would have been reimposed if the Bolsheviks had not acted. They saw no injustice in a fractional minority imposing its own will on the people. Reed's attitude toward the usurpation was summed up in the few words of the headline the New York *Call* put over a story published on November 26: BOURGEOISIE FORCED BOLSHEVIK UPRISING, JOHN REED SAYS.

The revolution, he wrote in another article for Eastman, was not merely entering a new phase, but "has just begun. For the first time in history the working class has seized the power of the state for its own purposes—and means to keep it. As far as anyone can see there is no force in Russia to challenge the Bolshevik power. And yet, as I write this, in the flush of their success, the new-born revolution of the proletariat is ringed round with a vast fear and hatred. The proletarian revolution has no friends except the proletariat."

Reed saw what he wanted to see. The revolution in Russia was his dream come true. His account of it was shaped by this bias, yet he was as much a reporter as he was a revolutionary, and he was committed to telling the truth. "He tried to see it all," as Bertram Wolfe has written, "put it all on paper. If he did not comprehend the meaning of the large events, what observer or participant did? He understood less and misunderstood more than many, so that one of the personages of whom he wrote would say to me of his book: 'The work of an innocent who did not know whether he was attending a wedding or a funeral!' It was a funeral —of Russia's newly won liberties, achieved after a century of struggle. If Jack thought he was witnessing the wedding of liberty and justice destined to live together happily ever after, so well does he report that we can see the acts of burial even as he sings of nuptials." [24]

An instance of this unconscious objectivity, drilled into him by his professional training, was his reportage on the Peasants' Congress convened in the Duma building in Petrograd the day he returned from Moscow. Somehow the loyalty of the peasants, who formed the bulk of the Russian population, had to be secured, and quickly. Admittedly they were largely anti-Bolshevik. They had to be whipped into line before a reaction to the latest revolution could set in. As Reed frankly stated, the Congress was summoned to session "over the heads of the Executive Committee of the Peasants' Soviet." Mere promises of land reform were not sufficient to enlist their support. Most of their leaders had been dismayed by the way their own party, the Social Revolutionary, had been thrown into discard at the Congress of Soviets.

"In the long run," as Reed explained, "everything depended upon the peasants. While the peasants had been politically backward, still they had their own peculiar ideas, and they constituted more than eighty percent of the people of Russia. The Bolsheviki had a comparatively small following among the peasants; and a permanent dictatorship of Russia by the industrial workers was impossible. . . . The traditional peasant party was the Socialist Revolutionary party; of all the parties now supporting the Soviet Government, the Left Socialist Revolutionaries were the logical inheritors of peasant leadership. . . ." The first vote at the Congress showed that more than half of the delegates belonged to that party, while only one-fifth were Bolshevik sympathizers.

Speaker after speaker, including Zinoviev, was hooted down when Bolsheviks came over from Smolny to argue their case for the peasants' support.

Then Lenin himself came, and "for ten minutes the room went mad. 'Down with him!' they shrieked." But Lenin simply waited on the podium, refusing to stalk out, as Zinoviev had done. When the delegates quieted down, Lenin addressed them calmly and simply: "This is class war. . . . Are you going to allow the ranks' of the proletariat to be divided? Which side will you be on? . . . The Soviets are the perfect representatives of the people—of the workers in the factories and mines, of the workers in the fields. Anybody who attempts to destroy the Soviets is guilty of an anti-revolutionary act. . . ." [25]

For several days, Reed observed, the Congress seemed to be deadlocked, but "None of us knew that a series of secret conferences were already going on between the Left Socialist Revolutionaries and the Bolsheviki at Smolny." What the Bolsheviks couldn't accomplish in open, democratic debate they would win in seclusion, when the peasant leaders could be privately harangued and bludgeoned into line. Day after day, on the floor of the Congress, there were "stormy debates," and "the Bolsheviki were twice on the point of quitting the assembly." On November 29, however, an agreement was reached behind the scenes, the peasants dropped their demands for a government composed of all the Socialist parties, and the Peasants' Soviets were joined with the Workers' and Soldiers' Soviets.[26]

Meanwhile, Trotsky was conducting what he later called "revolution by telegraph." From his offices in the Smolny went out telegrams to the administrative centers in all corners of Russia, from the Baltic States to the Ukraine, from the western borders to the maritime provinces of Siberia, notifying them of the change in government. Would 175,000,000 Russians submit to a Bolshevik regime based on a party membership of 240,000? It was to take years, millions of lives, and a civil war before the answer came.

Although an American citizen, Reed soon attached himself to the ruling apparatus. It was not that he now considered himself more a Russian than an American, but that he was a Bolshevik above all. Soon all national distinctions would be erased. He and everyone else worthy of inclusion in the new equalitarian society would be citizens of the world. Thus he went to work in the Bureau of the International Revolutionary Propaganda, a section of the Department of Foreign Affairs. The bureau was directed by Boris Reinstein, a friend of Reed, and part of its function was to publish newspapers and magazines in German, Hungarian, and Rumanian. Reed and another friend, Albert Rhys Williams, worked in a section directed by Karl Radek, one of the intellectual inner circle of Bolshevism, which produced a German-language paper, *Die Fackel*, and a magazine, *Die Russiche Revolution in Bildern*, which were spirited to the German lines.

Reed's involvement with a foreign government, which was beginning to attract an increasingly censorious attention from the American Embassy in Petrograd, was deepened shortly before he left Russia. Edgar Sisson, an envoy of the Committee of Public Information, the wartime American propaganda agency, warned him against getting in any deeper if he still hoped to consider himself an American citizen. Yet a few days later, with Sisson in the audience, Reed brashly (and on his own insistence) addressed the All-Russian Congress of Soviets meeting in the Tauride Palace. He promised that he would carry the revolutionary message back to the United States, where he would face trial with other editors of the *Masses* on charges of sedition, and help to free the "oppressed and exploited masses" in his native country.

"By his speech before the All-Russian Soviet," as Sisson later commented, "Reed became a factor, though a small one, in adding to a situation whereby Russia not only withdrew from the war but enabled Germany to move its eastern armies to the Western Front for the offensive of 1918, which theoretically should have won the war for Germany." [27]

A few days later Reed took an even bolder step, which the State Department was to regard as sheer mischief-making. He was appointed by Trotsky to be Soviet consul general in New York. How an American citizen could serve as the official representative of a foreign government was a matter neither Reed nor Trotsky, evidently, explored. When word of the appointment reached Washington, the State Department immediately announced that it would not be recognized, that he would have no standing, and a short time later Lenin canceled the appointment.

The day Reed received his short-lived appointment, Arno Dosch-Fleurot, the Petrograd correspondent of the New York World, waited in an anteroom of Trotsky's offices. Reed "came out," Dosch-Fleurot said, "his eyes full of merriment at the indignation it would arouse in Washington, and confided his appointment to me. I knew how he was regarded by our Government and told him he could not consider it. I tried to argue with him that he was a writer and not a propagandist, but he did not listen to me. . . . He looked at me smiling and said: 'When I am consul I suppose I will have to marry people. I hate the marriage ceremony. I shall simply say to them, "Proletarians of the world, unite." ' " [28]

Reed started for the United States early in February, a few weeks after Louise had begun the same journey. They had a few days together in Sweden before Louise boarded a ship at Christiania. Jack was supposed to take the same ship, but he was held up when the U.S. consul informed him that he had been instructed not to supply him with a visa. Thus Jack had to wait until the next sailing, in April.

In Stockholm he and Louise had met a remarkable and redoubtable woman who was to be their friend until the end of their lives. She was Angelica Balabanoff, the rebellious daughter of a Ukrainian landowner, who was then secretary of the Zimmerwald (Socialist) Movement, which was headquartered in Stockholm and was, as she later wrote, "the chief link between the new Russian government and the revolutionary labor movement of other countries." A short, heavy-set woman with black eyes and heavy hair worn in a braid coiled around her head, Miss Balabanoff was forty years old and a celebrated figure in international socialism. She had broken with her father when he refused to send her to college, had studied abroad, and become a Socialist in her youth. One of the rare distinctions of her career was her intimacy with the two great political figures of the nineteen-twenties—Lenin and Mussolini. Lenin personally endorsed her identity document as "the most outstanding militant representative of the Communist International." She singled Mussolini out of an audience of expatriate Socialists in Geneva, Switzerland, as one of the most pathetic youths she had seen. Then a Socialist firebrand, Mussolini was in exile, sleeping like a tramp under bridges. She got him work as a translator and befriended him.[29] "He needed someone to lean on, and his vanity would never permit him to lean on a man," she later said.[30] *

Angelica closely resembled both Jack and Louise in one respect: they were all blazing romantics. They all saw the Russian Revolution as the beginning of mankind's salvation, the first long stride toward a human paradise regained. A close friendship quickly formed among the three of them, a case of platonic love at first sight.

Jack Reed, as she recalled in her memoir *My Life as a Rebel*, came to her with a letter "from Chicherin or Lenin," and immediately impressed her as "one of the most devoted and genuine revolutionaries I had ever met. . . . I was amazed to find in an

---

* Angelica Balabanoff died in Rome at the age of eighty-seven on November 25, 1965, outliving by many years her associates in the revolutionary movement. For many years she lived in California and New York. She remained a Socialist, but was bitterly anti-Communist. Soviet leaders, she declared, had followed the path of least resistance—"the extermination of opposition in any form. The path of least resistance can very easily become a trap, and the price one pays for taking it may ultimately come too high."

American such love for the Russian masses . . . it was probably natural that he should have been stirred by the dramatic boldness of the Revolution itself. But there was something more than an appreciation of the colour and drama of the Revolution, hero-worship of its leaders and sympathy with its aims in Reed's enthusiasm for Russia. He loved the country itself and the great anonymous mass that had made the Revolution possible by its suffering and endurance." Louise Bryant was "a beautiful and radiant girl at this time . . . and her enthusiasm for the Soviets matched that of Jack. I was to know Louise in three different phases of her life— as Jack's courageous and adventurous comrade, fascinated by the Russian Revolution; as the broken-hearted woman of 1920, after Jack's tragic death, the reasons for which she fully understood; as the sick and shattered woman, without either the will or the strength to fight her own weakness, during her last years in Paris. In Stockholm, we had no intimation of the tragedy which our relation to the Russian Revolution would bring to all three of us within the next two or three years."

The friendship between Jack and Angelica intensified during the two months he spent waiting to be granted his visa and for the next ship to leave Christiania for New York. "We spent our evenings together, reading or talking, and on one occasion Jack induced me to go with him to the cinema to see a Charlie Chaplin picture."

To fill the hours of waiting, he began work on what was to be the classic account of the Russian Revolution, *Ten Days That Shook the World*, and he showed her several of the first chapters. Then, she said, "I understood to what extent Jack's intuition and creative art, his passionate love for the masses, had contributed to his understanding of the significance of the Russian events." [31]

During his two-month wait, all his letters from Louise were intercepted, and only one of his reached her. Robert Minor, later a considerable figure in American Communism, "has just come through here and brought me news of you," he wrote late in March, 1918, from Christiania. "I was so worried, and now I am relieved, but still worried to think of your having to work hard.

. . . I do so want you to come over here and be with me. . . . But how can we support ourselves, here or in Russia?" He added that he was selling articles on Russia to the Scandinavian news-papers. At the moment he still was not sure whether he would be allowed to return to the United States.[32] The letter was sent in care of Sonya Levien, then a member of the *Metropolitan Magazine* staff and later a highly successful screenwriter in Hollywood, and passed through the Allied censorship.

He also worked on a long Whitmanesque poem, "America, 1918," in which he expressed some of his feelings about his native land, which seemed so reluctant to receive him back. At least one of its stanzas might have served as the theme of the love-hate song of so many other expatriates:

> Deep within me something stirs, answers—
> (My country, my America!)
> As if alone in the high and empty night
> She called me—my lost one, my first lover
> I love no more, love no more, love no more. . . .[33]

11

"BREATH AND BLOOD

OF ME!"

On April 28, 1918, Jack Reed returned to an America with little
patience for dissenters, a wartime America quick to crush any
threat to national unity. As he landed in New York that April
morning, the war against Germany and her allies had entered a
crucial phase. The Germans had been able to transfer whole armies
from the eastern front, and late in March had hurled sixty-four
divisions against the Allied line in France. It was still not certain
that the Allies could withstand the successive German offensives
while waiting for the hundreds of thousands of American troops
to take their places in the battle as an integrated army; nor was
there any certainty that they could be trained, equipped, and organized in time to save the cause. Only a few days before Reed
arrived in New York, dispatches from France told of a sharp re-
verse suffered by American troops at Seicheprey, where elements
of the Yankee Division had been caught in a box barrage in a

supposedly quiet sector and suffered 634 casualties. Things did not look good for an untested army. And at home people worried about food rationing, German sabotage, and rising prices. Little sympathy could be spared for those who opposed what the majority considered America's righteous and self-sacrificing role in the war.

Thus Reed's reception committee when the ship docked was a squad of federal agents and Customs officials. He was held on board for eight hours while they searched him, his cabin, and his personal effects for revolutionary propaganda and messages to American sympathizers with the Bolshevik Revolution. They found nothing but his notes for *Ten Days That Shook the World*, which were confiscated, but later returned to him. He had, however, succeeded as a smuggler for the U.S. conduit of the Bolshevik underground. According to Benjamin Gitlow, in those years a comrade of Jack's, but later a vigorous anti-Communist, Reed smuggled in a "load of revolutionary propaganda and contraband. The authorities had taken every precaution and they were puzzled. They did not know that Reed had made friends with members of the crew, was helped by I.W.W. seamen and got direct aid from James Larkin, who put his Irish rebel network in New York harbor at Reed's disposal." [1]

Reed was informed that because he was under indictment in the *Masses* sedition case he would have to report at the Federal Building the next day.

Louise waited the long hours on the dock for him, and together they took a taxi to a hotel in the Village. No doubt she immediately filled him in on the first trial of Max Eastman, Art Young, and other codefendants. The day before, the jury had failed to agree on a verdict. A second trial had been ordered.

Reed had come home to face the possibility of imprisonment, to risk his person in the prevailing war hysteria, and yet New York, which he loved above all other inanimate things, still exercised its old imperial fascination. He transcribed some of his feelings about home-coming on a scrap of paper, in a poem titled "On Returning to the City (1918)," which was never published.

> To greet these towers where the morning
> First kindles from the rim of the sea
> Last pinnacles of sun's adorning,
> Manhattan! Breath and blood of me! [2]

Max Eastman admired him wholeheartedly for having come back to stand trial with the *Masses* group, an admiration undimmed forty-six years later when Eastman published another volume of his memoirs. To Eastman it was a simple case of loyalty to his old associates, a loyalty Trotsky thought "amusingly un-Marxian." Reed, Eastman was certain, "never subscribed any more than I did to the religion of immoralism that the Bolsheviks inherited from Marx and Nechayer." What brought him home to chance a prison sentence at the second *Masses* trial was a "sense of honor and good fellowship." He buoyed them all by the gaiety with which he faced that prospect. Eastman now felt that their roles had been reversed. "He had a reckless equilibrium in walking life's tightropes that abashed me a little, and made me feel secondary, as though he were my more muscular big brother who knew all about living and was equal to it, whereas I was still trying to grow up." [3]

But there may have been more to the gesture than simply a high sense of comradeship. Certainly it was true that Reed still possessed that archaic "sense of honor," which as much as anything else was to prove fatal to him; that element of true aristocracy which all his revolutionary experience, and all the dialectic in which he was drenched, could not extinguish. Yet his return to stand trial also served the purposes of the Communist International, which did not disdain the uses of martyrdom. He had taken Lenin and Trotsky into his confidence about his plans to return to the United States, and, as Benjamin Gitlow has observed, "The Bolshevik leaders were no fools. They appreciated the importance to Soviet Russia of getting the right publicity in the proper places. . . . Trotsky had been in America. . . . Lenin too had long ago recognized the power of the press. . . . They decided on a course that would dramatize Reed's return to his native land." Furthermore, Lenin and Trotsky appreciated "his intention to utilize his time back home for the Bolshevik cause." In prison, if it came to that, Reed would be a martyr to the U.S. government's suppression of the pacifist-Socialist cause; as a free man he would work diligently to promote Bolshevism in America—and he was one of the few Americans with the literary and journalistic reputation to be able to raise an effective voice.[4]

Immediately after his return, in fact, Reed flung himself into unceasing activity as an agitprop specialist. He and Louise took a small dingy apartment at 1 Patchin Place, an alley in Greenwich Village from which both sallied on speaking tours. Gitlow said Reed spent "twenty hours a day making America Bolshevik-conscious," and, thanks to Louise's lack of interest in housekeeping, they lived in several small rooms littered with undusted books and papers, ashes overflowing from the fireplace, unwashed dishes and unemptied ash trays.

Reed considered the Socialist Party, as a political apparatus, as an organism for causing a revolution, all but dead. "All the Socialist party needs," he said, "is an undertaker. . . ." The radical movement in America had to be revitalized, made worthy of the Bolshevik minority which had turned Russia upside down.

When he visited them at 1 Patchin Place, Gitlow remarked on Louise's beauty, "a miniature of well-shaped daintiness and charm, with large dreamy eyes that looked straight at you. Jack seldom talked about Louise, but Louise always talked about Jack." Louise did not accept the Bolshevik Revolution with anything like Jack's enthusiasm, was willing to work for the Soviet government's recognition by the United States, but was "positive that bolshevism was not good for America." [5]

During the months following Jack's return, they were often separated. On May 9, he spoke at a meeting to celebrate the hung jury at the first *Masses* trial; the following night at a mass meeting hailing the short-lived Finnish People's Republic. Other engagements included speeches before Socialist clubs, at a meeting in Carnegie Hall at which he defended Bolshevism against the accusations of moderate Socialists that it had established a dictatorship *over*, rather than *of*, the proletariat, at a dinner given by the

New York *Call* at which he was the guest of honor. Everywhere he stubbornly and often eloquently defended the new government of Russia. He talked down Harvard students who heckled him at a meeting in the Tremont Temple in Boston, and early in June addressed more sympathetic audiences in the Bronx, Newark, Brooklyn, and Detroit. His swing around the eastern cities was briefly interrupted by an encounter with the law in Philadelphia on June 1. He had been scheduled to speak in a hall there, but found its doors locked and about five hundred people waiting outside when he arrived. The city had revoked permission for the meeting. Reed suggested that the crowd follow him to a quiet street a block or two away, where the meeting would be conducted in the open air. He had just mounted a box to begin his speech when a police lieutenant, at the head of a squad, came up and kicked the box out from under him. A melee ensued, though Reed for once was not charged with swinging his own fists in his usual joyous fashion. There were plenty of other charges: breaking a municipal ordinance by speaking without a permit, inciting a riot (one of his would-be listeners had been arrested for assaulting four policemen), and inciting seditious utterances. He was released on five thousand dollars' bail, with a trial to be held later in the year.[6]

Later in June he and the genial cartoonist Art Young went to Chicago on an assignment from the *Liberator* to cover the trial of one hundred and one I.W.W. men charged with interfering with the conscription laws. There were none of the niceties of journalistic objectivity in Reed's account of the trial. It was, he said, an inquisition, presided over by federal judge Kenesaw Mountain Landis, who later was more famous as the first commissioner of baseball.

Reed wrote of Judge Landis: "Small on the huge bench sits a wasted man with untidy white hair, an emaciated face in which two burning eyes are set like jewels, parchment skin split by a crack for a mouth; the face of Andrew Jackson three years dead. A fighter, a sport, according to his lights, and as just as he knows how to be . . . Upon this man has devolved the historic role of trying the Social Revolution. He is doing it like a gentleman. The other day he ruled out of evidence the report of the Committee on Industrial Relations which the defense was trying to introduce in order to show the background of the I.W.W."

And of the defendants he said: "Inside the rail of the courtroom, crowded together, many in their shirt-sleeves, some reading papers, one or two stretched out asleep, some sitting, some standing up; the faces of workers and fighters, for the most part; also the faces of orators, of poets, the sensitive and passionate faces of foreigners—but all strong faces, all faces of men inspired somehow; many scarred, few bitter . . . One hundred and one *men*—lumberjacks, harvest-hands, miners, editors; one hundred and one who believe that the wealth of the world belongs to him who creates it, and that the workers of the world shall take their own." [7]

Bill Haywood and others he knew were among those on trial, and he went to visit them in jail and inspire them with his account of what had happened in Russia. To him their faces closely resembled those of the Executive Committee of the Congress of Soviets, and it took only the slightest effort to imagine that not they, but Judge Landis was on trial as an enemy of the United States. In the end, however, weeks after Reed and Art Young went back to New York, it was the I.W.W. men who went to prison; all were convicted, and Haywood and several other leaders got twenty years in Leavenworth.

During the Fourth of July recess in the I.W.W. trial, Reed and Young went down to Terre Haute to visit Eugene Debs, the titular head of the American Socialists, who also was awaiting trial on charges of sedition. They were sitting in Debs's living room while a Fourth of July parade was forming up the street. "The sound of the parade came drifting down," Reed reported in the same issue of the *Liberator* in which his account of the I.W.W. trial appeared. "Looking through the darkened windows we watched the people. As they passed the house they motioned or pointed toward it, with expressions compounded half of eager malice, and half of a sort of fear. 'That's where Gene Debs lives,' you could see them saying, as one would say, 'The House of the Traitor.'

" 'Come on,' Gene said suddenly. 'Let's go out and sit on the front porch and give 'em a good show, if they want to see me.' So we went out on the porch and took off our coats. And those who passed only looked furtively our way, and whispered, and when they caught Gene's eye, bowed over-cordially." He quoted Debs as saying that he was not afraid of being lynched by any of his more bloody-minded townspeople, because "as a rule they're cowardly curs anyway." [8]

The latter part of the summer of 1918 Reed spent mostly at his cottage on Mt. Airy Road, near Croton, a half-mile up from Eastman's. Eastman saw much of him during those weeks and was puzzled then—but not later—by his "almost somber" attitude. Jack, he believed, was a man split by the contradictions he faced. Well-educated, he found it difficult to reconcile himself to the "cloudy ideologies" of the men he admired so much in Russia. "It is like racing a car backward for a well-educated American to compete with a Marxian fundamentalist. That is what Jack had to do in order to fulfill his task of creating a Bolshevik party in the United States."

It was this "state of tension," Eastman believed, that was partly responsible for Reed's announcement one day that he intended to resign from the staff of the *Liberator*. He was also "disturbed by the pro-Wilson tone of my editorials," Eastman said.[9] In the same September, 1918 issue of the *Liberator* that carried his articles on the I.W.W. trial and the meeting with Debs, Reed's letter of resignation appeared.

"I'm going to resign as one of the contributing editors of the *Liberator*. I've thought about it for a long time, and I make this decision not without emotion, remembering our long work together on the *Masses*. But I feel I must take my name off the editorial page. The reason is, I cannot in these times bring myself to share editorial responsibility for a magazine which exists upon the sufferance of Mr. Burleson [the postmaster general]. Of course, this does not mean that I want to stop contributing to the *Liberator*. And in the happy day when we can again call a spade a spade without tying bunting on it, you will find me, as you have in the past, Yours for the Profound Social Change, John Reed."

Eastman replied in a letter published below it that he regretted Reed's decision and explained that he considered it "our duty to the social revolution to keep this instrument we have created alive toward a time of great usefulness," and added the riposte: "Personally I envy you the power to cast loose when not only a great deal of the dramatic beauty, but also the glamour of abstract moral principle, is gone out of the venture, and it remains for us merely the most effective and therefore the right thing to do." [10]

Reed continued writing for the *Liberator*, and his friendship with Eastman, outside the ideological arena, was fortunately undamaged.

He began devoting most of his journalistic efforts, however, to editing the *Voice of Labor*, which followed the Bolshevik line with considerable fidelity. The office of that organ, as well as that of the *Revolutionary Age*, which was edited by Louis Fraina, was in the Connolly Club, on Twenty-ninth Street near Broadway. There he spent much of his time. The club was named for James Connolly, known as the "Lenin of the Irish Radicals," who was executed after leading the Easter Rebellion in 1916. The club was the headquarters of Reed's close friend Jim Larkin, another of the Dublin revolutionaries and the man who had organized the Irish Transport and General Workers Union.[11] He had come to the United States to whip up anti-British sentiment, collect funds for the Irish revolution, and obtain the arms that would make it possible. In the blithe Celtic fashion, Larkin was both a Catholic and a Marxist, a flaming activist whose contradictions matched Jack Reed's. At his first public appearance in New York, before a radical audience in the New Star Casino, he had shocked them by dangling a gold cross and proclaiming, "There is no antagonism between the Cross and Socialism. A man can pray to Jesus and be a better militant Socialist for it. There is no conflict between the religion of the Catholic Church and Marxism. I belong to the Catholic Church. In Ireland that is not held against a Socialist. I defy any man to challenge my standing as a Socialist and a revolutionist." A man like that could hardly help endearing himself to Jack Reed; and besides, Larkin, with his influence on the New

York water front, was his means of egress, by the underground route, if and when a hasty and clandestine exit became necessary.

Reed still had his moments of prankishness, perhaps inspired by the mischievous Celtic atmosphere of the Connolly Club. According to Benjamin Gitlow, he would leave the door of his office ajar so he could overhear the arguments in the outer room. When they grew especially heated, he would rush out and demand excitedly, "Comrades, what do you think about the materialistic conception of history and economic determinism? Which is right?" That would usually bring an earnest student of Marxism to his feet. Reed would contradict him, reeling off quotations, with page numbers, from Marx's works. His opponent would insist that Reed produce Volume I of Marx to prove he had quoted correctly. "Oh, sorry, Comrade," Reed would reply with a condescending smile. "I did not comprehend the extent of your ignorance on the subject. I did not refer to Volume I containing the elementary postulates of Marx. I referred to Volume III which contains Marx's final and basic philosophical conclusions." Then, having delivered himself of an entirely imaginary quotation from the masterwork, he would duck back into his office, "excited as a young colt." It was a magnificent display of Marxist one-upmanship, but it would hardly have amused any dour and doctrinaire Bolshevik of the sort he admired so extravagantly in Russia.

"In his serious moments," Gitlow recalled, "Reed sometimes discussed the kind of communist movement he believed in. He wanted a rank and file movement backed up by an independent militant revolutionary trade union organization like the I.W.W. He had no use for a movement dominated by politicians. 'Ben,' said Reed, 'we've got to have a movement with guts, whose members will hoof it over the country and concentrate wherever they are needed. We must build a disciplined movement but not one bossed by politicians.' " [12]

The worry and fatigue lifted from Reed when he went up to his cottage in the hills overlooking the Hudson. A shed near the cottage, he said, was "my workshop, my sanctuary. Within its walls I meditate in a world of my own and write." He pointed southward and told Gitlow, "In that direction is Sing Sing Prison. When the siren's howl disturbs the stillness of the night you know that a prisoner has escaped. I've heard the warning a number of times. Each time I went out on the road hoping to meet the poor devil in order to hide him from his pursuers."

Imprisonment had a personal meaning for him that autumn of 1918. Eugene Debs had just been sentenced to ten years in federal prison on the same charges that confronted Reed. Eastman said that all the *Masses* defendants had made up their minds they would probably be convicted at their second trial. Yet Reed was undeterred; only two weeks before the second *Masses* trial was scheduled to open, he spoke at Hunt's Point Casino before a crowd of four thousand, charging that the British had been involved in a recent attempt at assassinating Lenin, and that President Wilson, by what means he did not make clear, could have blocked the German-Russian agreement at Brest Litovsk by which Soviet Russia withdrew from the war. He was arrested, again charged with sedition, and released on five thousand dollars' bail. He also still faced trial on the Philadelphia charges.

The second *Masses* trial, in which Reed was made a codefendant for having written the "Knit a Strait-Jacket for Your Soldier Boy" caption, opened in the federal court of the southern New York district before Judge Martin Manton. "The attitude of the defendants," as Reed described it later, "was different from what it had been at the first trial. Last Spring Germany was invading Russia; this fall the United States was invading Russia [the U.S. had sent an expeditionary force to Siberia nominally to protect the mountains of war supplies it had sent to Vladivostok before the revolution]; and Socialists were in a different frame of mind. Moreover the persecution of Socialists had grown more bitter, and it had become more and more clearly a class issue. I think we all felt tranquil, and ready to go to prison if need be. At any rate we were not going to dissemble what we believed. . . ." [13]

On October 3, Reed was called to the stand and testified at length on his experiences as a war correspondent—"very boyish and high-voiced and inept and uneasy in his clothes," Eastman described him, "but all the more likable and believable because of it." [14] This testimony was designed to show how personal acquaintance had turned him against war.

He described the nightmarish scene, from his viewpoint, in the German trenches on the western front, with the French positions only eighty yards away, visible under the bursting light of flares and star shells. "It had been raining for two weeks, two solid weeks of rain had come down, and in this mud midway between the two trenches—"

The defense attorney, Seymour Stedman, asked him to raise his voice.

"—between these two trenches, in the mud, forty yards from each trench, there lay a heap of bodies, all that was left of the last French charge, and these bodies were slowly sinking in the mud, had been left out there wounded to die. Nobody dared to come out, although they were only forty yards from the French trenches, and forty yards from the Germans. There had been no cessation of fighting. The wounded had lain out there screaming and dying in the mud, and they were sinking in the mud, and in some cases there wasn't anything left of those bodies but an arm or a leg sticking up out of the soft mud with the flesh rotten on it."

And when he returned to New York, he said, his voice sharpening with disgust, what "had happened while I went to war? At the time I came back . . . the society columns were full about people getting up war benefits, giving war plays, and the hotels and the houses of the upper West Side, upper Fifth Avenue, were full of knitting parties, knitting socks for soldiers. They were not knitting socks for soldiers because their sons were in the trenches, as they knit socks for soldiers now; they were knitting socks for soldiers because it was the thing to do. They had Caruso sing there in the afternoon while they were knitting socks for soldiers, and the talk was all of frivolity about the fact there was a war going on in Europe; England, France were in it, it was fashionable to be in it, and we were not in it—and why weren't we in it? It made me sort of sick."

Later, Judge Manton asked him if he were a Socialist. Reed replied that he "had been working with the Socialist movement for a long time. I did not become a Socialist until last summer."

The federal prosecutor, Earl Barnes, was fairly gentle in his cross-examination, perhaps sensing that the jury felt a certain amount of sympathy for Reed's boyish forthrightness. He asked whether he believed in a revolution of the proletariat against the ruling classes.

"Yes, sir," Reed replied. "All Socialists do."

"All Socialists do?"

"Yes."

"And that, in your mind, is the only war worth fighting in?"

"Well," Reed answered with an engaging smile, "to tell you the truth, it is the only war that interests me." [15]

Max Eastman observed that the jury seemed to be impressed by his testimony. "Some people, you look in their eyes and you say 'This man is honest and kind,' and you feel that no further questions need be asked. Jack had such eyes." Codefendant Floyd Dell remarked that Reed had "held the court-room spellbound."

Art Young was responsible for adding one of the lighter touches to the trial testimony when Prosecutor Barnes asked him under cross-examination: "Now, Mr. Young, you have told us a good deal about your beliefs in revolution and that you believe the American Revolution was justified, but, Mr. Young, do you believe in the theory of the class struggle?"

"If you've got the measles," Young replied in his mild, Pickwickian manner, "it doesn't necessarily mean that you believe in them." [16]

In his summation to the jury Prosecutor Barnes worked himself into a state of considerable eloquence by recalling a friend of his who had gone overseas with the American Expeditionary Force and had recently been killed in action. "Somewhere in France he lies dead, and he died for you and me. He died for Max Eastman, he died for Jack Reed, he died for Merrill Rogers [another co-defendant]. His voice was but one of a thousand silent voices that demand that these men be punished!"

Young had been dozing at the counsel table until the prosecutor raised his voice for that closing remark. "Who's he talking about?" Young whispered, leaning over toward Jack Reed. "Who is this hero who didn't die for *me?*"

Jack grinned and said, "Cheer up, Art. Jesus died for you."

The result of the trial was another hung jury, with eight jurors voting for acquittal, four for conviction. Reed credited the lack of a verdict to Max Eastman. "The jury was held tense by his eloquence; the Judge listened with all his energy." But there was another factor, as one of the jurors disclosed to Young. "It's a good thing for you boys that you were all American-born," he said. "Otherwise it might have gone pretty hard with you." [17]

"The second trial was over," Reed wrote. "We await the third with equanimity." But there was to be no third trial; the government gave up its case against the *Masses* defendants. Subsequently Reed was acquitted of the Philadelphia charges, and the government had dropped its case against him for his speech at the Hunt's Point Casino shortly before the second *Masses* trial.

During the succeeding months he continued his propagandizing in print and his agitation on the public platform. He contributed almost every month to the *Liberator*, edited the *Voice of Labor*, and wrote for other left-wing journals. He spoke before "labor lyceums" and Socialist and pacifist meetings all through the five boroughs of New York. Later in the year he resumed work on *Ten Days That Shook the World*. In addition to all these endeavors—which rarely brought him more than twenty dollars a week, according to Benjamin Gitlow—he was also drawn into a scheme for establishing a new magazine, to be called *These States*, with the vociferous and unpredictable Frank Harris, later notorious as the biographer of Shaw and Wilde. Floyd Dell was to be coeditor. The magazine, which Dell said was "to be full of the finest modernist literature now being produced in America," foundered on the rocky personalities involved—particularly Frank Harris.

As Dell recalled: "Jack collected together most of the contents of the first issue, but at that point Frank Harris, who had been very enthusiastic about it, read some of the contents of this modernist magazine of which he was to be one of the editors, and suddenly and furiously revolted." Harris had edited several polished and highly literate journals in pre-war Britain and prided himself, perhaps excessively, on his editorial taste. "What he disliked most," Dell recalled, "was Carl Sandburg's poetry—which we had been printing with pride in The Masses and the Liberator. 'No, no— good God!' he repeated violently. 'No, no—good God!' And so the whole project was abruptly abandoned." [18]

Thereafter, according to Gitlow, Reed took care to have nothing more to do with the abrasive Mr. Harris. Frank Harris frightened him. "When Reed came across the critic on the street, he became apprehensive and quickened his steps to avoid meeting a literary monster who made his blood curdle." [19] *

During their brief association in attempting to start These States, Dell said, Reed told him that he was going to "organize a Communist Party in America—which he subsequently did, though it turned out to be one of several, which later coalesced. It would be a disciplined party of professional revolutionists, he said. 'Then I shan't join it,' I told him; 'I'm a professional writer.' Jack wanted to be everything, artist, revolutionist, adventurer." [20]

That fall of 1918 Reed settled down to finish his day-to-day account of the Russian Revolution. According to Eastman, Jack, red-eyed and unshaven, working sixteen and eighteen hours a day, finished the manuscript of Ten Days That Shook the World in just about ten days. He had been given an advance by Boni & Liveright, and took an attic room in the Village to get away from the interruptions that would have occurred if he had settled down to the task at 1 Patchin Place or the cottage near Croton. He had the journalistic aptitude for doing his best work in white-hot haste.

---

* Harris was adept at bloodcurdling. Earlier in his career he published England or Germany?, in which he asserted that Britain had attacked Germany out of envy for its naval, military, and industrial establishments, and suggested that the Kaiser sink all food ships heading for England, which would shortly bring about a revolution and an end to the war. Britain could then subside into its rightful place as a third-rate power. Though claiming to sympathize with the Russian Revolution, he also attacked Lenin as a "dude, prig and sissy" who changed his silk underwear every few hours.

It was a fairly long book, but Boni & Liveright was able to send it to the press in January of 1919.

Once that was out of the way Reed resumed his whirlwind activities as a prophet of the revolution. His narrow escapes from imprisonment had not tempered his disposition to attack the government, though this was no safer early in 1919 than it had been before the armistice brought the war in Europe to a halt. Almost a stock headline in the daily newspapers was NEW ROUNDUP OF RADICALS. Attorney General A. Mitchell Palmer was beginning to press his campaign against foreign-born radicals, which was to sweep up six thousand "dangerous aliens," of whom a thousand were deported. The climate, chilled by news from Russia of continuing civil war and repression, was adverse to such statements as Reed made one evening in January, 1919, before a mass meeting guarded by one hundred policemen. "My family came to this country, both branches, in 1607; one of my ancestors was Patrick Henry, who signed the Declaration of Independence; another of my ancestors was a general under George Washington; and another was a colonel on the northern side in the Civil War. I have a brother, a major in the aviation corps, now in France. I am a voter and a citizen of the United States, and I claim the right to criticize it as much as I please. I criticize the form of it because I claim that it is not a democratic enough government for me. I consider the Soviet government a more democratic government at the present time than our own government." The war was finished, but civil liberties had not been fully restored to the people, he said. Free speech was suppressed, certain periodicals were banned from the mails, and militarism was still triumphant. The World War supposedly had been a contest of democracy versus autocracy; actually it was merely a war between competing capitalistic systems. Now a new war was beginning, and "this time it is a war between two ideas."

Although he detested Louis Fraina personally, he began contributing to *Revolutionary Age*. For the *Liberator* he eulogized Karl Liebknecht, the German Communist, who was murdered in

Berlin with Rosa Luxemburg during the postwar struggle between left and right for control of a beaten Germany which, according to Marxist-Leninist doctrine, would serve as the industrial base of world Communism. Liebknecht had been released from prison shortly after the war ended. "He must have known," Reed wrote, "as he was drawn in his flower-filled carriage through the shouting streets, that his hour was near. He must have known—when he cried to the throng from the balcony of the Russian embassy, the red flag floating over him, 'The future belongs to the people!'—that for him there would be no future." [21]

Perhaps he suspected that for Jack Reed as well as for Karl Liebknecht there would also be no future. Certainly he faced his official inquisitors in February, 1919, with something close to bravado.

The scene this time was a hearing room in the Capitol in which a judiciary subcommittee of the Senate was holding an inquiry into what was officially titled "Brewing and Liquor Interests and German and Bolshevik Propaganda." Shortly before the war ended, the subcommittee had been investigating connections between German-American brewers and distillers and pro-German activities in the United States. After the war the subcommittee decided there was a connection between pro-Germanism and Bolshevism and sought to prove it. A number of witnesses were summoned to testify to the horrors of the Russian Revolution, though they were unsuccessful in linking it with pro-German propaganda in the United States.

Reed and his wife and several others sympathetic to the Russian Revolution telegraphed to Senator Lee S. Overman, the chairman of the subcommittee, and asked to be heard in defense of the Soviet Union. Their request was granted. The first pro-Russian witness called was Louise, who visibly confounded the committee, whose members perhaps were expecting something along the lines of the well-weathered Emma Goldman, by being so sweetly formed and lissome an All-American Girl. Even her pertness and her saucy manner could not quite stir up indignation in the senatorial breasts.

First the senators questioned her on whether she believed in the sanctity of the oath.

Q. "Do you believe there is a God?"

A. "I suppose there is a God. I have no way of knowing."

Q. "Do you believe in the Christian religion?"

A. "Certainly not. I believe all people should have whatever religion they wish, because that is one of the things—"

Q. "You are not a Christian, then?"

A. "I was christened in the Catholic Church."

Q. "What are you now, a Christian?"

A. "Yes, I suppose that I am."

Q. "And you do not believe in Christ?"

A. "I believe in the teachings of Christ."

After more skirmishing on this issue, Louise complained, "It seems to me as if I were being tried for witchcraft."

She admitted under questioning that she had acted as a courier for the Soviet government on her return to the United States, but indicated that her enthusiasm for Communism was qualified.

Q. "Do you advocate a Soviet for this country?"

A. "No."

Q. "Do you approve a Soviet government for this country?"

A. "No, I don't think it will work."

Q. "Do you believe in a Soviet government for Russia?"

A. "It's none of my business. It's their affair and all I ask is that they be allowed to settle it themselves."

Q. "Are you a capitalist or a proletarian?"

A. "I am poor. I suppose I am a proletarian."

Her manner, alternately demure and spirited, the former when questioned about leaving her first husband for Reed, the latter when several of the committee members tried to pin her down on the subject of how Reed was employed by the Bolsheviks in their propaganda bureau, finally infuriated at least one senator.

She insisted on testifying about the German-language propaganda sent into the enemy lines—which, of course, would tend to contradict the subcommittee's theory that Bolshevik propaganda worked in favor of Imperial Germany—and Senator Nelson cut her off, saying, "Do not be so impertinent." Chairman Overton was annoyed when hisses and applause came from the audience and said, "I do not want any more noise or we will have an executive session. . . . I want to treat this lady respectfully."

"I hope you will," Louise responded. ". . . I am a free American citizen. I expect to be treated with the same courtesy as former witnesses, and I have not gotten it so far."

Again there was a mixture of applause and hisses from the audience, and the chairman ordered the hearing room cleared. Reed then stood up in the rear of the chamber, identified himself, and asked that he be allowed to stay. His request was granted.

Louise testified quite freely all that day, February 20, and the following morning. At the close, she insisted, "I do not think the Russians are such beasts and fanatics as many of the witnesses have tried to make out."

"Has any witness," inquired one of the senators, "referred to the Russian people in any but the most kindly way?"

"When they say that people are murdered by the thousands," Louise replied, "and that people are starved, and all those conditions exist, I would consider it just exactly the same thing." She added that her purpose in volunteering to testify was that Americans were "prejudiced against the Russians. . . . We think that everything they do is bad and immoral, and I have wanted to protest." [22]

Reed followed her as a witness that afternoon. "There was a hint of swagger in his gait," observed Stanley Frost, of the New York *Tribune*, "the glint of steel behind his gray eyes and a general air of you-be-damnedness. . . . Reed thoroughly enjoyed himself while he told the committee about his views on Russia, revolution and life in general. He reveled in his own dialectic skill and found pleasure in the atmosphere of opposition." [23]

Again there was an opening skirmish over the oath-taking, with Reed insisting that he would "affirm" but not swear to tell the truth. Somewhat wearily, Major E. Lowry Humes, the subcommittee counsel, finally agreed to the affirmation.

Reed testified for three and a half hours, ranging over his experiences in Russia, his work as a Soviet propagandist, the way the Bolsheviks organized food supply and control of the press. He delighted in evading the traps his inquisitors laid and in embarrassing them considerably by introducing testimony favorable to the Soviet system as compared to the American. He would have been a more effective witness for Communism if he had not so openly enjoyed his own nimbleness.

He admitted under questioning by Major Humes that he believed extraconstitutional methods might, under certain circumstances, be necessary to change the American political system, but he denied that he advocated overturning the government by force.

Q. "Have you in any of your public speeches advocated a revolution in the United States similar to the revolution in Russia?"

A. "I have always advocated a revolution in the United States."

Q. "You are in favor of a revolution in the United States?"

A. "Revolution does not necessarily mean a revolution by force. By revolution I mean a profound social change. I do not know how it will be attained."

Q. "Do you not in your speeches leave the impression with your audiences that you are talking about a revolution by force?"

A. "Possibly."

Reed insisted that the coming of the Bolshevik rule brought law and order to Petrograd, that "for the first three weeks of the Bolshevik regime the city was excellently policed and excellent order was kept in it." Shortly after that period came what the American press called the "wine pogroms." Several regiments went on a roaring mass drunk after locating a number of huge wine cellars.

"Well," Reed explained to the subcommittee, "it was very cold, and these soldiers were out in the streets most of the time fighting, etc., and they yielded to temptation—some of them—and broke into the wine cellars. For about two weeks you would hear of a sudden in the night a terrible crash—somebody would smash a window in—and the soldiers would go in and pass out bottles, and there would be a crowd of about 200 soldiers around the wine cellars, and they would drink this wine and go around town firing off guns in the air. . . .

"The soviets stopped the wine pogroms themselves. They sent first the Kronstadt sailors and tried to stop the looting of the cellars by argument . . . but the plundering of the wine cellars still continued, especially by two regiments—the lowest element of the regiments—so the soviets saw that something had to be done immediately . . . they sent out trucks with machine-guns strapped on them, and they stopped this business. The commissars would go in and give three warnings to the men who were looting the wine cellars, and if the men left the wine cellars, the commissars would go in and smash all the bottles out in the street and let the wine flow. That is what they did with the Winter Palace wine cellar, which was worth about $4,000,000. . . . If the soldiers did not leave the wine cellars, they would shoot."

Regarding his own efforts as a propagandist in Russia, he testified that half a million copies of *Die Fackel,* the paper published for clandestine distribution to German troops, were printed daily. The paper, he testified, launched "fierce attacks on German militarism" and encouraged the German people to revolt—thereby inferring that his work as a Bolshevik propagandist assisted the Allied war effort. (It was not included in his testimony, but General Max Hoffmann, the German commander on the eastern front who presided over the peace conference at Brest Litovsk, complained that his troops were "conquered" by Bolshevik propaganda. "Our victorious army on the eastern front became rotten with Bolshevism.") The subcommittee, however, was not interested in any proof that Bolshevism was antipathetic to German militarism, and Major Humes hastily changed the subject.

Reed's reply to questions about freedom of the press in Russia was a masterpiece of evasion. He admitted that the Bolsheviks "sought to destroy the monopoly of the press by the propertied classes." Their method, in effect, was to deny ink, paper, and the use of presses to any opposition journals. This, however, was the way he described the process: "They [the Soviets] took over the monopoly not of the newspapers but of the ink-printing presses and paper in Russia. A commission was elected, a nonpartisan commission . . . to decide upon the distribution of this paper and ink and presses. The municipal elections determined what proportion of constituents each party had, and the proportion of constituents of each political party determined the amount of ink, paper, and presses which were awarded to that party. . . ."

Major Humes brought up the embarrassing matter of Reed's having fired a German rifle in the direction of the French trenches while a correspondent on the western front. A German officer, Reed replied, asked him if he wanted to see how a Mauser worked. "It would not have occurred to my mind to shoot at anyone. I am entirely opposed to anything of that kind. Besides, I have lived in France myself, and have more affection for the French people than any other people except my own people. Dunn wrote an article in the *Evening Post,* in which he called himself and me franc-tireurs in the trenches; he said that the Germans had offered us a gun to shoot through a peephole, and he took a gun, and he did not take it until after I, who was a pacifist —and that is not true, by the way—until I had shot it. He knew my aversion to such things and, as a matter of fact, neither of us shot. I do not know how many times this thing must be contradicted, but I am perfectly willing to keep on contradicting it." *

Q. "That is one of the harrowing tales of war correspondents that is mere fiction?"

A. "Pure fiction, as far as I am concerned."

Q. "It is some satisfaction to get a light on war correspondents."

Reed declared that he had been misquoted in a Christiania newspaper interview on February 8, 1918, on leaving Russia, that "Conditions in the United States have long ago become worse than in Russia. Freedom of speech has been suppressed and every vestige of democracy has disappeared." He said it was "slightly exaggerated." He also denied having stated in a speech the previous Sunday that "very shortly there would be 3,000,000 rifles in

---

* More than a quarter-century later, however, Robert Dunn still affirmed, in his memoir *World Alive,* that both he and Reed fired the German rifle.

the hands of 3,000,000 workingmen in the United States, to be used in the same manner that they were used in Russia."

Major Humes asked him, "Are you in communication with the officers of the Bolshevik government?"

"Why," Reed replied, treading water for a moment, "I see people who are going abroad sometimes, and I send notes by them."

"You have never undertaken to represent the Soviet government officially in this country?"

"No, I never have."

"I think that is all," said Major Humes curtly.

Several of the senators on the subcommittee then took up the questioning. They wanted to know how Reed would bring about a revolution if not by force. With an impudent grin he replied that it could be done if the American people would demand an amendment to the Constitution abolishing the Constitution. Had he been advocating the redistribution of land in America and the nationalization of all industry? No, he had simply said that it would be a good idea, because "I don't think a capitalist can be efficient at anything."

The senators were also appalled by his statement that shortly after returning from Russia he had had the inspiration to open a pro-Bolshevik "bureau of information" in New York City. "I went around to some people in New York from whom I thought I might get money—and I think I may get some yet. You know," he added with a confidential smile, "there are some wealthy women in New York who have nothing to do with their money except something like that."

He left the hearing room well pleased with himself, and with the memory of Senator Wolcott's confession, "Your mental agility is, I confess, too much for me." [24]

A few weeks later there was cause for even more satisfaction. On March 19, *Ten Days That Shook the World* was published, and was generally acclaimed, even in the "bourgeois" press Reed disdained (with the notable exception of Charles Edward Russell's review in the New York *Times*, which dismissed it as "Russian propaganda," to which Reed replied that "the great majority of people who learn the truth about Russia become convinced Bolsheviki"). The book sold well in the bookstores, too.

It was a dismal early spring, but Reed went up to the cottage above the Hudson alone. Louise had started off on a lecture tour of the Pacific Northwest, and they exchanged frequent letters in which Jack signed himself "Big" and Louise "Small." On March 16, he wrote to her that he had found the cottage in a mess, the rats had pulled jars and packages from the kitchen shelves and books from the bookcases, and "everything was like a cesspool." Two days later he mentioned her future husband, whom she had not yet met, when he asked in a letter, "And did you see that President Wilson has sent Lincoln Steffens, Bill Bullitt and two or three of that sort to Russia on a destroyer to investigate the Soviets?" It was on returning from this mission to Russia that Steffens made his famous proclamation that he had seen the future in Russia—"and it works!"

On March 25, Reed wrote Louise, "My book is out, and seems to be selling like hotcakes." In the three months after publication, in fact, nine thousand copies were sold, and millions more were sold all over the world in succeeding years.

Though it was wet and dismal, he spent as much time as possible up in Croton, more than a little weary, judging from his letters to Louise, of political activity and controversy in the city. On April 1, he enclosed an article about her from the New York *Tribune*, explaining, "It is the second of a series; No. 1 was about me—and equally stinking. But I know this sort of thing does us no harm, and them no good." He had just returned to Croton "after two hectic days in town, spent speaking at meetings, attending the Executive Committee of the Left Wing. . . . How I hate to leave the country. . . ."[25]

The reception of *Ten Days That Shook the World* evidently caused him to think wistfully of giving more time to his literary career. To Max Eastman he remarked, "The class struggle certainly plays hell with one's poetry, doesn't it?" Running into Sherwood Anderson in the Village one evening, he discussed the problem of trying to be both a writer and a political activist. His voice trailing off, he remarked to the novelist, as Floyd Dell reported, "If I could be dead sure that I had something on the ball as a poet . . ."

That summer he and Louise spent a few days on Cape Cod, and one afternoon he lay out on the dunes with George Cram Cook and talked about his future. "I wish I could stay here," he told Cook. "It may surprise you, but what I really want to do is write poetry."

"Well, why don't you?" Cook asked bluntly.

"I can't," Reed replied, sadly shaking his head. "I've promised too many people."

One night while Louise was still on her lecture tour, Reed met the young red-haired poetess Edna St. Vincent Millay, who rather resembled Louise in her delicacy and vibrant eagerness for experience. Accompanied by Floyd Dell, they boarded a Staten Island ferry and rode it for hours, back and forth between its lower Manhattan pier and the island. The three quoted poetry to each other. Then Reed began talking about his experiences as a war correspondent and revolutionary. Jack and Miss Millay, Dell observed, had eyes only for each other. It seemed to Dell, who suddenly felt excluded, that they were falling in love. It was a "damnably awkward situation for me," he later said. Close to dawn, he saw Miss Millay look up at Jack and heard her murmur, "I love you for the dangers you have passed." [26] *

If he was momentarily smitten by Miss Millay, however, the hurly-burly of American Communism's internal stress and intrigue soon absorbed him to the exclusion of everything else. The left wing in America was then undergoing an explosive fragmentation. Not only were the sympathizers with the Russian Revolution splitting away from the Socialist Party, but also the pro-Bolshevik element was divided into two camps. One, headed by Louis Fraina, who was of Baltic origin and whom Gitlow describes as "vain, graspingly ambitious, spoke a Marxian gibberish that sounded like Greek to Americans," regarded itself as the true

---

* In his *Improper Bohemians*, Allen Churchill says that "Old Villagers like to think that John Reed and Edna St. Vincent Millay . . . enjoyed a brief, Village-type love affair after this ferry ride."

standard-bearer of the revolution because it was composed of the Russian bloc of the Slavic Federations of the Socialist Party. The other, led by Reed, Gitlow, and others, was opposed to the Slavic dominance.

Reed was easily outmaneuvered by Fraina in his efforts to unify the Communist factions. "He failed to grasp the basic relations of bolshevism to the individual," a failure that was to lead to a crushing disillusionment, as Gitlow has written in *The Whole of Their Lives*, a work essential to any understanding of American Communism. "Jack was no politician. Circumstances, the accident of place and time pushed him to the top of the American communist movement. He never sought personal power. But the communist leaders around him were different. They had not, like Reed, seen bolshevism in action, but they understood it better and came more completely under its influence. The American communist leaders recognized in bolshevism essentially a movement for power," and held to the premise that "power is in itself the essence of morality."

The showdown came at the emergency convention of the Socialist Party in Chicago on August 30. The scene was Machinists' Hall, on South Ashland Avenue. At the outset Reed tried to seize control of the convention for the left wing, but the right-wing Socialists on the platform read him and his comrades out of the party and summoned police to eject them from the hall. Art Young arrived shortly after the melee and found Reed elated over his scrimmage with Julius Gerber, one of the right-wing leaders. "Chuckling as he described it, he told me that it began like a boxing match and that, after a few rounds, he held Julius off at arm's length clutched by his neck. 'It was a great fight. Too bad you missed it,' he said." [27]

Infighting with Fraina and the Russian-Slavic faction continued. This group refused to be reconciled with Reed and his faction, and held their own convention as the Communist Party.

"I am willing to accept the proposal of unity," Reed said, "but not on the basis of submission to the Russians and the purging of Gitlow and others who made the fight with me." [28]

While the newly styled Communist Party convened at Smolny Hall, Reed and his followers assembled nearby at the I.W.W. Hall. They decided to call themselves the Communist Labor Party. Both factions read each other out of the Bolshevik movement. During the next two days the Communist Labor Party adopted a program in line with the principles of the Third International, and proclaiming the dictatorship of the proletariat, which was essentially the same as that adopted across town by the Communist Party. It was a footling affair, an impasse brought about by Fraina's ambitions and Reed's determination to block them. Victor Berger, the old-line Socialist, summed it up when he met Art Young and cracked, "You tell Jack he'd better write another book, and call it *Three Days That Shook the Left Wing*." [29]

Just after the convention ended, Reed met with other members of the Central Executive Committee of the Communist Labor Party and brought up the necessity of racing to Moscow—now the "Third Rome," the administrative headquarters of Soviet Russia —and obtaining recognition for their group against the claims of their rivals. "Comrades," he told the committee, "we are in the unfortunate position of having two communist parties in the United States. One we control. The other the Russian-Slavic bloc controls. That Communist party will survive which gets the endorsement of the Bolsheviks. It is therefore most important that I get to Moscow before Fraina does. I propose to leave for Moscow as soon as arrangements for my departure can be made." [30]

It took several weeks for those arrangements to be made, mostly through the efforts of Jim Larkin and his left-wing Irish revolutionaries on the New York docks.

During that time Reed, who had returned to New York, found himself under constant surveillance by federal agents. To support his faction's claims to recognition by Soviet Russia, he felt it necessary to bring out another issue of the *Voice of Labor*. His usual haunts were so closely watched by Attorney General Alexander M. Palmer's operatives that he virtually went underground, and edited his paper in a deserted building in the Village also used by Carlo Tresca in publishing a left-wing Italian-language paper. Occasionally he got away, with Louise, to their cottage near Croton, on the country road where Eastman, Dell, and so many other sympathizers had their hideaways that Reed called it the Mt. Airy Soviet.

Any day he expected to be indicted again on the initiative of the federal government, and by staying out of sight he hoped to avoid arrest long enough to slip out of the country.

One afternoon Don Marquis, the newspaper columnist and humorist, met him strolling along Fifth Avenue in the threadbare gray Norfolk suit that had been his daily uniform ever since returning from Russia. "This is a hell of a place to hide," Marquis commented, gesturing at the throngs swarming past them.

"None better," said Reed cockily. "Besides, the Red-hunters never catch anybody."

By the time the Attorney General's agents got around to raiding the Communist Labor Party's offices, appearing with a warrant for Reed and confiscating all the papers they could find, he had slipped out of the country. He had outwitted the "Red-hunters," but also, and fatally, himself. He would never again see the towers of "Proud New York" which had continually inspired the poet in him. The poet was the sacrifice of the revolutionary.

12

MAN UNDERGROUND

Jack Reed's departure from the United States one night late in September of 1919 was managed with efficiency but without style or comfort. In no way did it resemble the gay leave-takings, punctuated by the pop of champagne corks and the cries of *bon voyage*, of previous Atlantic crossings, or even the insouciance of his first trip to Europe, just nine years before, as a hired hand on a cattle boat. The Communist underground route to and from Europe was well established, but its accommodations were on a proletarian scale.

His travel agent was Jim Larkin, who provided him with a seaman's identification card as Jim Gormley; occupation, stoker. This was necessary because the State Department had refused to issue him another passport.

Wearing the roughest clothes he could find and carrying a seaman's bag slung over his shoulder, Reed went down to the water front and boarded a Swedish freighter. Several friends accompanied him, watched a couple of Irish longshoremen of Larkin's "rebel network" in New York Harbor slip out of the shadows of the pier shed, and waved good-by as he was escorted aboard the freighter. Jim Gormley then descended to the stokehold and began earning his passage across the Atlantic.[1]

It must have been the toughest voyage of his life. At not quite thirty-two, Jack, underneath the boyish demeanor, was beginning to look older than his age. The last two years had been ones of constant strain, tension, and anxiety. His irregular habits of eating, drinking, sleeping, and working were not the sort that doctors would prescribe for a man with one kidney. He had never led a really dissipated life—he rarely drank to excess—but he was reckless with his health as with the other aspects of his life.

The Swedish freighter docked at Bergen, where Reed jumped ship and took a train to Christiania, which, with its colony of left-wing Socialists, had become a principal way station on the underground route to Russia. On October 21, 1919, he wrote a long letter to Louise, part of which contained details of how they could keep in touch through Communist couriers. The present letter, he wrote, would be taken to the United States by courier, and others would take the same route, "but not many by open post." He wanted her to write to him as soon as possible. "Get ——— to send your letters to me care of ——— in Stockholm, my courier. Do not write any more letters care of Chabrow, and tell Key not to also. He is watched." *

He told her that he had had to "desert the ship at Bergen and skip down here without permission. At present, however, I am in a safe place, and this goes forward by a safe man. Tomorrow I must get across the Swedish frontier on foot by night, and then we shall see. If I were caught nothing could be done except to deport me to the U.S. . . . I have my papers in a safe place and shall not be caught with them on me." The Scandinavian police had been very active, he reported; they had arrested a number of

---

* The letter is in the John Reed Collection at Harvard's Houghton Library. The names have been cut out, by whom it is impossible to say.

couriers and broken up the organization, but there were some Hungarians, Finns, Russians, and Letts who "have performed prodigies of heroism going back and forth from Russia."

Much of the letter concerned the political and military situation. Communist Russia was now ringed by enemies, who had set up a *cordon sanitaire* to isolate her. In Scandinavia the left wing controlled the Socialist parties, but "there can be no revolution in Scandinavia, and other small countries until the great capitalist countries go, for these small countries have to import their food and could be starved at once." In Finland there had been a counterrevolution, led by Baron Mannerheim, and his "white terror" had made the Finnish egress to Russia highly dangerous.

Meanwhile, Communism's motherland was in great peril. "The Russian situation has been heartrending. When I came here there was news of Petrograd and Kronstadt's fall . . . the White Guards are close to the city and Denikin [the leader of the counterrevolutionary forces to the south, who was supported in his efforts by the British and French] seems to be advancing. It is a last desperate effort to crush Russia, and may succeed. Something appears to be wrong internally. . . ."

Despite all these forebodings, he said that he was in excellent health, and boasted, "I am the big cheese in these parts." By this he meant, apparently, that his status as an American Communist leader and the author of *Ten Days That Shook the World* made him a preferred and honored client on the underground, which would attempt to forward him to Russia. He closed his letter with the hope that he would be "back before Christmas."

The clandestine journey, however, took him much longer than he had expected. He was delayed a week in Stockholm while arrangements for his secret landing in Finland were being made. It was November 1 before Swedish members of the underground managed to slip him aboard a ship bound for Finland. He was hidden away in a compartment near the engine room and crossed the Baltic lying on a pile of oil-soaked waste. Finnish police boarded the ship as it docked at Abo. But a seaman led him up to the snow-covered deck, where two cranes were beginning to unload crated parts of tanks to be used in operations against Petrograd, and onto the dock. He pushed his way through Customs as one of a group of longshoremen.

A couple of Finnish Communists picked him up and led him to a "safe house," the home of a woman writer with Bolshevik sympathies, where he was sheltered for the few days until he took a train for Helsinki. There another refuge had been prepared for him. On November 9 he was able to send off another letter to Louise by courier, this one less reassuring and testifying to the strain of hiding out in a country where Communists were now being hunted down with counterrevolutionary fervor. "Terrible police raids at Viborg . . . all our organization there was broken up. If I had gone there when I expected I should now be in the jug. . . . Tell Eugen [Boissevain] that I lost his letter of credit when I jumped my last frontier . . . very well and happy and still expect to be with you before Christmas. . . . Don't try to come this way. It would be ghastly for you just now." [2]

The letter was written one day after the police raided the offices of the American Communist Labor Party in New York, as well as other Communist headquarters, seized bales of propaganda and documents, and arrested thirty-five men. Only then was it discovered that Jack Reed had skipped the country. The police learned that fact from the records seized in his New York headquarters.

The Finnish section of the underground succeeded in smuggling him to the Russian frontier, passing him along from one safe house to another, until he reached the headquarters of a Red Army unit on the border. He found Russia gripped in the crisis of its postrevolutionary period. There were three main counterrevolutionary forces still in the field. General Nikolai Yudenitch's advance on Petrograd had been blunted by a proletarian force, such as had saved the city just after the Bolshevik coup, which had poured into the fieldworks around the city. General A. I. Denikin's army was operating in the Ukraine, and Admiral A. V. Kolchak's white forces in Siberia. All were eventually defeated, but at a cost that was almost to destroy the Soviet regime. There were food shortages in the cities, the transportation system had broken down, and the Allied blockade deprived the country of supplies from the outside.

From Petrograd Reed hastened to Moscow to present his case for recognition of the Communist Labor Party. He appeared before the Executive Committee of the International. Lenin, Trotsky, and Kamenev listened to him with friendly interest, but gave no indication of what line the Comintern would take in settling the dispute of the American party factions. At that moment in Soviet history, with the government struggling for its existence, the problems of factionalism in distant America must have seemed utterly remote and unimportant.

The vain and dictatorial Zinoviev, Chairman of the Comintern, finally ordered Reed to submit a written report on the dispute and include in it a thorough survey of political, social, and economic conditions in the United States.

Reed was offered a fairly comfortable apartment and a card that would allow him to obtain the best food available, but he turned them down and insisted on taking a room in a working-class district and cooking his food over a small iron stove. He wandered around the city and marveled at the heroism of the people in surviving near-starvation, unheated homes, endemic diseases, and lack of medicines, which were not permitted to be shipped through the *cordon sanitaire*. Commissar for Education Lunacharski impressed him with his plans to create opportunities for the people to enjoy art and literature; Lenin, whom he often saw privately, lectured him about neglecting his health, the signs of which were growing more visible daily. At Lenin's suggestion he wrote an article for the Comintern's official organ on the possibilities of a revolution in America, in which he claimed that capitalism was entering the last stages of decomposition, and "what will come in its place depends on the power of the workers. If the workers are not prepared to resist, the capitalists will set up a military dictatorship and reduce the proletariat to slavery." The workers' power to resist, he said, was contained largely in the more militant sectors of the labor movement, particularly the I.W.W., with its tradition of activist struggle; the Socialist Party was degenerating almost as fast as capitalism and was incapable of mounting or even effectively participating in any revolution. The I.W.W., which he had admired ever since the Paterson silk-mills strike, was the "vanguard of the American proletariat" and would "lead the assault against capitalism in America." [3] Here Reed was not a first-rate prophet; the I.W.W. movement withered away long before the Socialist Party.

With the blessings of the Comintern, he took a journey through the Russian countryside in the dead of winter, traveling eastward as far as the Volga. Often he went across the ice-locked steppe in a sleigh. He stopped in the widely separated villages and observed the activity in district soviets, schools, collectives, and workers' theaters. The peasants, he noted, had more food than the people in the cities, but they were still slower to accept the revolution than were the industrial workers. [4]

When he returned to Moscow, he was informed that the Executive Committee of the Communist International had come to a decision on the split in the American Communist movement. The opposing factions must settle their differences; there could be only one party in America. The decision could hardly have surprised Reed, and, lacking any practical alternative, he could only agree to it.

Soon after his return to Moscow he also learned that he and thirty-seven other members of the Communist Labor Party, as well as eighty-five members of the Communist Party, had been indicted by a federal grand jury in Chicago for plotting the overthrow of the government. He immediately began requesting permission of the Comintern to return to the United States and stand trial with his comrades, although the Executive Committee, at first, objected.

During this time, Emma Goldman and Alexander Berkman, among two hundred and forty-nine foreign-born radicals who had been arrested, taken to Ellis Island, and deported from the United States, arrived in Moscow. Miss Goldman's memoir, *Living My Life*, provides a grimly objective portrait of the Soviet capital and its leaders. A lifelong anarchist, she was disenchanted with the Communist experiment in her native land almost from the day she arrived in mid-January, 1920. What particularly bothered her was that, in passing through Petrograd, she found the people of the old czarist capital freezing for lack of fuel even though vast forests were within easy reach. She first sought an answer to this in an interview with Zinoviev, who explained that the government lacked the means of transportation to bring firewood into the cities. Then, Miss Goldman wanted to know, why could not the workers of Petrograd, who had twice saved the city by going out and manning its defenses, be enlisted to march out en masse with the necessary axes, ropes, and sledges? It would help them through the winter, Zinoviev admitted, but it would interfere with carrying out the government's main policies, which were not chiefly concerned with chilblains and frostbite. Instead of offering a solution, Zinoviev fired off a barrage of revolutionary slogans: "Concentration of all power in the hands of the proletarian avantgarde . . . the Communist Party . . . the dictatorship of the proletariat is the only workable program during a revolutionary period. . . ." What did that have to do with heating people's homes? "One city, with a million and a half inhabitants reduced to four hundred thousand!" Miss Goldman wrote later. "A mere bagatelle in the eyes of the Communist political program! Disheartened, I left the man so cock-sure of his party's wisdom, so ensconced in the heavenly Marxian constellation and self-conscious of being one of its major stars." [5]

Hopeful of hearing a more sensible discussion of how to solve the physical problems of the people's existence, she looked up Jack Reed immediately on reaching Moscow. Reed, however, was still dazzled by the light of the red star he had followed eastward; but his enthusiasm had all the warmth of the idealistic true believer as contrasted with Zinoviev's chilling obsession with the exercise of power. "Jack Reed had burst into my room like a sudden ray of light, the old buoyant adventurous Jack that I used to know in the States. He was about to return to America, by way of Latvia. Rather a hazardous journey, he said, but he would take even greater risks to bring the inspiring message of Soviet Russia to his native land."

He said, "Wonderful, marvelous, isn't it, E.G.? Your dream of years now realized in Russia, your dream scorned and persecuted in my country, but made real by the magic wand of Lenin and his band of despised Bolsheviks. Did you ever expect such a thing to happen in the country ruled by tsars for centuries?"

"Not by Lenin and his comrades, dear Jack," Miss Goldman replied, "though I do not deny their great part. But by the whole Russian people, preceded by a glorious revolutionary past. No other land of our days has been so literally nurtured by the blood of her martyrs, a long procession of martyrs who went to their death that new life may spring from their graves." [6]

Reed insisted that the older generation of revolutionaries had been a hindrance to the Bolshevik achievement, that many had even betrayed it. "Look at your old pioneers, the Breshkovskayas and Tchaikovskys, the Chernovs and Kerenskys and the rest of them; see where they are now! With the Black Hundreds, the Jew-baiters, and the ducal oblique, aiding them to crush the revolution. I don't give a damn for their past. I am concerned only in what the treacherous gang has been doing during the past three years. To the wall with them! I say. I have learned one mighty expressive Russian word, *razstrellyat* [to the firing squad, roughly translated]."

Miss Goldman remarked that she had been awakened by sounds of shooting at night, and had asked a Communist official what it was. He explained that it was the *kursanty*, young Communists under training for the Red Army officers' corps, holding target practice. Reed said he knew nothing about the shots, but recalled that on the eve of the day the decree against capital punishment went into effect five hundred prisoners, accused of being counter-revolutionaries, had been executed by firing squads. "He was surprised to see me so worked up over the death of a few plotters. As if that mattered in the scales of the world revolution!"

Although she was twenty years older than Jack and had been conditioned in a much harsher school, having arrived in America in 1889 with only five dollars and a sewing-machine to her name, Miss Goldman and he had always been close personal friends. Until now her anarchism and his Communism had not divided them, and she felt that she could still speak frankly to him.

She begged him not to let the word *razstrellyat* roll so glibly off his tongue: "This word is terrible enough in the mouth of a Russian. Since when do revolutionists see in wholesale execution the only solution to their difficulties? In time of active counter-revolution it was no doubt inevitable to give shot for shot. But cold-bloodedly and merely for opinion's sake, do you justify standing people against the wall under such circumstances?"

Reed, perhaps reflecting that his old friend had not experienced the revolution itself, and that she was one of those humanists who refused to see the connection between the omelet and the eggs, said he believed a certain amount of shooting was necessary.

Miss Goldman insisted that, hard as she had worked in revolutionary causes, "I certainly never believed that it would signify callous indifference to human life and suffering, or that it would have no other method of solving its problems than by wholesale slaughter. Five hundred lives snuffed out on the eve of a decree abolishing the death penalty! I call it a dastardly crime, the worst counter-revolutionary outrage committed in the name of the Revolution."

She recalled that Reed tried to calm her by saying, "That's all right; you are a little confused by the Revolution in action because you have dealt with it only in theory. You'll get over that, clear-sighted rebel that you are, and you'll come to see in its true light everything that seems so puzzling now. Cheer up, and make me a cup of that good old American coffee you have brought with you. Not much to give you in return for all my country has taken from you, but greatly appreciated in starving Russia by her native son."

She was amazed by his sudden change of mood. "It was the same old Jack, with his zest for the adventures of life. I longed to join in his gay mood, but my heart was heavy. . . ." [7]

That may well have been the last time anyone saw Jack Reed cheerful or optimistic in Russia. His own time of disillusionment was fast approaching.

Soon after his reunion with Emma Goldman he was notified

that he would be permitted to return to the United States. On the trip through the underground he would act as a courier, carrying propaganda material, money, and jewels to finance Communist activities abroad. In February he made two attempts to find a hole in the Allied *cordon sanitaire*. The first, as he told Miss Goldman, would take him through Latvia. When he reached the Latvian front, however, he was caught in a sudden withdrawal of the Red Army, and the attempt had to be abandoned. Later in the month he set out on a second journey, which would take him through Finland and across the Swedish frontier if his plans worked out. The second attempt was foiled by his arrest by the Finnish police. According to Emma Goldman and Benjamin Gitlow, Zinoviev, in particular, did not want Reed to leave Russia, and he was deliberately betrayed to the Finnish police. Miss Goldman wrote that on his second effort to leave the Soviet Union he was "betrayed to the Finnish authorities by a Russian Communist, a sailor whom Zinoviev had sent with him as a companion." Reed himself later told her this, Miss Goldman declared. By Gitlow's account, though he cited no source, "Zinoviev placed many obstacles in his way in order to prevent his immediate departure." Either the Comintern suspected his loyalty or it was regarded as inadvisable that he stand trial and thus cost the American Communist movement a valuable adherent. He would almost certainly have been convicted and sent to prison. Others tried on the same charges were sentenced to terms of two to five years. Reed blamed himself for getting caught in his second attempt to get home, and, Gitlow wrote, "concluded that he was slipping in his technique of crossing hostile borders. . . . He did not stop to question why the proficient Comintern apparatus for smuggling persons and revolutionary propaganda and contraband out of Russia had failed in his case." [8]

Another reason may have been simply that the Communist underground in Finland had temporarily broken down. Under Baron Mannerheim's "white terror," as Reed himself had observed in passing through Finland several months before, the Finnish secret police had become even more proficient at smashing clandestine activity than the Communists were at conducting it. It would also seem strange that Zinoviev, inimical though his feelings about Reed evidently were, would have sacrificed him to the enemy along with the small fortune in money and jewels he was carrying with him as a Communist courier.

According to the account Eadmonn MacAlpine, who was in Russia at the time and knew Reed well, wrote for Louise Bryant in Paris fourteen years later, Reed crossed the Finnish frontier without trouble late in February, 1920. He managed to evade arrest for "several weeks" while wandering around looking for an exit from Finland. "A passport was needed to travel from one town to another," so tight was Baron Mannerheim's security against Bolshevik infiltration, as MacAlpine later learned from Reed. Finally he reached the port of Abo and stowed away in the coal bunker of a Finnish freighter about to sail for Sweden. There he was discovered by the police.

The Finns proclaimed an important arrest and reported that they had found 880,000 Finnish marks and a quantity of unset diamonds in Reed's possession, in addition to letters to Soviet agents and Communist leaders in America, instructions on how to proceed with the revolution in the United States, copies of Comintern decisions handed down to the American section of the party, and propaganda material. He was immediately placed in solitary confinement and held incommunicado.

"Despite severe beatings and threats of torture and death," MacAlpine wrote, "he refused to talk and was thrown into a dungeon. . . ." This may have been a touch too melodramatic—since the Finnish authorities were not likely to treat an American citizen too brutally—but he was kept in a basement cell in the Central Police Station in Abo, and for a man in his now precarious health the conditions of his confinement were wretched. He subsisted on a diet of salt herring, which no physician would prescribe for a man with only one kidney. His cell was wet and cold.

For weeks he was unable to communicate with any American. Oddly enough, considering his attitude toward his government, it was the Americans he depended upon to get him out of the Finnish jail. Through one of his jailers, according to MacAlpine's account, he managed to get word to an American press-association correspondent in Helsinki that he was under arrest. The press association's wires carried the first news of it to America. Then, no longer incommunicado, he arranged for a Finnish sympathizer to spread the report that he had been executed in Finland. This, of course, forced the State Department to begin an investigation.[9]

As soon as Louise heard the news, she launched an energetic campaign in Washington to obtain his freedom. She enlisted the help of many persons with influence—Bernard Baruch, William Hard, Carl Hovey, Arthur Garfield Hays, Bourke Cochran, Senator Charles McNary—to put pressure on the State Department on Jack's behalf. Secretary of State Bainbridge Colby finally agreed to order the American legation to obtain a lawyer for him as soon as Louise cabled the necessary funds.

On May 3, Reed was allowed to write a letter to Louise. "I have been so fearfully worried—about your health, about whether you had anything to do, enough to eat, etc.—whether you were well or ill. . . ." He did not mention the perilous state of his own health after eight weeks in solitary confinement.

Regarding his case, he said, "At present I am in jail, waiting for something to happen. Up to now no charge has been laid against me, except that of smuggling. This case has been tried, the diamonds all confiscated, and I have been fined five thousand marks (about $250-$300). I have appealed. But this is not what keeps me in prison. It is the question of whether I have committed treason towards the Finnish state. It appears that there are 'diplomatic negotiations' going on between the Finnish government and the United States government. Why, I do not know.

"Now, honey, I wish you *please not to influence the American government*. I mean this very seriously. I want this case decided on its merits."

He told her that "the thought of you drags at me sometimes until my imagination plays tricks, and I almost go crazy. Please, please write me about everything. . . ."

Ten days later he wrote to her that he had heard that the American authorities in Finland had demanded that he be turned over to them. ". . . why I cannot understand. But I do not think the Finnish authorities can do this without accusing me, trying me, and finding me guilty. However, it is impossible to say what a bourgeois government cannot do. . . .

"I heard that you are planning to come here. If it is for the sake of helping me, I beg you not to do so. But if it is because you want to come abroad, and possibly to be with me in case I am delayed—and, of course, if you can find the money—do it by all means. But wait for a cable before you actually sail.

"I am very well. Have given up smoking for the last two months here, and am allowed a little walk in the yard every day. The police master here has really been most friendly and generous to me. As for the American authorities, they have of course not been near me, or sent any word all the time I have been here. But I am thankful for that. I do not want any help from the authorities as regards myself."

He closed the letter by asking her to tell his publisher, Horace Liveright, that the "big chief," Lenin, "thinks my book the best." [10]

Two days later he wrote, "I am surprised you have received no direct word from me, because I have also cabled you three times, and two days ago I sent you about $300." The Finnish government, he said, "has absolutely no case against me. It dares not bring me to trial." Her account of the efforts being made in the United States to secure his release, as detailed in a letter he had just received from her, was astonishing to him. *"And it will surprise you to hear that I am informed by the Finns that I am kept in prison at the request of the United States government."* He complained that he had been "neglected" by the U.S. government, even though in previous letters he had strongly urged Louise not to seek its intercession, and that a letter he had written to the U.S. Minister in Helsinki had not been answered. (In the letter to Minister Magruder he had evidently asked that a U.S. passport be issued to allow his return to the United States.) With all his other troubles, he remembered that the previous summer, when they were low in funds, Louise had pawned his watch in a hockshop at Sixth Avenue and Twenty-ninth Street, and he asked her to be sure to pay the interest on it, "not redeem it, just pay the interest."

On May 19, he wrote to Robert Hallowell, his Harvard classmate and the artist who painted the portrait of him presented to the university by the Harvard Alumni John Reed Committee many years later, that he had just been informed that because of lack of evidence the Finnish government had decided against bringing his case to court. "The Finns are asking the American minister, Magruder, to give me a passport. If he does—which is practically impossible—I shall start for Stockholm immediately, and from there, after learning the situation at home, I shall act accordingly. If he does not give me a passport, the Finnish government will give me notice to leave the country in twenty-four or forty-eight hours. The idea is, of course, if I then go to Sweden, I will be hustled to America without any opportunity to look around—more or less deported, in fact. So I have demanded, if I am to be told to leave the country, to go to Esthonia; I am asking a permit from the Esthonian government." He asked that the letter be forwarded to Louise.

During the weeks in his stone-walled cell, he occupied himself much of the time by writing scraps of verse and making outlines for two novels he planned to write. One of them was purely autobiographical. The hero, named Robin, had a father like Jack's, whom he admired intensely, and a mother, also like Jack's, whom he described as "loving, narrow, maternal."

Robin was a Middle Westerner who came to New York, then, according to notes, "Meets Steff. Gets job on magazine. . . . Dutch Treat. Harry Kemp comes with poem . . . Brevoort. Hippolyte Havel. Henrietta Rodman. Mary Vorse . . . 42 Washington Squ. Seeger. Bobby Rogers. Red Lewis. Bobby Jones. Seeger lost in curious English poets . . . Wash. Sq. Players Prov. Players . . . The coming of Gene O'Neill . . . Robin in love with the doctor's wife—her salon. She rich, old. He poor. Conflict. He tries to leave. Wretchedness. Break . . . Death of Osgood. Death of Adams . . . Leo Stein's talk . . . Long poem (mine) on the city

. . . *New Republic* . . . . . Harold Stearns. Randolph Bourne. Walter Lippmann . . . Gift-shops, guides, and village riff-raff. A scene in Frank Shay's book-shop . . . Free-speech fight. Tannenbaum and unemployed—churches . . . Haywood, Gurley . . . Collapse of the I.W.W. Joining Socialists. Branch meetings, street speaking, Jim Larkin. Bayonne, the break with his paper. Freelancing. Poverty. Marriage. The war. Conscientious objector but registers. Not called. Russian revolution and the new Socialism . . . Tortures, deportations, raids, soldier-mobs, fearful sentences. The raid on People's House. The Communist Party . . . Peace and Bolshevism."

On May 30, he started a serial letter to Louise reporting that "here I still sit, going on the twelfth week of imprisonment. But the end is in sight. The Finnish government has already notified me that I shall not be tried, but turned loose. I asked the American minister here for a passport home. He did not reply—as he has refused to answer all communications from me. But he told a Finnish government official that he would on no circumstances give me a passport. Therefore, rather than be brutally deported, I have asked the Esthonian government to allow me to go through Reval to Russia . . . it is now *ten days* since I requested permission. And still I sit here, in the bright June weather, spending most of my time worrying about my honey and longing for her.

"I shall return for the present to Russia. If you can come abroad, do so. Get ready, but don't start until later word from me! I shall send you much more definite instructions as soon as I leave here. . . ."

On May 31, June 1, and June 2, he added paragraphs to the letter, reporting that no permission had been received from Esthonia granting him transit privileges on his way back to Russia. "I have nothing to read, nothing to do. I can only sleep about five hours, and so am awake, penned in a little cage, for nineteen hours a day. . . ."

The last paragraph, dated "8 p.m., June 2," informed Louise, "Just this minute *word came!* I am to go to Reval on Saturday's boat from Helsingfors—or maybe I must wait until Tuesday."

He reached Reval, Esthonia, on June 7, and cabled Louise immediately: "PASSPORT HOME REFUSED TEMPORARILY RETURNING HEADQUARTERS COME IF POSSIBLE."

His release was secured, finally, by the Soviet government, when it got around to negotiating an exchange with Finland. The deal was rather flattering to Reed: three anti-Communist Finnish professors held in the Soviet Union in exchange for him. Weeks later, when he returned to Moscow, according to Eadmonn MacAlpine, in the account he wrote for Louise, "Lenin told him in my presence that the Finns had made a bad bargain as he would have exchanged a whole jail full of Finns—not merely three professors —for Jack."

When he reached Petrograd, he was a very sick man, suffering from malnutrition and its accompanying diseases. Emma Goldman hastened to look him up at the Hotel International, where she found him "alone and without anyone to take care of him," and suffering not only physical but also mental anguish. Despite the determinedly cheerful tone of his letters to Louise, Miss Goldman's account indicates that he had entered the first painful stage of disillusionment with the new masters of Russia.

"I had found him in a deplorable condition," Emma Goldman wrote later, "his arms and legs swollen, his body covered with ulcers, and his gums badly affected as a result of scurvy acquired in prison. The poor boy suffered even more spiritually, because he had been betrayed to the Finnish authorities by a Russian Communist, a sailor whom Zinoviev had sent with him as a companion. . . .

"It was Jack's second failure of the kind and he took it much to heart. Two weeks' nursing helped put him on his feet again, but he remained fearfully distressed over the methods of Zinoviev and others in jeopardizing the lives of their comrades.

" 'Needlessly and recklessly,' he kept saying.

"He himself had twice been sent on a wild goose chase without any trouble having been taken to find out whether there was any possibility of the venture's succeeding. But at least he could take care of himself and he went into it with open eyes. Moreover, as an American he did not run the same risks as the Russian comrades. Communists, mere youngsters, were being sacrificed by the score for the glory of the Third International, he had complained.

" 'Perhaps revolutionary necessity,' I had suggested; 'at least your comrades always say so.'

"He had believed it also, he admitted, but his experience and that of others had made him doubt it. His faith in the dictatorship was still fervent, but he was beginning to doubt some of the methods used, particularly by men who themselves always remained in safety. . . ." [11]

Still weak and ailing, with his teeth wobbly in his scurvy-weakened gums, Reed proceeded to Moscow late in June. His presence was required there for the great propaganda showpiece of the Second Congress of the Communist International, opening on July 2. As the train carried him to that mecca for Communist pilgrims from all over the world, he must have brooded over his situation, which, outward form aside, was exchanging Finnish for Russian captivity. Increasingly, Mother Russia's embrace would become less maternal and more possessive, demanding and suffocating. He would have to tread carefully, mind his tongue, learn (at this late date) discretion. Otherwise he might find himself sacrificed to "revolutionary necessity," the full meaning of which was now part of his experience.

Yet his courage and his rage for living courageously and speaking the truth no matter what it cost—whether in "free" Russia or "oppressed" America—were undiminished. So was his lack of discretion, his inability to conceal what he thought and felt. He was as much the Storm Boy in Moscow, the stage managers of the Second International were to learn shortly, as he had been in his Greenwich Village youth.

He made no secret of his bitterness to Angelica Balabanoff, with whom he was reunited in Moscow just as the delegates to the Second International began gathering. ". . . It was John Reed who put into words that which I had already begun to suspect," she wrote in her memoirs.

Fortunately, the Dictograph and other more sophisticated listening devices had not yet been discovered by the Soviet secret police. It was still possible for malcontents to discuss their grievances behind closed doors. "The fact that he talked with me of such matters," Miss Balabanoff recalled, "was not due to caution or diplomacy, but to the fact that he knew that I, too, was in the same mood. He was merely thinking out loud."

Reed confided in her even more than in Emma Goldman. "I do not think that any foreigner who came to Russia in those early years," she recalled, "ever saw or came to know as much about the conditions of the people as did Reed in the spring and summer of 1920. He was becoming more and more depressed by the suffering, disorganization, and inefficiency to be found everywhere, but like the rest of us who saw these things he understood the difficulties of the situation—enhanced by the blockade, sabotage, the shortage of materials—and his irritation and discouragement were directed not at the government itself, but at the growing indifference and cynicism of the bureaucracy of all gradations. He was particularly discouraged when he saw his own efforts and those of other friends of the Revolution defeated by indifference and inefficiency. Sensitive to any kind of inequality and injustice, he would return from each of his trips with stories that were heart-breaking to both of us."

She remembered meeting him at one of the entertainments arranged by the trade unions in a sumptuous building inherited from the former aristocracy. The entertainment was to distract people from the food and fuel shortages with musical and dramatic performances. "Though some of the artists who performed on this occasion were among the best in Russia . . . there was something about the quality and manner of their performance that irritated me. They were obviously giving inferior performances, playing down to a working-class audience which was not supposed to know any better. I was all the more irritated when I saw that the officials who had organized the affair were so radiant and proud of their achievement. 'Parvenus, petit-bourgeois,' I thought to myself. 'They don't see how the artists are insulting these workers.' I rose and started to leave the hall, and as I did so, Jack Reed came over and joined me. 'Let's go,' he said. I have never heard a voice so full of humiliation and sadness." [12]

There was enmity in the atmosphere of the higher echelons of the party, Reed believed, toward foreign-born Communists or Russians who had been outside the country long enough to compare, perhaps unconsciously, the administrative talents of the new rulers of Russia with those of the leaders of governments under which they had formerly lived. This was not true of Lenin and Trotsky, perhaps, but was true of the lesser lights who were presiding over the vast and growing bureaucracy. Miss Balabanoff thought it strange that "Jack, a foreigner, should have understood both my own and the general situation before a Russian like myself."

Shortly after her return from a meeting of the Petrograd Executive, she recalled, Reed warned her, "They want to get rid of you before the foreign delegations arrive. You know too much."

Miss Balabanoff said she did not see how "they"—the Zinovievs, Kamenevs, and Radeks—could possibly doubt her loyalty.

"Of course not," he replied, "but neither do they doubt your honesty. It is that they are afraid of."

Miss Balabanoff thought that she was in bad grace with the leaders of the Comintern because she had refused to obey an order from the Executive Committee to go to Turkestan and work for the party in that wild and remote province, which was one of several racked by Moslem dissidence. "In the 1930's," she noted, "a similar breach of discipline would probably have resulted in my imprisonment or worse. In 1920 the Soviet leaders were still responsive to the working-class opinion abroad." [13]

About a week later Reed asked, "Tell me, Angelica, are you still the secretary of the International or not?"

"Of course I am, at least nominally," she told him.

"If that is so, why aren't you attending the Executive meeting?"

Miss Balabanoff said she had not been told about it, and wanted to know where it was being held.

"Well, I know," he said. "Those cowards are meeting in Litvinov's commissariat so that you won't know where they are."

She hurried over to Maksim Litvinov's offices and broke into the secret session. Zinoviev turned pale; the other members of the committee looked embarrassed. She waited until the meeting ended, then demanded to know why she had been excluded. "Oh," Zinoviev said, "we thought that Trotsky had told you. The Executive Committee has already decided to remove you—because of your refusal to go to Turkestan."

Miss Balabanoff said later that she felt a "sense of liberation" on learning of her removal, but "what impressed me most at this moment was the cowardice of this man who, pretending to be a revolutionary leader, had not even the courage to face an individual or to assume responsibility in an unpleasant situation."

Despite her initial relief, Miss Balabanoff suffered what she called "a sort of physical and mental breakdown in which my whole organism was shaken." It was a psychic shock—one that was to be experienced by so many hopeful idealists who would make the same pilgrimage—which she believed was caused by her "realisation of the means" by which her removal had been accomplished, "the motives behind it, and the suspicion of how widespread and pervasive these methods had become." She was greatly heartened during this ordeal to receive a photograph from Reed of himself. "In the corner he had written: 'To the best revolutionary I have known in Russia.' I knew when I read these words what John Reed must have suffered—he who had known and worshipped the leaders of the Revolution." [14]

As the Second Congress of the Communist International opened, Reed resolved to pit himself openly against the triumvirate of Zinoviev, Kamenev, and Radek, who in terms of accumulated bureaucratic power stood only slightly below Lenin and Trotsky. Perhaps it was only natural, in view of his open defiance, that the triumvirate welcomed Louis Fraina, his chief rival for leadership in the United States, with open arms. (It must also have impressed Zinoviev in Fraina's favor that the Communist Party of America claimed a membership of fifty-eight thousand to ten thousand claimed for Reed's Communist Labor Party. Both claims were greatly exaggerated.)

It may have aided Fraina's cause that he "fawned before the seats of the mighty and became an intimate of Zinoviev," as Benjamin Gitlow observed, but Fraina, with his suppleness and his understanding of how power must be grasped and wielded, his respect for it, in fact, as contrasted with Reed's innate and indelible contempt for authority, would obviously have been more acceptable to the Comintern's leaders. Reed's spirit was anarchistic and idealistic; Fraina was a realist. Nor did it help Reed's cause that he worked openly against the leaders of the Comintern just at the moment, with all the world watching, they wanted to make a great show of unity at the Second Congress. Perhaps he overrated the value of his influence with Lenin and Trotsky, his prestige as the author of the definitive account of the Ten Days, and underrated the determination of Zinoviev and his collaborators. Zinoviev was feminine-looking but a bitter-end antagonist in any fight for power, and he had worked with Lenin for years before the revolution and was one of the passengers on the famous sealed train from Switzerland. With that background, he could only look upon Jack Reed as an amateur, a summer soldier of the revolution who might desert when wintry realities of governing confronted him.

The opening session of the Congress was held in Petrograd, with considerable pageantry and ceremony, at the Tauride Palace and the Field of the Martyrs of the Revolution, and was designed to impress and inspire the foreign delegations. Then the Congress adjourned to Moscow, and on July 23 got down to the business of drawing up programs and planning how to foment revolution abroad.

Shortly after the Congress was called to order, in the Throne Room of the Imperial Palace in the Kremlin, Reed popped up and made two motions. With the backing of twenty-nine other delegates, he proposed that the question of how to deal with the trade unions in other countries be placed closer to the top of the agenda. He also moved that, at least for discussion of the trade-union question, English be made one of the official languages of the Congress. Both motions were quickly voted down. The Congress appointed a special committee to decide on the policy to adopt toward trade unions, before which Reed carried his opposition to the Zinoviev line.

It was a hopeless cause, Angelica Balabanoff believed. "As I was the only translator available for the Congress, I was able to judge more clearly than most of the delegates the character and trend of that event. Through the interminable discussions [the Congress lasted for three weeks] I was forced to repeat lengthy polemics in Russian, German, French, Italian, to translate hundreds of questions and answers. I had a feeling that I was participating not merely in a political, but also a personal, tragedy involving some of my dearest friends. It was obvious that for Jack Reed, waging his own particular battle with Radek and Zinoviev, that tragedy lay not so much in his inability to defend himself effectively against these men, as in the realization that he was struggling against a *system* which had already begun to devour its own children." [15]

Americans attending the Congress noted how ill Reed looked— flabby, gray-faced, new lines on his face and around his mouth, and lacking his former exuberance. He fought feverishly, despairingly, rather than with the old joy of battle, to impose his views on the trade-union committee. All day he spent in the committee rooms of the Kremlin, and half the night, arguing with other delegates. Communist though he was, he still had a vestigial faith in the democratic process, a wisp of hope that logic and truth would prevail over the dogmatic and dictatorial methods of his opponents. He insisted that the American Communists must take a forthright and unequivocal stand against the American Federation of Labor and all other union organizations that refused to join the revolutionary movement. The A.F.L. must be destroyed.

The Zinoviev-Kamenev-Radek program was subtler and would employ the techniques of subversion against the trade unions. Their policy was for Communists to pretend to co-operate, to infiltrate the unions and capture control of them from within, then convert them to revolutionary purposes.

Reed argued that, unlike the labor unions of Western Europe, those of the United States were so tightly organized that subversion was impossible, and that the union leaders were able to restrain their members from carrying on revolutionary activity.

The issue was regarded as so critical that Lenin himself was appointed to the trade-union committee. Radek stated the case for the triumvirate. Reed spoke for his faction, contending that the Communists could no more work within the A.F.L. than within the "bourgeois state," and that both must be destroyed before the real work of Communism could begin. Lenin settled the matter by agreeing with Radek and his collaborators. The committee, over Reed's bitter and continuing objections, voted him down and presented its majority report to the Congress, which accepted it.

A less celebrated figure than Reed would probably have been shuffled into the discard for his rebellious attitude, but he could still count on Lenin's almost paternal attitude toward him. Lenin, at least, was not dismayed by his fiery spirit; it would take firebrands like Jack Reed to prevail in the reactionary and complacent nations of the West. He had a private talk with Reed in which he agreed that the leadership of the A.F.L. should be driven out of power, but he maintained that the organization itself should not be smashed.

It must have taken all of Reed's quite visible influence with Lenin to offset the ill will he had aroused in many of Lenin's closest associates. "Reed put up a last-ditch fight against the Comintern's line and leadership that was unique even in 1920," Theodore Draper has written. "He never gave the slightest indication of repenting his own position and, indeed, went to the opposite extreme of publicizing his opposition. His personal relations with the Comintern leadership had degenerated into an ugly feud. He made no secret of his contempt and hatred for Zinoviev and Radek, whose authority in the Comintern was then pre-eminent. On at least one occasion—when and why may be debatable but the fact is not—his anger or embarrassment or both brought him

to the edge of lese majesty, as that crime of extreme insubordina-
tion was understood in the Comintern—he proffered his resignation from its Executive Committee. . . ." [16]

Aside from the trade-union policy, Reed, at Lenin's request, delivered to the Congress a report on how the American Negroes
might be made a part of the revolutionary movement. Probably
his interest in the Negro as a factor in the hoped-for overturn of
established authority dated back to his only trip through the
South, when he went to Florida to interview William Jennings
Bryan. On that journey he had written to Louise, "The bloated
silly people on this ridiculous private rich man's train throw pen-
nies and dimes and quarters to be scrambled for by the Negroes
whenever we stop at a station. Lord, how the white folks scream
with laughter to see the coons fight each other, gouge each other's
eyes, get bleeding lips, scrambling over the money. All the whites
in this section look mean and cruel and vain. Have you ever seen
Jim Crow cars, colored waiting rooms in stations, etc.? . . . Just
make me feel sick. I hate the South." [17]

Late at night, between committee meetings and sessions of the
full Congress, he labored over the report he would make. Using
a typewriter, he outlined Negro attitudes as he understood them,
and the history of their mistreatment in America. His notes, on
odd lengths of checked paper, testify that he had given considerable thought to the revolutionary power that might be generated
among millions of disaffected and disenfranchised black Americans.

Under NEGRO DEMANDS, he wrote: "Not a trace of Nationalist
movement. Feel are Americans. 'Back to Africa.' Social and political equality . . . Negro Revolutionary movement. Racial and
partly Socialist. Negro capitalism. Mostly real estate."

Under AWAKENING NEGROES: "Spanish War. First experience as
fighters.* . . . European war. Conscription. Brigaded with French

---

* He was referring to the two Negro cavalry regiments, with white officers,
which fought so valiantly in Cuba, particularly in the charge up San Juan Hill.
Actually, of course, both infantry and cavalry regiments composed entirely of
Negro enlisted men had played a much more considerable role than that which
they have been credited for in the conquest of the West. Moreover Negro

troops. Treated white. Orders from American headquarters. . . . Negroes decorated by foreign governments. Return Negro army. Decorated shot in streets, lynched, etc. Negroes migrate from South to war industries. High wages but high prices. Speeded up. Caught in general labor movements . . . strikes, etc. Proletarization. Flowed out of Negro quarters into cities.

"All reform movements stop at Mason-Dixon line . . . At present Southern whites united Democratic, Negroes Republican . . . If dare vote assassinated. Conventions held where Negroes can't enter. Fictitious Republican representation."

Under CONDITIONS NEGROES: "Lynchings, Rape, Jim Crow. Hotels, Schools, Churches. Segregation in districts. Laws against marriage, etc. Educational. Position in industry. AFL and IWW. But cannot be driven like whites. Cotton mills . . . Internal imperialism. West like any undeveloped backward country. But other Imperialisms found colonial populations waiting for them."

Under SUGGESTIONS: "Negro leaders invited to visit Russia. Call Negro World Congress. Solidarity with white workers." Among the names of Negro leaders he jotted down were "DuBois, Randolph, Garvin." It would be necessary, he wrote, to strike hard at Southern capitalism in the United States and "especially create unbridgeable gap between petty-bourgeois north and southern Negroes." [18]

On July 26 he addressed the Congress as a whole on the subject, his speech generally following the notes he had made, and it is apparent that his recommendations became part of the official party line on the American Negro. The situation of the Negro, he said, was "that of a strong racial and social movement, and of a proletarian labor movement advancing very fast in class-consciousness." Alluding to the futile Marcus Garvey back-to-Africa movement in terms that ruled out any prospects for Negro nationalism or separatism, he told the Congress: "The Negroes have no demands for national independence. All movements aiming at a separate national existence for Negroes fail. . . . They consider themselves

---

regiments had fought for the Union in the Civil War. Negroes, too, had fought for their country in the American Revolution.

first of all Americans at home in the United States. This makes it very much simpler for the Communists. . . .

"As an oppressed and downtrodden people, the Negro offers to us a twofold opportunity: first, a strong race and social movement; second, a strong proletarian labor movement. . . . In both the northern and southern parts of the country the one aim must be to unite the Negro and the white laborer in common labor unions; this is the best and the quickest way to destroy race prejudice and develop class solidarity. . . ."

The Communist Party, he emphasized, should not stand aloof from the Negroes' surge toward social and political equality, but should bend every effort to convince them they would never achieve it under a capitalistic system and that a special revolution would be necessary to free them as well as all other workers from oppression.

Lenin was fascinated. He saw the Negro problem as a fulcrum by means of which the whole American nation could be tilted leftward. Some months later, he sent a directive to the American Communist Party ordering that the Negroes be made a strategically important element in future party activity.[19]

Some years later Sen Katayama, a Japanese Communist who served on the Second Congress' national and colonial commission, recalled that Lenin had told American members of the commission that he "considered the American Negroes as a subject nation, placing them in the same category as Ireland." Lenin went no farther, however, in suggesting that the Negroes be urged to press for "self-determination." [20]

The Second Congress adjourned on August 6, 1920, and most of the delegates were able to return to their homelands. Reed was making his own plans and keeping them a secret from the Comintern, as he indicated in a letter sent to Louise shortly before the Congress began meeting. It was written on a scrap of ruled paper and marked "Please hand to Louise Bryant—DO NOT MAIL.—" and read: "Did you get the $100 I sent you? More money is coming soon. I am doing all I can. If you haven't arranged to leave America don't do so. You will soon know why. . . . If you'll just hold out, my dearest, we'll soon be together all right and safe." [21]

13

STATE TRAIN
TO BAKU

A Socialist from Milwaukee named Jacob H. Rubin made the pilgrimage to Moscow that summer, and the way he remembered it fourteen years later, the American exiles in the Soviet Union were more overcome by homesickness than awe for the achievements of the new rulers of Russia. One of the first he met was Emma Goldman, who implored him to "get me out of this and I'll promise to be a good little girl."

In a book he wrote later, Rubin recalled that he met Jack Reed one evening in Red Square and that they went to Rubin's room and talked until four o'clock in the morning.

Reed, he said, was raging with bitterness and frustration, and complained that he had "sacrificed my friends, my family and myself" in a cause he now mistrusted. With the honorable exception of Lenin and Trotsky and a few others, the Communist leaders, he quoted Reed as saying, were "grafters, politicians, theorists or hopeless fools." The freedom to express oneself freely had been snatched away, and the country was in the hands of tea-swilling bureaucrats. Reed also told Rubin, whom he had met at the Socialist convention in Chicago the previous summer, that he thought he was being spied upon by the secret police.[1]

Some doubt has been cast on the accuracy of Rubin's account, because he also claimed that Reed referred to Joseph Stalin as his best friend, that he spoke of going to the Caucasus with Stalin to recuperate from his months in the Finnish prison. Reed and Stalin were undoubtedly acquainted, but they were never friends. Rubin, however, quoted Reed as saying that Stalin would eventually win the struggle for power in the Kremlin: "He's got the will power and he's going to be on top of the pile some day." [2]

Undoubtedly Rubin's quotations, whether accurate or not, expressed Reed's mood during the Second Congress and after. He had said much the same thing, in even stronger terms, to Emma Goldman and Angelica Balabanoff. After the Second Congress adjourned, and he was appointed to the Executive Committee of the Comintern as a concession to his standing with revolutionaries abroad, he continued to fight for his views on how Communists should grapple with the "reactionary" trade unions.

By his persistence he persuaded the Executive Committee to modify its directives on how the trade unions were to be approached. He argued that "dual unionism," supporting a rival to the A.F.L., such as the I.W.W., for instance, might be permissible in some cases. But he persuaded the committee to bend only slightly in its "revised theses," since foreign Communists were still required to join the available trade unions, to bore from within and attempt to seize the leadership, and were to stay unless thrown out. On at least one occasion the deliberations became so heated, with Reed opposing Zinoviev and Radek, that he resigned from the Executive Committee. It was a startling instance of indiscipline to his fellow members, and he was persuaded not only to withdraw his resignation but also to apologize to his comrades. Obviously the Comintern had further use of him, particularly to spread Communism in the United States. He was still precious as a symbol, if not as a disciplined and entirely reliable party functionary like Louis Fraina. He must be made to work with Fraina. "Fraina was the ideological brain, the Marxian iceberg of dialectical abstractions," Benjamin Gitlow observed. "A living movement could not enthuse around Fraina alone. John Reed supplied American communism with the heart and soul." [3]

The outlines of the Leninist strategy were made clear by the directives of the Second Congress of the Communist International. They called for deception and depended for their success on the unquestioning obedience of the party underground in the nations of the West—the sort of obedience that did not come naturally to Reed. The surface apparatus of Communism—the Soviet government—would press for peace and collaboration with the Western governments in hopes of obtaining the economic assistance the Soviet Union needed to recover from the war against Germany and the civil war. At the same time, the Comintern would be working under the surface of events to overthrow those governments: first in Germany, always the number-one target for Marxism, for its industrial base; then Britain's imperial system was to be corroded and national revolutions encouraged in its colonies. Soviet Russia would take Britain's place as the leading world power. Then would come the turn of the United States.

In furtherance of these objectives, particularly in the matter of British hegemony over the Middle East, the Politburo ordered the Comintern, as the agent of the external revolution, to convene a Congress of Oriental Nations at Baku, the oil port on the northern shore of the Caspian Sea. Leaders of the peasants and workers in such borderlands as Persia (now Iran), Mesopotamia (now Iraq), Turkey, Syria, and Arabia were summoned to Baku by an "Appeal to the Enslaved Masses" of those countries. The purpose was to inflame the Middle East against Britain, which had picked up most of the pieces when the Ottoman Empire collapsed. Beyond that the congress looked to the revolutionary possibilities of almost a billion turbulent people in the rest of Asia. It did not seem to have occurred to Lenin or the leaders of the Comintern that in practice dialectical materialism was incompatible with the mysticism and feudalism of the Moslem populations. The Congress of Oriental Nations was designed, as Lord Kinross wrote, "at once to flatter and to menace their Moslem neighbours." [4] The Russians hoped to secure the alignment of Turkey, which was fighting to expel the Greek armies from what was left of its territories, and its new ruler, Mustapha Kemal, agreed to send a sizable delegation to Baku.

Perhaps, too, the Russians were overimpressed by Enver Pasha, one of the Young Turks who had formerly ruled Turkey and who had fled to the Soviet Union, along with Jemal Pasha, in hopes of realizing his dream of a Pan-Islamic dominion extending from Constantinople to the frontiers of India. The two pashas were received with flattery in the councils of the Comintern and were regarded, despite the ruin they had brought to Turkey, as charismatic leaders who would encourage millions of Moslems to revolt. Suspicious as the Turks had always been of the Russians, and embroiled in a dispute over the possession of the Armenian provinces, Mustapha Kemal and his advisers were toying with the idea of entering into a partnership with the Soviets after the exiled Enver Pasha wrote them from Moscow that he and the Russians were working for "the establishment of an organized Islamic world and the delivery of our country." [5]

In its official Appeal to the Enslaved Masses of the Middle East, the Comintern implored the delegates it invited to Baku, "Do not spare any effort, and let as many of you as possible come to Baku on September 1. Formerly you used to make pilgrimages across the desert to the Holy City; now cross mountains, rivers, and deserts to meet one another. Let the Congress show your foes in Europe, America, and in your own country that the time for slavery is over, that you have risen, and that you will conquer."

To his surprise and dismay, Reed was among those bidden to attend the conclave at Baku. He was to be the American delegate, and, in addition, all members of the Comintern's Executive Committee were required to attend.

He protested to Zinoviev that he was still ailing from his experiences in the Central Police Station at Abo, and that he was not well enough to make the long journey to the Caspian. Besides, Louise was finally on her way to Russia, they had been separated for months, and he wanted to be in Petrograd to meet her. (Louise was indeed en route. She had dressed herself in a man's clothes and been smuggled on a ship disguised as a seaman, complete with the required papers. Despite word from Jack that it might be better if she stayed in the United States, she was determined to reach his side, alarmed as she was by reports of his failing health.)

Zinoviev would not listen to Reed's protests. Both his health and his emotional life had to be sacrificed to "revolutionary necessity." An American's presence was required in Baku, and he was the available American.

"The Comintern has made a decision," Zinoviev snapped at him in German. "Obey." [6]

Thus Reed, in his lifelong search for freedom and truth, found that his options had been narrowed down to one: obey. Weary, ailing, sick with disillusionment, he boarded the State Train bound for Baku with the hierarchy of the Comintern. Before he left he wrote a letter to be handed to Louise on her arrival in Moscow. "I am so disappointed not to be able to meet you when you enter Russia," he wrote in a subdued tone, explaining that he had intended to greet her in Petrograd. "But yesterday," he continued, "I was informed that I must go to Baku in the Caucasus, with the rest of the Executive Committee, to attend the Oriental Congress. . . . I asked permission to stay here and come later with you. But they refused.

"Then I asked that you be sent after me. That also cannot be done, because there is a civil war going on down south, and we are going in an armored train, which is the only one to go."

He left careful instructions on where she was to go and who she was to see. She must check into the Dielovoy Dvor Hotel, where a room had been reserved for her. She was to see "Rosenberg at the Foreign Office, also Boris Reinstein at the National Hotel, also Angelica Balabanoff and Aleksandra Kollontai.

"I am longing to see you more than I can tell," he assured Louise. "It seems years. I am worrying about only one thing. I must soon go home, and it is awfully difficult to get out of here, especially for a woman. That is why I tried to get word to you to wait for me outside. . . ." [7]

This letter may have been intended as a warning, to tell her their true situation as guests of the Soviet Union. If Louise could make her way into Russia via the underground route, it was equally possible—if the Comintern leaders were of a mind to permit it—for them to leave the same way.

The State Train, with its armor-plated cars and its heavily armed troops riding on the roofs, carried Reed and his companions across the Volga plains and through the Ukraine, in which the Red Army was still campaigning against Baron-General Wrangel and his White forces. Banners on the train proclaimed it the "Near East Revolution Limited." Once, a band of White guerrillas tried to disrupt its passage through the Ukraine, but they were driven off by machine guns mounted on the cars. Many of Reed's traveling companions, as he later told Louise, were "adventurers who represented nobody but themselves," a group that no doubt included the dapper little chocolate soldier, Enver Pasha, who, during the war against Russia in 1915, had abandoned a whole Turkish army in the Caucasus to die in the snow-locked mountains while he hastened back to the comforts of Constantinople.

The journey only deepened his doubts as to the purity of his fellow revolutionaries' motives and conduct. No one ever accused him of being a prig, but the orgiastic behavior of his fellow delegates, catered to by the stage managers of the Baku conclave, disgusted him immeasurably. If there was a Puritan element in Reed, it centered around the use of prostitutes, whose plight had touched him deeply ever since, as a youth just out of college, he had spent nights talking to them on his rambles around the lower East Side.

"On the way," as Louise later repeated what he had told her, "the train picked up delegates dressed in various oriental garments, tough-looking wild men, who guzzled vodka by the tumblerful, most of them unaware of the purposes for which the conference was called. As soon as the train entered the Caucasus, Radek outdid himself in providing suitable entertainment for the delegates."

He reflected that the proletarian revolution's methods of cajoling those it wanted to impress were not essentially different from a group of lobbyists catering a congressional junket, only a little cruder. He was shocked, he told Louise later, when "old Mohammedan women boarded the train followed by beautiful Caucasian girls. Some of the girls were barely fourteen years old. The old women disrobed the girls before the eyes of the delegates. The nude beauties stood before the gaping eyes of those who called themselves communists, who were prepared to tear down the rotten structure of capitalist society in order to build a new, a better world. What followed turned out to be an orgy of drunken lasciviousness in which Radek was the central figure."

Louise, in recalling what Jack told her, said the spectacle "thoroughly sickened and disgusted him. . . . He told me that there were many fine Russian girls who went along to act as secretaries and stenographers. Had any of these chosen to engage in sexual intercourse with the delegates, it would have been perfectly all right with him, but he objected to the use of prostitution by the leaders of the Comintern on the strictly capitalist basis of buying and paying for the commodity." [8]

The train reached Baku the day before the Oriental Congress was to open. The old Tartar city, its battlements now sprouting with oil derricks and pipelines, was thronged with the colorfully robed representatives of most of the eastern nations, some from as far away as Hindustan, China, and Chinese Turkestan. Superficially it must have seemed that all of Asia was rising to the summons from the "Third Rome," and the physical fact of the convocation, drawing in so many disparate nationalities, rang alarm bells in the Western chancelleries much as the Bandung Conference did many years later.

To dramatize this ingathering of the Oriental nations, the Comintern's propagandists staged a crude little morality play in the main square of Baku. It was to impress what they took to be simple nomadic mentalities with how easily a victory over the West could be won. "In the middle of the square stood a scaffold," as the scene was described to Robert Dunn. "Under it were Lloyd

George, Mitterand, and Wilson, in effigy. They were well made, with black coats, medals, ribbons, which the sea breeze blew curiously.

"The hangman held under their noses a bottle of the petroleum which they had so liked to receive (as mementoes of the Congress) at Baku. Then he poured it on the figures, and fire appeared. Lloyd George's portfolio fell blazing. The crowd shrieked with joy. He toppled from his chair like a man whose heart was broken. The head of Mitterand fell off, like Louis Capet's rolling under the guillotine. But Wilson lasted longer, since America is not so near revolution as France or England." [9]

For the important personalities attending the Congress there were more sophisticated diversions, as Louise remembered from Jack's account. "Though the Russian people were suffering badly from the lack of bare necessities and starvation was rampant, the delegates . . . were lavishly supplied with rich food and liquor, including rare wines and champagnes. Reed saw no excuse for flaunting such extravagance in the faces of the poverty-stricken masses. When he complained Radek and Zinoviev laughed at him." [10]

The conference itself was a mockery of shouted slogans, speeches which few of the delegates could understand, even though they were translated into four languages, and the droning of interpreters. "The meeting became a babel," Robert Dunn wrote. "Moscow forbade talk of religion or caste, though the subjects were afire in the hearts under Asia's flowing robes."

Reed agreed that the Congress bore only the slightest resemblance to a serious forum at which the problems of half the world were to be discussed, if not solved. "He witnessed a conference," Louise recalled from her subsequent conversations with him, "in which Kurd, Caucasian and oriental chiefs, gangster leaders, smugglers and adventurers mingled with European communists and communists from the United States, to shout approval of all the prearranged motions and resolutions worked out by the Politburo of the Communist Party of Russia. Radek and Zinoviev did most of the engineering of the conference and most of the talking.

Delegates were shoved up on the platform from all the countries to greet the conference in their native tongues. But it did not matter to Zinoviev and Radek what they said or didn't say. The wires carried only Radek's manufactured version of what they said. Often the versions of what was said at the conference sent out to Germany, Britain and the United States differed from what was sent out to the Russian people.

"Jack had sharp verbal encounters with Zinoviev and Radek. He warned them not to garble his speeches. Radek laughed at him. Told him not to be naïve. Zinoviev, his vanity hurt by Jack's persistent opposition, warned him that a revolution must be carried on with the material one has on hand."

Zinoviev, by Louise's account, even had to deliver a lecture to Reed, somewhat along the lines of the Leninist dictum that any means were justified by the revolutionary end, and was quoted as telling him: "A Bolshevik is a hard realist, one not moved by cheap maudlin sentiments; neither is he concerned whether what he does conforms to bourgeois ideas about justice and morality."

Such backstage bickering between producers and one of the star performers thus was the muted counterpoint to Reed's own message for the delegates to the Congress of Oriental Nations. However much he may have detested his role in the proceedings, he took the platform and read his lines. The speech—which may or may not have been doctored by Karl Radek's press bureau—was greeted with a dutiful enthusiasm by the assemblage, not more than a score of whom could understand English. The official transcript says he said:

"I represent the revolutionary workers of one of the great imperialistic powers—the United States of America. You have not yet tasted American domination. You know and hate English, French and Italian imperialists, but you probably think that 'free America' will rule better, will liberate the colonial peoples, will feed and protect them. But the workers and peasants of the Philippines, the peoples of Central America and of the islands of the Caribbean Sea—they know the meaning of the domination of 'free America.'"

He outlined the history of the American occupation of the Philippines and declared that even when the islands were cut loose from formal ties to the United States they would still be dominated economically by American capitalism. The same thing had happened in the American occupation of Cuba, Haiti, and Santo Domingo. The ten million American Negroes were still held in bondage only different in form from slavery. Could the peoples of the Middle East expect any better treatment when the United States inevitably moved into that sphere of influence?

He warned the Armenians—then the subject of intense propagandizing by the Russians, who were establishing a Soviet Republic of Armenia—that the administrator of American relief to the hundreds of thousands of Armenians who had been "deported" by the Turks and driven into the deserts to be massacred by tribesmen (largely Kurds, some of whom may have been sitting with their curved daggers in the audience) was one Cleveland Dodge. In his own country, Reed was quoted as saying, Dodge was known as a copper magnate who drove his own workers out on the desert if they dared to strike against his mines. The Americans' Near East Relief was a monstrous hoax; their food and medicines would be distributed in a manner such as to advance the imperialistic designs of the United States. In Hungary, where a Communist revolution had been countered by the Horthy dictatorship, American relief supplies had been used to bring about the downfall of Béla Kun, the Hungarian Communist leader, who was among the delegates to the Congress.

"No, comrades," Reed was supposed to have declared, "Uncle Sam never gives anything free of charge. He comes with a sack of hay in one hand and a whip in the other, and whoever believes his promises will pay in blood.

"Don't trust American capitalists. There is but one road to freedom. Unite with the Russian workers and peasants, who overthrew their capitalists and whose Red Army conquers the troops of the foreign imperialists. Follow the Red Star of the Communist International!" [11]

Zinoviev, Radek, and Béla Kun also addressed the Congress,

which included among its delegates 235 Turks, 192 Persians and Parsis, eight Chinese, eight Kurds, 157 Armenians, 100 Georgians, and a number of Arabs. Like Reed these three were greeted by a roar of acclaim and a waving of swords and daggers, and the dutiful responses led by those who had been coached in the Soviet litany.

Zinoviev, in the opening address, made an emotional appeal, an essay in demagoguery that made Reed writhe in disgust. "Comrades! Brothers! The time has come when you can start on the organization of a true and holy people's war against the robbers and oppressors. The Communist International turns today to the peoples of the east and says to them: 'Brothers, we summon you to a holy war, in the first place against English imperialism!' May today's declaration be heard in London, in Paris, in all cities where the capitalists are still in power! May they heed the solemn oath, taken by the representatives of tens of millions of toilers of the east, that in the east the might of the oppressors, of the English, the capitalist yoke which weighs on the toilers of the east shall be no more!"

"Stormy applause" followed, noted the official transcript. "Prolonged hurrahs. The members of the congress rise from their seats and brandish their weapons. The orator is unable for a long time to continue his speech. The delegates stand and clap applause. The cry rings out: 'We swear it!' "

Undoubtedly Zinoviev's words were fervently received, because many of the delegates were embittered victims of French and British colonialism, but later in the convocation Zinoviev, perhaps made overconfident by the reception of his opening address, proceeded to blunder. He underestimated the hold their religion had over the Moslems, the difficulty of shifting their polarization from Mecca to Moscow, and their deep respect even for traditions that had betrayed them.

"Turks," he declared, "must drop their adoration of sultans and other superstitions."

He attacked Mustapha Kemal for not adhering to Soviet policy in driving the British and the French out of the Middle East, and further offended the Turks present by his sponsorship of Enver Pasha, whom many regarded as a defector, and who had declared to the congress that he regretted having been "compelled to fight on the side of German imperialism," which only recalled to many of the Turks present how poorly he had fought in the Caucasus before abandoning his army to the mountain snows.

The Turkish delegation decided to walk out, and were followed by many other Moslems. Later in the month, in any case, military movements on the Turkish-Russian border mocked the show of unity put on at Baku. Kemal's troops moved into the Armenian districts formerly part of the Ottoman Empire, and Moscow dispatched cavalry regiments to push them back. The Soviet move to replace the Western imperialisms in the Middle East and gain control of a lion's share of the world's oil reserves would have to wait upon another season.

Most of the Moslem delegations had drifted away earlier, affronted by suggestions from the presidium that Allah was dead, that there was no God but Marx and that Lenin was his prophet. As Robert Dunn wrote, "Some set up bazaars to sell the silks, rugs and rice they'd brought. The devout washed themselves by Koran rule, and Khiva envoys stole what rugs they could lay hands on. So fizzled Lenin's first try to fire the East." [12]

Baku had been an Arabian Nights entertainment—commissars trying to teach a new religion to nomads among whose ancestors had been the Three Wise Men, who clicked away at their prayer beads while pale intellectuals tried to explain the meaning of dialectical materialism. Jack Reed, according to Dunn, began working on the scenario of a musical play about the conclave at Baku. It was to be a farce, but he never finished it. [13]

14

"DEATH COMES LIKE THIS,
I KNOW . . ."

In mid-September the State Train returned to Moscow with its high-ranking delegates, commissars, and propaganda-makers, fresh from their futile effort to stir up a holy war in the Middle East against the Western nations slicing away at the carcass of the Ottoman Empire. Among them was one raging dissident: Jack Reed. Perhaps there were others, but they were cautious enough to conceal their dissidence.

Nothing can be found among Reed's surviving papers and notes to indicate exactly what happened or what was said on that last journey of a restless life; he had learned too much from the tactics of his opponents to trust his thoughts to paper. The evidence of what happened on that dolorous journey probably would not stand up in a court of law. Whether it can be judged credible in an extralegal sense, as historical truth, is a matter of opinion. Perhaps the only tentative verdict possible is that it seems to fit.

This evidence consists of what Louise Bryant remembered of his conversations on his return to Moscow—admittedly filtered through the mind of a subsequently hostile witness—and what she told their friends Max Eastman and Benjamin Gitlow, and the published testimony of Angelica Balabanoff and of Emma Goldman. All of them became bitter anti-Communists, though Miss Balabanoff remained a Socialist to the end of her life. The fact that they were disillusioned does not discredit their testimony —what happened to Jack Reed, in fact, was partly the cause of their disenchantment—but it does have to be taken into consideration. So does the fact that it appears highly unlikely that, acting and speaking independently of each other, they could have contributed to a wholesale fabrication.

Eastman has recorded that Louise told him the story twice, once in Paris, while she was the wife of William C. Bullitt, and a half-dozen years later, when she returned to the cottage at Croton she had shared with Jack and was attempting to write the story of his life.

Louise told Eastman that Reed quarreled with Zinoviev and Radek all the way back to Moscow on the luxurious train, the blinds of which were drawn when they passed through the towns of southern Russia so the populace could not see the tables overflowing with food and drink. Reed was unable to contain his "indignation at Zinoviev's demagogic harangue, in which he presented the revolution as little but a Mohammedan war on Christian Europe. Zinoviev was, notoriously, the very incarnation of a demagogue. He became excited to inebriation by his own oratory, and by the hypnotic effect that his high tenor, half-chanting, madly lucid utterance had upon his auditors. He could not resist the temptation to stir them yet more . . . working them up to an orgasmic rapture which must end in his touching, at the expense of whatever rationally conceived purpose he may have set out with, the very quick of their emotional life."

Zinoviev's manipulation of mass emotions—self-defeating as it had been at Baku—was the essence of fraud and deceit to Reed. Even a demagogue of his previous acquaintance, William Jennings

Bryan, was worthy of a certain respect by comparison, because he believed what he was saying and had proved it. To Reed, Zinoviev's cynical harangues all but made a lie of the revolution. As Max Eastman analyzed Reed's attitude, "He did not want to sit aloft in a new priesthood, a new cult of intellectual complaisance, knowing what is good for the masses, because Marx had explained it to him, and he had been superior enough to understand Marx, and was therefore justified in hoodwinking and cheating the masses, and arousing them any way he could to the action called for by an esoteric conception of history."

Reed told Zinoviev, "I don't think a real revolutionist would talk that way," referring to Zinoviev's speechmaking at Baku. And when Zinoviev, with Radek chiming in as a cospokesman for what they maintained was revolutionary necessity, defended the position, "Jack got up on his two feet and let them have it from the shoulder. He told them what he thought of them in forty different ways, and the fight lasted all the way back to Moscow." [1]

As soon as the State Train rolled into the station Reed hastened to the Dielovoy Dvor Hotel and his long-anticipated reunion with Louise.

She saw immediately that she had been wise in coming, despite the dangers and hardships of her underground journey. Jack was pale, weary, and sick; he complained of severe headaches and a weakness he had never experienced before. In her account of their reunion to Benjamin Gitlow, whom she visited in prison a year or two later, she related much the same story as she did later to Max Eastman. It seemed to her that his "great personal disillusionment" was crushing the life out of him. "He was no longer sure of his bearings. The cause for which he was prepared to give up his life did not measure up to his expectations. Ever since his return to Soviet Russia from Finland, from his horrible experiences in Abo prison, an inner conflict raged within him—between what he believed in and what he saw and experienced—that played havoc with his peace of mind." These privations were "nothing compared to the hours Jack spent trying to figure out why Zinoviev had such little regard for the safety of a comrade bound on an important mission as to attach to him a man who on the first opportunity betrayed him to the police."

As Louise recalled from their long and despairing conversations after their reunion, "Jack noticed how power and the lust for power affected the Bolshevik leaders. . . . He was terribly afraid of having made a serious mistake in his interpretation of an historical event for which he would be held accountable before the judgment of history. He lacked confidence in himself; was not sure of the ground on which he stood. He blamed himself for becoming a politician; he was not cut out for one. Perhaps Zinoviev and Radek were right and he was wrong. They were, after all, revolutionaries, politicians who had been hardened by years of activity and strife.

"I tried to argue with him; to bolster up his morale. 'Pull yourself together, Jack,' I pleaded. 'When you get back to the States you can do the things you set your heart on doing.' But he kept looking at me through his saddened eyes and ended up by saying, 'Honey, it's no use.' " [2]

For about two weeks late in September and early in October Jack and Louise enjoyed a sort of second honeymoon. In those brief days they came to a realization of how much they meant to each other, how insignificant had been the strayings and misunderstandings of the past. Undoubtedly they hoped that, once out of Russia, they would be able to make something of a conventionally—if not entirely bourgeois—happy marriage out of their freshly discovered attachment to each other.

They attended the ballet and visited the art galleries, and Jack took her to meet Lenin and Trotsky, Kamenev and other Soviet leaders, as well as Enver Pasha, the current darling of the inner circle. (Enver was to betray the hopes of his sponsors shortly. He made his way to Turkestan and launched a guerrilla war against the Red Army's occupying forces. For a short time he reigned as the Emir of Bokhara, but in the summer of 1922 the Russians sent a sizable expeditionary force to Bokhara, and Enver died with his Moslem partisans, defending the city.) Possibly Reed's private conversations with Lenin helped to open Lenin's eyes to the evils of the bureaucracy which had begun strangling the country in the same fashion as that which operated under the Czars. The following year Lenin issued a series of decrees ordering government officials of all ranks to behave as servants of the people rather than their masters. One decree directed that every government building post signs listing the days and hours when the offices within were open to the public, "not just inside the building, but outside as well, so that the people can avail themselves of this information without a pass." [3]

Jack and Louise also made the rounds of the small Anglo-American colony of exiles and expatriates, journalists and sightseers. Among them was Emma Goldman, who later wrote, "Ordinarily I would not have looked her [Louise] up. I had known Louise for years, even before she was with Jack. An attractive, vivid creature, one had to like her even when not taking her social protestations seriously. On two occasions I had realized her lack of depth. During our trial in New York, Louise had studiously avoided us. They were planning to go to Russia and she was evidently afraid of having her name connected with ours during that dangerous war period. . . . A much graver offence, and one that had angered me considerably, was her misrepresentation of anarchism in her book on Russia. My niece Stella had sent me the volume at the Missouri prison and I was indignant to find repeated in it the stupid story of Russia's nationalizing women that had made its rounds in the American press. Louise charged the anarchists with having been the first to issue the decree. She had taken no trouble to adduce any evidence for her wild assertions, nor had she done so in reply to my letter demanding it. . . . I decided to have nothing more to do with Louise." [4]

Miss Goldman, however, decided not to hold past differences against Louise, particularly since she was the wife of a man she herself wholeheartedly admired.

They also saw much of Angelica Balabanoff, having looked her up immediately after Reed's return from Baku. "Both of them looked unhappy and tired," she remembered, "and we made no effort to hide from each other what was in our minds. Jack spoke bitterly of the demagogy and display which had characterized the Baku congress and the manner in which the native population and Far Eastern delegates had been treated." [5]

They became acquainted with Clare Sheridan, an English sculptress, who had come to Moscow to make busts of Lenin, Trotsky, Zinoviev, and other Soviet leaders. Miss Sheridan's artistic activity immediately drew the disapproval of Angelica Balabanoff, to whom it appeared frivolous in the midst of all the difficulties the government was then attempting to surmount. Miss Balabanoff was even more annoyed when many of the Bolshevik leaders "seemed rather flattered by the attention of this glamorous and adventurous cousin of Winston Churchill," who had been doing all in his power to promote intervention by the Allied powers on the side of the White armies. "I disapproved of the whole idea of thus 'immortalizing' the leaders of the proletarian revolution and suggested to her that it would be far more fitting to take as her models typical representatives from among the workers and peasants—particularly the working women whose suffering and heroism were expressed so graphically in their faces. Shortly after this, when I mentioned to Lenin that I had met Clare Sheridan, he shrugged his shoulders and smiled. It was obvious that he, at least, was not seriously impressed." [6]

Miss Sheridan, unmoved by Miss Balabanoff's objections, went ahead with her work, and was beginning on a bust of Kamenev on the morning of September 22 when Jack Reed, just back from the Baku conference, stopped in at Kamenev's office.

She was puzzled by Reed, as she confided to her diary. "We were delayed in starting by John Reed, the American Communist; a well-built, good-looking young man, who has given up everything at home to throw his heart and his life into the work here. I understand the Russian spirit, but what strange force impels an apparently normal young man from the United States? I am told by the Russians that his book, *Ten Days That Shook the World*, is the best book on the Revolution, and that it has become a National classic and is taught in the schools."

Under a later date Miss Sheridan noted in her diary, "Everyone liked him and his wife, Louise Bryant, the war correspondent. She is quite young and had only recently joined him." [7]

Jack spent as much time as possible with Louise, almost as though he had a premonition that something stronger than the exigencies of a revolutionary's career would soon separate them. The last message to her that can be found in the collection of his papers was a note scrawled on blue paper and left for her return to their hotel room: "Louise! I'll be right back! Reed."

About two weeks after the Baku conference ended it was apparent to Louise and others that he was sicker than he would admit—and it was not merely the continuing ill effects of his imprisonment in Finland. That had weakened him, but a proper amount of food and rest should have helped by now, almost four months later. "When Jack first complained of being ill he did not take it seriously," Louise later told Benjamin Gitlow. "I did not like his looks. He said it was nothing to worry about." [8]

Just as his health took a sharp decline, the minutes of the Congress of Oriental Nations were published, and Reed was outraged. His speech to the Congress was garbled, either deliberately, by Radek's press bureau, or in the process of translation from English into German, German into Russian, and, finally, from Russian to English. Once again, and for the last time, he argued with Zinoviev and Radek. He had resolved to hold his tongue until the minutes of the Congress had been published, and hope that he and Louise would soon be allowed to leave the Soviet Union. He was determined to return to America and answer the federal indictment, even though he was almost certain to be sentenced to five years in prison. If he continued to defy Zinoviev, he believed, he would be kept in Russia to prevent him from spilling the truth as soon as he crossed the border.

But what had happened in the minutes was too much. He was proud of his record as a revolutionary, and he would not have it smirched by a false report of his remarks to the Congress of Oriental Nations. "Zinoviev and Radek got him aside," Louise told Eastman, "and Zinoviev said to him: 'Reed, you can't afford to do this—we'll destroy you. You can't fight the organization.

We'll destroy you, Reed. You're with us and you've got to stay with us.' "

The eruption from Zinoviev came after Reed had hotly offered his resignation from the Executive Committee of the Communist International.

Reed replied, "It hasn't worried me when American capitalists threatened to destroy me, and I'm not afraid of you either—go ahead and do your worst."

Then, Louise recalled, he "just came home, hot and angry and tragically discouraged and lay down on the bed and turned his face to the wall, and would hardly speak." [9]

Soon he was racked with fever. A doctor summoned to their hotel room diagnosed his ailment as influenza, but Louise was certain that it was something more serious. Other doctors were called into consultation as he began rambling in delirium. Louise was appalled at the obvious incompetence of the medical assistance she had been able to obtain. She went to Lenin and told him how sick Jack was, and Lenin ordered that everything possible be done for him. "A whole week had been lost before the physicians agreed in their diagnosis," Emma Goldman later learned from Louise.[10]

Then it was decided that he had contracted typhus, probably during the days he spent in Baku, and he was hurried off to a hospital on Lenin's orders. It seems almost incredible, with all the typhus epidemics that had raged through Russia during the war and after, that the doctors should have been so slow to recognize the symptoms of the fever.

When Reed was taken to the hospital, Louise begged to be allowed to stay at his bedside and help nurse him. But she was not allowed to stay in his room, perhaps for her own protection. "What I saw on my visits to the hospital alarmed me. He did not receive the care he should have been given. I knew he needed me desperately. Only when delirium set in was I allowed to be at his side. I spent horrible days and nights with him, days and nights I can never forget. He raved and he cried. . . ." [11]

For three days, from October 14 to October 17, the doctors and nurses fought to save his life, but the typhus was raging unchecked through his system. The proper drugs were not available, and later his friends back home suggested that his life would have been saved if the United States had not joined in the blockade, which included a prohibition on the shipment of medical supplies. It was an assertion almost as far off the mark as any accusation that the Comintern's chieftains murdered him by ordering him, against his will, to go to Baku, where he probably picked up the typhus germs.

In his last hours, as Louise told both Emma Goldman and Benjamin Gitlow, Jack kept muttering in his delirium, "Caught in a trap . . . caught in a trap. . . ."

Toward the end, in a moment of clarity, he spoke to Louise of the stories and poems he intended to write, and, rather strangely, said, "You know how it is when you go to Venice. You ask people —Is this Venice?—just for the pleasure of hearing the reply." [12]

On the morning of October 17, 1920, death reached out for him, the death of which he had written in one of his best poems:

> Snow-soft and gently cold;
> Impalpable battalions of thin mist,
> Light-quenching and sound-smothering and slow . . .
> How vast your voice has grown,
> That was so silver-soft. . . .

The news spread quickly through Moscow, then out to the world. Angelica Balabanoff had heard that he was seriously ill and wanted to see her, but "to my everlasting regret I postponed my visit, not realising how ill he was. On the very morning that I was preparing to go to the hospital I received the news of his death. . . ."

Louise Bryant, widowed at the age of twenty-five, was shattered, not only by the fact of his death, but also by her conviction, as she later expressed it, that "he died because he did not want to live." She had pleaded with him "not to give up. He didn't respond." She was convinced, she told Gitlow, that he "died because of his great personal disillusionment" with the integrity of Communism as it was practiced in the motherland of the revolution.

On hearing the news of Reed's death, Emma Goldman went to Louise's room in the Dielovoy Dvor Hotel and found her "a wreck, completely shattered. She broke down in convulsive weeping that no words could allay. I took her in my arms, holding her quivering body in a silent embrace. She quieted down after a while and began relating the sad story of Jack's death. . . ." Louise told her how he had kept muttering "Caught in a trap" in his delirium, and Miss Goldman wondered, "Had Jack also come to see that all was not well with his idol . . . or had it only been the approach of death that had for a moment illumined his mind?" [13]

The Soviet government decreed a state funeral, with all the proletarian pomp and Red Square pageantry that since have become traditional for the passing of a Communist dignitary. He was honored far more in death than he had been in life. For seven days his body lay in state at the Trades Union Hall, with Red Army soldiers standing as a guard of honor day and night.

Thousands attended the funeral services on October 24. First they assembled at the hall where his body lay. Emma Goldman was among those standing in the cold autumn rain and thought it a pity that there was "No beauty for the man who had loved it so, no colour for his artist-soul. No spark of the red-white flame of the fighter to inspire those who in bombastic speeches claimed him as their comrade." [14] Angelica Balabanoff was not among those present, because "I knew I could not bear to listen to the speeches that would be made over his coffin. Any speech that I might make which did not allude to the tragedy of the last months of his life would be a lie and a profanation." [15]

The best account of the ceremonies that sent John Reed to his grave under the Kremlin Wall was that Clare Sheridan wrote in her diary immediately afterward. It was the first funeral she had ever attended without any religious service, and it struck her as "peculiar" not to hear God mentioned, even more to observe how the occasion was used principally as a propaganda-making device. The walls of the Trades Union Hall were covered with huge revolutionary cartoons in bright colors. The coffin stood on a dais and was covered by wreaths. Looking closer, she saw that the wreaths were made of painted tin flowers and apparently "did service for each Revolutionary burial."

The hall was crowded with a murmuring throng. "I noticed a Christ-like man with long fair curly hair, and a fair beard and clear blue eyes; he was quite young. I asked who he was. No one seemed to know: 'An artist of sorts,' someone suggested. Not all people with wonderful heads are wonderful people."

A procession formed to follow the coffin as it was borne through the streets to Red Square. It was accompanied, Miss Sheridan said, by a band playing a funeral march she had never heard before. "Whenever that Funeral March was struck up (and it had a tedious refrain) everyone uncovered—it seemed to be the only thing they uncovered for. We passed through the Place de la Revolution, and through the sacred gate to the Red Square." The procession halted at the grave site. On the wall behind it, serving as a backdrop, was a large red banner with gilt lettering that read, "The leaders die, but the cause lives on."

Those words—the theme, in fact, of the lengthy tributes spoken over his grave—were of little consolation to his young widow. Louise Bryant was deathly pale and hardly seemed conscious of what was taking place. The ceremony was not planned with her grief in mind, and went on interminably, with speeches and translations of speeches in English, French, German, and Russian. It was, after all, a drama staged by and for the Communist International.

Bukharin spoke, and Radek and other party figures, but not Lenin or Trotsky. The occasion, as Clare Sheridan dryly noted, "was one for speeches." They spoke as the rain and snow fell, and Louise swayed on her feet, and thousands listened with blank faces. "I marvel continually at the blank faces of the Russian people," she wrote in her diary that night. ". . . Russia seems numb. I wonder if it has always been so, or whether the people have lived through years of such horror that they have become insensible to pain." She was also struck by the fact that the burying ground of the revolution's heroes was so unadorned. "There was not a memorial, a headstone or a sign, not even an individual mound. The Communist ideal seemed to have been realized at last; the Equality, unattainable in life, the equality for which Christ died, had been realizable only in death."

The handsome and eloquent Aleksandra Kollontai was the only speaker to bring to the occasion any sense of the fact that a human being, not merely a cog in the revolutionary machine, had died. It was while she was speaking of Reed and his human qualities and what his death meant to his friends that Louise, unable to endure any more, suddenly collapsed. The show went on, following the scenario written for it. The widow could not be removed, unconscious though she was, because it would prove a distraction.

"It was extremely painful to see this white-faced unconscious woman lying back on the supporting arm of a Foreign Office official, more interested in the speeches than the human agony," Clare Sheridan observed. "The faces of the crowd around betrayed neither sympathy nor interest, they looked on unmoved. I could not get to her, as I was outside the ring of soldiers who stood guard nearly shoulder to shoulder." [16]

All continued to stand at attention until the leaders had finished speaking and the coffin was lowered into the ground. Then, when the honor guard broke ranks, Louise's friends were permitted to reach her side. Emma Goldman and Alexander Berkman carried her to an automobile.*

Louise survived Jack by sixteen years—most of them unhappy ones. In 1923 she married William C. Bullitt, later American ambassador to France and to Soviet Russia, and seven years later was divorced by him for "personal indignities." She stayed on in Paris, pathetically incapable of finding herself after Jack died. She was a "sick and shattered woman," Angelica Balabanoff said of her last years in Paris. "Poor Louise committed slow suicide—went the sad road of narcotic escape," Art Young wrote shortly after

* Commenting on Jack's funeral, Mabel Dodge Luhan maliciously and inaccurately observed, "Louise, draped in crêpe, the wife of a hero, threw herself on his bier long enough to be photographed for the New York papers." (Movers and Shakers, pp. 421-422.)

her death in 1936, at the age of forty-one, from a cerebral hemorrhage. A short time before she died, Young received a letter from her. "I suppose in the end life gets all of us. It nearly has got me now—getting myself and my friends out of jail—living under curious conditions—but never minding much. . . . Know always I send my love to you across the stars. If you get there before I do—or later—tell Jack Reed I love him." [17]

It is an unquiet grave that lies in the shadow of the Kremlin wall, in earshot of the speeches that have reverberated through the world and the thunderous displays of Red Army power and intercontinental missiles brandished for the benefit of Western nations still resisting, after half a century, the ideology supposed to overwhelm them. John Reed's name has been used in that curious life-after-death accorded the members of the Communist pantheon, with a Byzantine religiosity, as an example to the proletarian youth of the world.

Shortly after his death he was deified by the Communist International as the great poet and historian of the Ten Days who gave up the promise of a brilliant career in capitalistic America to fight for the revolution. When Stalin came to power, however, Reed's ikon was discreetly curtained off, his book on the revolution thoroughly "edited," then suppressed, because he had mentioned Stalin only twice, glancingly, in *Ten Days That Shook the World*.

He was resurrected again during the years when Stalin was constructing a totalitarian state, with accompanying purges and deportations and executions, as a symbol of respectability to impress Americans being recruited into the Communist Party. On the Comintern's orders, John Reed Clubs were formed in every sizable city across the United States, to the greater glory, not of their patron saint, but of Joseph Stalin. The John Reed "of this second apotheosis, or rather the glossy glass-eyed teetering simulacrum which was carted about this country between 1925 and '35 with the label 'John Reed' hanging round its neck," Max Eastman wrote, was presented as a sort of American Lafayette of the Russian Revolution.[18]

During that resurrection, Jack's mother was still alive and bitterly protested the use of her son's name in that fashion. She wrote his old friend Lincoln Steffens, asking what she could do to prevent it. He referred her to Francis J. Heney, whom her husband had assisted in the land-fraud prosecutions, and then added a few words which could hardly have comforted her:

"The last time I saw Jack he blew me hard, eloquently, rather bitterly for not myself doing what he had done: come out straight for the Communist Party and the world revolution. . . . The point here is that Jack did go completely over; he ceased to be the free soul that you (and I) remember. He lived the life of a party Communist to the end. . . . He became a hero in Russia; he will be for ages a Soviet Russian hero. And, Mrs. Reed, I'm afraid that you are wrong about his not standing for the use of his name by the clubs. My impression is that Jack would approve of that or, if he objected, he would have complained only that the John Reed Clubs do not go far enough. He might say to them what he said to me that night on a street corner in New York: 'Go on—the limit!' " [19]

Sensitively attuned as his ear was to such matters, Steffens may not have heard of Reed's final disenchantment.

In any case, John Reed was figuratively laid to rest again in the mid-nineteen-thirties when the John Reed Clubs were allowed to wither away in the milder climate of the popular-front movements sponsored in the Western democracies by the Soviet Union.

But the afterlife of a Communist legend is never a quiet one. John Reed's example, or what the Communist International chooses to make of it, may be exhumed again. He was essentially an old-fashioned romantic among the hard-eyed revolutionaries of a later breed, yet in spirit he resembles many of the impressionable young who form the New Left today.

He deserves the compassion and understanding of a later generation. The meaning of his life, particularly why he turned to Communism in a raging despair over what he considered the irretrievable failures of democracy, and equally why, in the end, he was disillusioned by the first practical application of Communist theory, should not be lost in the rush of events that have occurred since his life prematurely ended. That meaning was perceptively recaptured some years ago by Max Lerner, who believed that John Reed's life was important for something more than its excitement and its eager quest for experience. "Through all its apparent gyrations it had order, sequence, and inner logic. Actually it was one of the most deadly serious attempts ever made by an American to organize his experience into something that had meaning and stature . . . it takes on a meaning that places it high in the history of the American consciousness. . . ." [20]

In his consideration of the meaning of Reed's life, George F. Kennan also found a "blazing honesty and a purity of idealism" that reflected credit on the society that so unwittingly produced him. "Perhaps it is too much to ask that the America of that time should have accepted this foolish and rebellious child and treated him with gentleness and understanding merely for the sake of his sincerity and talents. . . . Even his immature opinions deserved reasoned, patient argument rather than emotional indignation. And his provocative behavior would have been better met by an amused sympathy than by criminal indictments. Had such consideration been shown, a gifted nature might have been preserved for the time when its talents could mature and yield their full flower, instead of being thrust out to find a premature death in Moscow and an interment, more ironic than fitting, alongside the various revolutionary figures whose ashes repose in the Kremlin wall." [21]

The men in the Kremlin did not permit themselves the sentimentality of an epitaph for the black plinth placed over his grave. That was most affectingly supplied by Max Eastman in a sonnet he published in the *Liberator* shortly after Jack's death, in which he recalled "The pulse of the young lion and the fire / In that bright engine of extreme desire / That could never be tired or quieted. . . ." [22]

It was that pulse and the spirit it animated that made the thirty-three years of John Reed's life one of the most remarkable American chronicles. That it ended "caught in a trap," as he murmured in his delirium, was its bitter irony and mocking waste.

Bibliography

Aaron, Daniel, *Writers on the Left*, New York, 1961

Adams, J. Donald, *Copey of Harvard*, New York, 1960

Balabanoff, Angelica, *Impressions of Lenin*, Ann Arbor, Mich., 1964

——, *My Life as a Rebel*, London, 1938

Beatty, Bessie, *The Red Heart of Russia*, New York, 1918

Berkman, Alexander, *The Bolshevik Myth*, New York, 1918

Brenner, Anita, and Leighton, George R., *The Wind That Swept Mexico*, New York, 1943

Brinnin, John Malcolm, *The Third Rose: Gertrude Stein and Her World*, Boston, 1959

Brooks, Van Wyck, *The Confident Years: 1885-1915*, New York, 1952

Churchill, Allen, *The Improper Bohemians*, New York, 1959

Dell, Floyd, *Daughter of the Revolution and Other Stories*, New York, 1927

——, *Homecoming: An Autobiography*, New York, 1933

Dos Passos, John, *Nineteen Nineteen*, New York, 1930

Draper, Muriel, *Music at Midnight*, New York, 1929

Draper, Theodore, *American Communism and Soviet Russia*, New York, 1960

——, *The Roots of American Communism*, New York, 1957

Dunn, Robert, *Five Fronts*, New York, 1915

——, *World Alive*, New York, 1959

Eastman, Max, *Enjoyment of Living*, New York, 1948
——, *Heroes I Have Known*, New York, 1942
——, *Love and Revolution*, New York, 1964
Farson, Negley, *Way of a Transgressor*, New York, 1936
Francis, David R., *Russia from the American Embassy*, New York, 1921
Gitlow, Benjamin, *The Whole of Their Lives*, New York, 1948
Goldman, Emma, *Living My Life*, New York, 1931
Hard, William, *Raymond Robins' Story of Bolshevist Russia*, New York, 1919
Haywood, William D., *Bill Haywood's Book*, New York, 1929
Hicks, Granville, with the assistance of John Stuart, *John Reed: The Making of a Revolutionary*, New York, 1936
Holbrook, Stewart H., *A Far Corner: A Personal View of the Pacific Northwest*, New York, 1952
Kaltenborn, H. V., *Fifty Fabulous Years*, New York, 1950
Kennan, George F., *Russia Leaves the War*, Princeton, N.J., 1956
Kinross, Lord, *Ataturk*, New York, 1965
Kornbluh, Joyce L. (editor), *Rebel Voices: An I.W.W. Anthology*, Ann Arbor, Mich., 1964
Kramer, Dale, *Heywood Broun*, New York, 1949
Lasch, Christopher, *The New Radicalism in America*, New York, 1965
Luhan, Mabel Dodge, *European Experiences*, New York, 1935
——, *Movers and Shakers*, New York, 1936
Madison, Charles A., *Critics and Crusaders*, New York, 1948
May, Henry F., *The End of American Innocence*, New York, 1959
Myers, Gustavus, *History of the Great American Fortunes*, New York, 1936
O'Connor, Richard, *Jack London: A Biography*, Boston, 1964
Parry, Albert, *Garrets and Pretenders*, New York, 1933
Parton, Mary Field (editor), *Autobiography of Mother Jones*, Chicago, 1925
Payne, Robert, *The Life and Death of Lenin*, New York, 1964
Quirk, R. E., *The Mexican Revolution*, Bloomington, Ind., 1960
Reed, John, *The Day in Bohemia*, Riverside, Conn., 1913 (privately published)
——, *Insurgent Mexico*, New York, 1914
——, *Sangar*, Riverside, Conn., 1913 (privately published)
——, *Ten Days That Shook the World*, New York, 1919
——, *The War in Eastern Europe*, New York, 1916
Rubin, Jacob H., *I Live to Tell*, Indianapolis, Ind., 1934
Scott, H. W., *History of Portland, Oregon*, Syracuse, N.Y., 1890
Sheridan, Clare, *Mayfair to Moscow*, New York, 1921
Steffens, Lincoln, *The Autobiography of Lincoln Steffens*, New York, 1931
——, *The Letters of Lincoln Steffens*, New York, 1938
——, *Lincoln Steffens Speaking*, New York, 1928
Steiger, John H., *Memoirs of a Silk Striker*, Paterson, N.J., 1914
Tarbell, Ida, *All in the Day's Work*, New York, 1939
Wolfe, Bertram D., *Strange Communists I Have Known*, New York, 1965
Yellen, Samuel, *American Labor Struggles*, New York, 1936
Young, Art, *Art Young: His Life and Times*, New York, 1939
——, *On My Way*, New York, 1928

MAGAZINES

American Heritage
American Magazine
American Mercury
The Liberator
Literary Digest
The Masses
Metropolitan Magazine
The Nation
The New Masses
The New Republic
The Outlook
Poetry
The Saturday Evening Post
The Seven Arts
Survey Graphic
Time

NEWSPAPERS

El Paso *Times*
New York *Call*
New York *Daily Mail*
New York *Herald Tribune*
New York *Times*
New York *World*
Portland *Oregonian*

Notes

CHAPTER 1

1. John Reed in his autobiographical essay, "Almost Thirty." The manuscript is in the John Reed Collection of the Houghton Library at Harvard University.
2. From an unpublished and untitled manuscript, apparently written while Reed was a student at Harvard, in the John Reed Collection.
3. "Almost Thirty."
4. Obituary of Henry D. Green in the Portland *Oregonian*, April 12, 1885.
5. H. W. Scott, *History of Portland*, p. 182.
6. Quoted in Gustavus Myers, *History of the Great American Fortunes*, p. 664.
7. Letter (undated) from C. J. Reed to John Reed, in the John Reed Collection.
8. "Almost Thirty."
9. *Ibid.*
10. Recollections of Lee Sing from the unpublished and untitled essay cited in note 2.
11. *Ibid.*
12. "Almost Thirty."

13. *Ibid.*
14. *Ibid.*
15. *Ibid.*
16. *Ibid.*
17. From an essay Reed wrote at fifteen, in the John Reed Collection.
18. "Almost Thirty."

CHAPTER 2

1. "Almost Thirty."
2. Quoted in Granville Hicks, *John Reed: The Making of a Revolutionary*, p. 19.
3. "Almost Thirty."
4. *History of the Great American Fortunes*, pp. 689-690.
5. *The Autobiography of Lincoln Steffens*, p. 549.
6. Lincoln Steffens, *The New Republic*, May 20, 1936.
7. Lincoln Steffens, *Lincoln Steffens Speaking*, p. 312.
8. "Almost Thirty."
9. *Ibid.*
10. Van Wyck Brooks, *The Confident Years: 1885-1915*, p. 481.
11. Quoted in Hicks, *John Reed*, p. 22.
12. "Almost Thirty."
13. In the John Reed Collection.
14. "Almost Thirty."
15. "Prophets of Rebellion," *The Outlook*, March 18, 1925.
16. "Legendary John Reed," *The New Republic*, December 16, 1914.
17. "A Soviet Saint," *The Saturday Evening Post*, September 13, 1930.
18. Unpublished essay, "The Harvard Renaissance," in the John Reed Collection.
19. *Ibid.*
20. H. V. Kaltenborn, *Fifty Fabulous Years*, p. 43.
21. Quoted in Hicks, *John Reed*, pp. 34-35.
22. "Legendary John Reed."
23. "Prophets of Rebellion."
24. *Fifty Fabulous Years*, p. 45.
25. Quoted in J. Donald Adams, *Copey of Harvard*, p. 187.
26. *John Reed*, pp. 41-42.

CHAPTER 3

1. "Almost Thirty."
2. *Ibid.*
3. *Ibid.*
4. *Ibid.*
5. *Ibid.*
6. *Ibid.*
7. "A Soviet Saint."

8. "The Cattleboat Murder," unpublished account in the John Reed Collection.
9. "A Soviet Saint."
10. Unpublished essay, "A Dash to Spain," in the John Reed Collection.
11. Quoted in Hicks, *John Reed*, p. 62.
12. Stewart Holbrook, *Far Corner: A Personal View of the Pacific Northwest*, pp. 190-191.

CHAPTER 4

1. Quoted in *The Autobiography of Lincoln Steffens*, p. 653.
2. "Almost Thirty."
3. Max Eastman, *Enjoyment of Living*, p. 427.
4. *Copey of Harvard*, p. 189.
5. "Almost Thirty."
6. From Reed's privately printed *The Day in Bohemia*.
7. *The Autobiography of Lincoln Steffens*, p. 654.
8. *The Letters of Lincoln Steffens*, Vol. I, p. 285.
9. "Almost Thirty."
10. "Playboy," *American Mercury*, June, 1934.
11. *John Reed*, p. 71.
12. "A Soviet Saint."
13. *Ibid.*
14. *The Confident Years*, p. 482.
15. *The Letters of Lincoln Steffens*, Vol. I, p. 304.
16. Quoted in Harriet Monroe's article "Two Poets Have Died," *Poetry*, January, 1921.
17. "A Soviet Saint."
18. "Almost Thirty."
19. *Enjoyment of Living*, p. 406.
20. *Ibid.*, p. 406.

CHAPTER 5

1. Mabel Dodge Luhan, *European Experiences*, p. 453.
2. Described in Allen Churchill's lively survey of Greenwich Village history, *The Improper Bohemians*, p. 39.
3. *Enjoyment of Living*, pp. 522, 523.
4. *The Autobiography of Lincoln Steffens*, p. 654.
5. *Movers and Shakers*, p. 216.
6. Quoted in *Movers and Shakers*, p. 187.
7. *Ibid.*, p. 189.
8. See *Rebel Voices*, edited by Joyce Kornbluh, pp. 197-225.
9. Reed, "War in Paterson," *The Masses*, June, 1913.
10. *Ibid.*
11. *Ibid.*
12. *Movers and Shakers*, pp. 200, 203-205.
13. "A Soviet Saint."

14. *Movers and Shakers*, p. 216.
15. *Ibid.*, p. 205.
16. John H. Steiger, *Memoirs of a Silk Striker*, p. 183.
17. Quoted in *John Reed*, p. 103.
18. *Memoirs of a Silk Striker*, pp. 224-225.
19. *Movers and Shakers*, p. 213.
20. *Ibid.*, p. 216.
21. *Ibid.*, p. 217.
22. Muriel Draper, *Music at Midnight*, p. 123.
23. Letters to Edward Hunt are in the John Reed Collection.
24. *Movers and Shakers*, p. 229.
25. Quoted in *John Reed*, p. 107.

CHAPTER 6

1. *Enjoyment of Living*, pp. 524-525.
2. *Movers and Shakers*, p. 232.
3. *Ibid.*, p. 233.
4. *Ibid.*, p. 245.
5. *Enjoyment of Living*, p. 443.
6. Max Eastman, *Love and Revolution*, pp. 22-23.
7. *Enjoyment of Living*, p. 455.
8. "Legendary John Reed."
9. "A Soviet Saint."
10. Quoted in Richard O'Connor, *Jack London: A Biography*, pp. 351-352.
11. *Movers and Shakers*, p. 247.
12. See Robert E. Quirk, *The Mexican Revolution*, and Anita Brenner and George R. Leighton, *The Wind That Swept Mexico*.
13. *The Mexican Revolution*, p. 7.
14. "Reed, Villa and the Village," *The Outlook*, May 6, 1925.
15. *Ibid.*
16. John Reed, *Insurgent Mexico*, pp. 7-8.
17. *Ibid.*, pp. 115-116.
18. *Ibid.*, p. 130.
19. *Ibid.*, pp. 127-133.
20. *Ibid.*, pp. 142-144.
21. "El Cosmopolita," *Metropolitan Magazine*, September, 1914.
22. *Insurgent Mexico*, pp. 157-160.
23. *Ibid.*, pp. 51-52.
24. *Ibid.*, pp. 83-87.
25. *New York World*, March 4, 1914.
26. *Insurgent Mexico*, p. 177.
27. *The Mexican Revolution*, p. 21.
28. *Insurgent Mexico*, p. 227.
29. *Ibid.*, pp. 257-258.
30. "Legendary John Reed."
31. Quoted in *Copey of Harvard*, p. 190.

CHAPTER 7

1. Quoted in John Malcolm Brinnin, *The Third Rose: Gertrude Stein and Her World*, p. 168.
2. Christopher Lasch, *The New Radicalism in America*, p. 128.
3. *Movers and Shakers*, p. 256.
4. *Ibid.*, p. 257.
5. *Ibid.*, p. 261.
6. "A Soviet Saint."
7. Max Eastman, *Heroes I Have Known*, which contains the most perceptive and affectionate portrait of Reed written thus far, pp. 208-209.
8. "Almost Thirty."
9. "Bryan on Tour," *Collier's*, May 20, 1916. The original draft, containing some material edited out of the published article, is in the John Reed Collection.
10. From the unpublished account of Reed's interview with Wilson in the John Reed Collection.
11. Quoted in *Jack London: A Biography*, p. 360.
12. Floyd Dell, *Homecoming*, pp. 326-327.
13. See Samuel Yellen, *American Labor Struggles*, pp. 205-250.
14. *Enjoyment of Living*, p. 452.
15. "The Colorado War," *Metropolitan Magazine*, July, 1914.
16. *Autobiography of Mother Jones*, p. 185.
17. "The Colorado War."
18. *Movers and Shakers*, p. 263.
19. "An Englishman," *Metropolitan Magazine*, October, 1914.
20. *The Masses*, September, 1914.
21. Robert Dunn, *Five Fronts*, a collection of war correspondence, p. 183.
22. Robert Dunn, *World Alive*, p. 291.
23. Unpublished article, "Rule Britannia," in the John Reed Collection.
24. *Ibid.*
25. *World Alive*, p. 215.
26. "German France," *Metropolitan Magazine*, March, 1915.
27. *World Alive*, p. 215.
28. "In the German Trenches," *Metropolitan Magazine*, April, 1915.
29. *World Alive*, p. 216.

CHAPTER 8

1. *World Alive*, p. 221.
2. Letter to *The Saturday Evening Post*, March 2, 1915.
3. *World Alive*, p. 221.
4. *The Letters of Lincoln Steffens*, Vol. I, p. 353.
5. Quoted from the *Metropolitan Bulletin*, an interoffice publication, in an article by Sonya Levien, "Col. Roosevelt in Our Office," March, 1916.
6. "A Soviet Saint."
7. *Metropolitan Magazine*, March, 1915.

8. *Movers and Shakers*, p. 354.
9. *Ibid.*, p. 357.
10. "Legendary John Reed."
11. Quoted in *John Reed*, p. 183.
12. "A Soviet Saint."
13. John Reed, *The War in Eastern Europe*, p. 10.
14. *Ibid.*, pp. 45-46
15. *Ibid.*, p. 92.
16. *Ibid.*, pp. 110-117.
17. *Ibid.*, pp. 163-164.
18. "A Soviet Saint."
19. *The War in Eastern Europe*, pp. 170-171.
20. *Ibid.*, p. 210.
21. "A Soviet Saint."
22. *The War in Eastern Europe*, pp. 182-183.
23. Quoted in Negley Farson, *The Way of a Transgressor*, p. 188.
24. *Ibid.*, p. 181.
25. *Ibid.*, p. 183.
26. *Ibid.*, p. 187.
27. *Ibid.*, p. 190.
28. *The War in Eastern Europe*, p. 246.
29. *Ibid.*, p. 250.
30. *Ibid.*, pp. 262-263.
31. *Ibid.*, pp. 280-281.
32. *Ibid.*, pp. 312-320.

CHAPTER 9

1. *Enjoyment of Living*, p. 537.
2. *Ibid.*, p. 565.
3. *John Reed*, p. 205
4. *Movers and Shakers*, p. 421.
5. *Enjoyment of Living*, p. 565.
6. *The Improper Bohemians*, p. 139.
7. Quoted in *John Reed*, p. 208.
8. Quoted in the Brooklyn *Eagle*, February 18, 1916.
9. Emma Goldman, *Living My Life*, Vol. II, p. 569.
10. *Collier's*, May 20, 1916.
11. *The Masses*, July, 1916.
12. "A Soviet Saint."
13. *Ibid.*
14. *The Masses*, August, 1916. His article for the *Metropolitan Magazine* appeared in the August, 1916, issue.
15. *Enjoyment of Living*, pp. 565-566.
16. *The Improper Bohemians*, p. 202.
17. "Fog" was not published until three years later, in *Scribner's*, May, **1919**.

18. Quoted in *John Reed*, p. 224.
19. New York *Times*, April 13, 1917, and record of the House Judiciary Committee, 65th Congress, Serial 3, Part II.
20. Quoted in *John Reed*, pp. 235-236.
21. Letters to Louise in June and July are in the John Reed Collection.
22. "Almost Thirty."

CHAPTER 10

1. Quoted in Max Eastman, *Love and Revolution*, p. 551.
2. *Ibid.*, p. 63.
3. "A Letter from John Reed," *The Masses*, November, 1917.
4. Quoted in *John Reed*, p. 259.
5. John Reed, *Ten Days That Shook the World*, Modern Library Edition, p. 3.
6. *Ibid.*, pp. 7-8.
7. *Ibid.*, p. 9.
8. *Ibid.*, pp. 12-14.
9. David R. Francis, *Russia from the American Embassy*, p. 166.
10. *The Way of a Transgressor*, p. 288.
11. *Ibid.*, p. 295.
12. *Ten Days That Shook the World*, pp. 36-37.
13. *Ibid.*, pp. 170-171.
14. *Ibid.*, pp. 75-84.
15. *Ibid.*, pp. 98-102.
16. *Ibid.*, pp. 138-144.
17. *Ibid.*, pp. 149-150.
18. *Ibid.*, p. 167.
19. *Ibid.*, pp. 170-186.
20. *Ibid.*, pp. 211-215.
21. *Ibid.*, p. 254.
22. *Ibid.*, p. 317.
23. *Love and Revolution*, p. 70.
24. Bertram Wolfe's introduction to the Modern Library edition of *Ten Days That Shook the World*, p. xxxv.
25. *Ten Days That Shook the World*, pp. 409-410.
26. *Ibid.*, pp. 418-419.
27. Quoted in "A Soviet Saint."
28. *Ibid.*
29. See the New York *Herald Tribune*, November 26, 1965, and Angelica Balabanoff's books, *Impressions of Lenin* and *My Life as a Rebel*.
30. *My Life as a Rebel*, p. 177.
31. *Ibid.*, pp. 177, 178.
32. Letter dated March 17, 1918, in the John Reed Collection.
33. Published in the *New Masses*, October 18, 1935.

CHAPTER 11

1. Benjamin Gitlow, *The Whole of Their Lives*, one of the more important documents in the history of personal disillusionment with Communism.
2. In the John Reed Collection.
3. *Love and Revolution*, p. 105.
4. *The Whole of Their Lives*, p. 17.
5. *Ibid.*, p. 22.
6. *John Reed*, p. 306.
7. *The Liberator*, September, 1918.
8. *Ibid.*
9. *Love and Revolution*, p. 107.
10. *Ibid.*, p. 109.
11. *The Whole of Their Lives*, pp. 37-44.
12. *Ibid.*, p. 24.
13. *The Liberator*, December, 1918.
14. *Love and Revolution*, p. 119.
15. *Ibid.*, p. 120.
16. Art Young, *On My Way*, pp. 293-299.
17. *Ibid.*, p. 298.
18. *Homecoming*, pp. 326-327.
19. *The Whole of Their Lives*, p. 28.
20. *Homecoming*, p. 327.
21. *The Liberator*, March, 1919.
22. *Report of the Judiciary Committee of the United States Senate*, 66th Congress, 1st session.
23. New York *Tribune*, February 22, 1919.
24. *Report of the Judiciary Committee of the United States Senate*, 66th Congress, 1st session.
25. Letters to Louise are in the John Reed Collection.
26. *Homecoming*, p. 327.
27. Art Young, *Art Young: His Life and Times*, p. 362.
28. *The Whole of Their Lives*, p. 28.
29. *Art Young: His Life and Times*, p. 363.
30. Quoted in *The Whole of Their Lives*, p. 29.

CHAPTER 12

1. *The Whole of Their Lives*, p. 29.
2. Letter is in the John Reed Collection.
3. *John Reed*, pp. 374-375.
4. *Ibid.*, p. 376.
5. *Living My Life*, Vol. II, p. 849.
6. *Ibid.*, Vol. II, p. 739
7. *Ibid.*, Vol. II, p. 741
8. *The Whole of Their Lives*, pp. 18-20.
9. MacAlpine wrote his account for Louise Bryant in Paris in 1934, when

she was planning to write a book about Reed. It is in the John Reed Collection.

10. All the letters are in the John Reed Collection.
11. *Living My Life*, Vol. II, pp. 850-852.
12. *My Life as a Rebel*, p. 244.
13. *Ibid.*, p. 245.
14. *Ibid.*, pp. 245-246.
15. *Ibid.*, pp. 274-275.
16. Theodore Draper, *The Roots of American Communism*, p. 284.
17. *John Reed*, pp. 208-209.
18. The notes are in the John Reed Collection.
19. Theodore Draper, *American Communism and Soviet Russia*, pp. 192, 387.
20. *Ibid.*, p. 387.
21. Letter dated June 29, 1920 is in the John Reed Collection.

CHAPTER 13

1. Jacob H. Rubin, *I Live to Tell*, p. 218.
2. *Ibid.*, pp. 219-220.
3. *The Whole of Their Lives*, p. 17.
4. Lord Kinross, *Ataturk*, p. 278.
5. *Ibid.*, p. 278.
6. *The Whole of Their Lives*, p. 33.
7. Letter dated June 26, 1920 is in the John Reed Collection.
8. Louise Bryant gave this account to Benjamin Gitlow, which he published in *The Whole of Their Lives*, when she visited him in prison not long after returning to the U.S. Gitlow had been arrested during Attorney General Palmer's "red raids," and served three years before he was pardoned. He had insisted that Clarence Darrow defend him solely on the basis of an American's "right to revolution."
9. *World Alive*, p. 366.
10. Quoted in *The Whole of Their Lives*, p. 34.
11. Quoted in *John Reed*, p. 397.
12. *World Alive*, pp. 366-367. Dunn was then serving as an intelligence officer of the U.S. government at Constantinople. One of his duties evidently was to collect information about Soviet intentions in the Middle East, particularly as they affected that region's oil deposits.
13. *Ibid.*, p. 367.

CHAPTER 14

1. Quoted in *Heroes I Have Known*, p. 230.
2. Quoted in *The Whole of Their Lives*, p. 36.
3. Robert Payne, *Life and Death of Lenin*, p. 539.
4. *Living My Life*, Vol. II, p. 850.
5. *My Life as a Rebel*, p. 291.

6. *Ibid.*
7. Clare Sheridan, *Mayfair to Moscow*, pp. 160-161.
8. *The Whole of Their Lives*, p. 36.
9. *Heroes I Have Known*, p. 236.
10. *Living My Life*, Vol. II, p. 851.
11. *The Whole of Their Lives*, p. 36.
12. Quoted in *Love and Revolution*, p. 260.
13. *Living My Life*, Vol. II, p. 851.
14. *Ibid.*, Vol. II, p. 854.
15. *My Life as a Rebel*, p. 291.
16. *Mayfair to Moscow*, p. 163.
17. Quoted in *Art Young: His Life and Times*, p. 389.
18. *Heroes I Have Known*, p. 208.
19. *The Letters of Lincoln Steffens*, Vol. II, p. 922.
20. Max Lerner, *The Nation*, April 29, 1936.
21. George F. Kennan, *Russia Leaves the War*, p. 69.
22. *The Liberator*, February, 1921.

Index